OPENING UP
MY AUTOBIOGRAPHY

Mike Atherton

Hodder & Stoughton

Copyright © 2002 by Mike Atherton

First published in Great Britain in 2002 by Hodder and Stoughton
A division of Hodder Headline

The right of Mike Atherton to be identified as the Author of the
Work has been asserted by him in accordance with the Copyright,
Designs and Patents Act 1988.

2 4 6 8 10 9 7 5 3

A CIP catalogue record for this title
is available from the British Library

ISBN 0 340 82232 5

Typeset in Stone Sans by
Rowland Phototypesetting Ltd,
Bury St Edmunds, Suffolk
Printed and bound in Australia by
Griffin Press, Netley, Australia

Hodder and Stoughton
A division of Hodder Headline
338 Euston Road
London NW1 3BH

To Mum and Dad

CONTENTS

ACKNOWLEDGEMENTS

I would like to thank Jon Holmes for encouraging me to write this book, and more generally, for his advice throughout my career; and Scyld Berry for his encouragement throughout my early attempts at journalism with the *Sunday Telegraph*, and during the process of writing this book. Vic Isaacs collated the statistics, Christine Forrest checked my occasionally hazy memory for facts, Marion Paull is an eagle-eyed copy editor and Gabrielle Allen came up with a fine selection of photographs.

Isabelle de Caires read the manuscript carefully and always made sound suggestions, while Roddy Bloomfield's patience and wisdom was greatly appreciated throughout the winter of 2001–02.

My thanks to all.

The quotations on pages xi, 252 and 295 are taken, respectively, from *Slouching towards Bethlehem* by Joan Didion, *Lincoln* by Gore Vidal and *Beyond a Boundary* by C.L.R. James.

Photographic Acknowledgements

The author and publisher would like to thank the following for permission to reproduce photographs:

AllSport/Getty Images, Philip Brown, Colorsport, Patrick Eagar, the *Guardian*, *Manchester Evening News*, Mirror Syndication, Graham Morris, News International, Popperfoto/Reuters, Press Association, Topham Picturepoint.

All other photographs are from private collections.

PREFACE

'It is easy to see the beginnings of things and harder to see the ends.' Well, for me, the end was easy to see. In fact, it slapped me squarely in the face on 19 June 2001, half an hour after the end of the first day's play of Lancashire's championship match against Essex. I had batted through the day for an unbeaten 100, my first really long innings of the season. As usual after such exertion, I lay on the physiotherapist's bed for some emergency repair work from Laurie Brown. When he had finished I stood up and the upper third of my body was at a near 45 degree angle to the rest, and my back was in complete spasm.

I kneaded my lower back and felt the tightness but I wasn't too worried; it had happened often before although it was a more frequent occurrence of late. I knew that a double dose of Voltarol that evening and the next morning, and a soluble Voltarol before I resumed my innings the next day would straighten me out and enable me to carry on, even if my stomach would pay the price later. If they didn't do the trick, there was always recourse to another cortisone injection. Things would be all right.

But I knew at that moment it was time to put an end to such nonsense, to excessive doses of painkillers and quick-fix steroid injections. The First Test against Australia was only a fortnight away and the Ashes, in any case, represented the final frontier for me as a cricketer. Win or lose, there didn't seem any point in going on after that. Once before (as England captain) I had made the mistake of going on too long and damaging my reputation. I wasn't going to make that mistake again. There and then I knew that the current season would be my last.

Although I had made up my mind, I didn't want to announce it until after the last Test. It was not that I was keen on suspense, but I had played in matches where players had announced their retirement beforehand – notably Mike Gatting and Graham Gooch in Perth in 1995 – and the fuss had overshadowed the game itself. I wanted to bow out in a low-key fashion, in a way that more accurately reflected my character and career. I decided upon a statement the day after the last Test when I knew the announcement of the winter squads would overshadow my news. I could then slip away quietly.

Despite these plans, there was some public expectation of my impending retirement. I also made my intentions clear to both Nasser Hussain and Duncan Fletcher once the Ashes had been lost after the Third Test at Trent Bridge, just in case they wanted to blood a new player for the winter tour. Fletcher was firmly of the opinion that long-serving players must be treated properly. 'You've been a great servant for England,' he said, 'and you should go out in a manner that reflects that.'

During my last Test at The Oval, I contemplated Fletcher's remark. The perfect way to bow out would be with a memorable innings, something typical – a battle with the opposition's fast bowler, probably not pretty, but effective. But Glenn McGrath would open the bowling for Australia. He was the only bowler I truly felt uncomfortable facing throughout my career and he was the one who consistently had the better of me. Of course, there were plenty of other bowlers who got me out, and frequently. Curtly Ambrose and Courtney Walsh dismissed me seventeen times each, but I could also claim my share of victories – in three out of the five series I played against them I scored more runs than any other English batsman. McGrath was different; I had few, if any, happy memories to fall back on to help me through.

My penultimate day in Test cricket dawned overcast and wet, and as for most of the summer, we began the day struggling to avoid defeat, needing 33 to prevent the follow-on with only three wickets in hand. A tailend of Gough and Tufnell didn't inspire much confidence and as an opener I would normally have conditioned myself to the follow-on and prepared to bat again. Now, secretly, I hoped Mark Ramprakash would steer us to safety; I rested my hopes on this blind and desperate act of faith.

Steve Waugh, Australia's captain, relied on McGrath and Shane Warne for the breakthrough, which eventually came, as did the follow-on. McGrath, though, had bowled for a long spell and there was a slim chance that he wouldn't take the new ball the second time around. Throughout my career I had always looked forward to the prospect of the contest – the raw, personal confrontation between a batsman and a bowler. Now I secretly wanted to avoid it and I hoped Waugh would throw the new ball instead to Jason Gillespie and Brett Lee, two bowlers with whom I felt much more comfortable.

I realised then that fifteen years at the top had begun to take their toll mentally. I had crammed in 115 Tests, fifty-two as captain (and two more when Hussain was injured) without any lengthy break. That was unusual for recent English Test batsmen. Graham Gooch missed three years of international cricket having been banned for going on the rebel tour to South Africa in 1982, while Graham Thorpe was the most recent high-profile case of a player taking a winter off to recharge his batteries. I had enjoyed no such break and the effects, both physical and mental, were obvious. In June I had recognised that my body was crying 'enough'. Not wanting to bat again or face McGrath were sure signs that mentally I had nothing left to give.

Mental strength and preparation had always been the keys to my success as an international cricketer. I always relished the challenge, and had the ability to clear my mind and think coolly and calmly of what lay ahead. Now, as I walked to the crease for the last time, with Marcus Trescothick, my mind was a maelstrom of conflicting emotions. I remember little – a pull and a cut off two uncharacteristically loose balls from McGrath and then the inevitable nick, which Shane Warne gobbled up at first slip – caught Warne, bowled McGrath, an entirely predictable end.

Disappointment would usually last all the way back to the pavilion and for at least a couple of hours afterwards. This time it was fleeting. Above all, I felt relief. I was glad it was all over. Halfway back to the pavilion I was jolted out of my self-absorption by the realisation that the whole ground had risen to me. What to do? I had scored a miserable 9, but it was clear that the applause was for much more than that and needed to be acknowledged. A raise of the bat, then, to the pavilion, and a half-turn to the rest of the ground (as I did so I saw the Australians, to a man, clapping me off). Then it was up the stairs and off the stage for the final time.

I sat in my corner with a towel over my head for an age. When I finally emerged it was to see on the television screen that since January 1990 I had scored more Test runs than anybody else. The two Waughs (Mark and Steve), Alec Stewart, Sachin Tendulkar, Brian Lara, Mark Taylor, Michael Slater, Inzamam-ul-Haq and Aravinda de Silva completed the top ten. I was, at least, in good company. There was a tap on my shoulder.

'Can I have your last shirt and bat for my benefit, Athers?' Darren Gough always had half an eye on a money-making opportunity, and since I kept few mementos I willingly obliged. My contribution was over and all I could do now was sit and watch as we vainly tried to avoid defeat.

The next day Philip Tufnell edged McGrath and Australia wrapped up their 4–1 series victory. I emerged on to the balcony to sign autographs. What struck me then, very suddenly, was the essential decency of the game. Nobody had stormed the playing area and the crowd had stayed behind to applaud and admire this outstanding Australian team as they did a lap of honour around the ground, bathed in sunlight. I viewed such things differently now, as a cricket lover rather than a cricket player – they ought to be the same thing but occasionally, sadly, are not. All of a sudden, Australia's victory wasn't important at all. That was very strange because for the last fifteen years winning and losing had mattered so much.

1

OFF THE MARK

Woodhouses Cricket Club is a small village club on an ever-narrowing strip of greenbelt that separates Manchester and Oldham. It is where I started playing, and the contrast with where I finished could not have been sharper – the changing rooms were small and, until the mid 1980s, showerless; there was no groundsman and the pitch was marked and rolled during the interval by the players in rotation while the rest enjoyed tea made by the players' wives or girlfriends or, in my case, my mum.

When I was young, our proud boast was that Woodhouses had more pig farms per square mile than any village in England. I don't know whether it was true, and if it was, it is certainly not any more, but nevertheless it was our claim to fame. Looking out from the pavilion at midwicket, flush to the boundary fence, was one such. Every Saturday afternoon at four, often at a critical stage in the game, the farmer, Len, would feel the need to feed his swine. There weren't many disincentives to batting, but the ensuing noise and smell, which settled over the ground like a wet blanket, was certainly one.

Opposite the pavilion was a small, brick scorebox. Before I was old enough to play, I could be found there on most Saturdays 'doing the tins'. I seemed to take an unnaturally keen interest in the game even then. While other boys would be gathered around the pornographic magazines that mysteriously appeared underneath the bales of hay at the back of the box, I would be at my cubbyhole, watching the cricket intently.

Woodhouses played in the Lancashire and Cheshire League. This was not quite as good as the Lancashire or the Central Lancashire Leagues, but one of the better competitions in the area nonetheless. Memory can play dangerous tricks but it seems to me that the standard was better back then. There were some good players. Tony Opatha, the Sri Lankan international, opened the bowling for Unsworth. He was a poor man's Mike Procter. He charged in with his lank black hair flowing, a slight beer gut wobbling, and bowled off the wrong foot. At the other end was the curiously named Neville Neville, father of Manchester United's Philip and Gary.

Sidath Wettimuny, another Sri Lankan international, came to Poynton for a couple of years. He was no more than twenty, but it was clear to me, even though I was not yet half his age, that he was a player on a different plane from the rest in our league. He was small and slight and played in a beautifully orthodox way. It was the first time I had seen somebody play in a manner that closely resembled the coaching books I was devouring.

We had our stars, too. A year after his retirement from the first-class game Farokh Engineer came to play for us. After years of back- (and finger-) breaking work, he didn't fancy keeping wicket any more; instead he bowled dreadful leg-breaks and in two years with us he barely scored a run. He was good for the odd autograph sheet though. T.E. Srinivasan, a swashbuckling batsman from Madras, also played for us. He was everything that Wettimuny was not – wild, aggressive and totally unorthodox. He was a stalwart for Tamil Nadu, in India, for many years and went on to play one Test and two one-day internationals for his country. Many years later I asked Sunil Gavaskar about him and he told me he would have played much more had it not been for his low-caste status.

It was Srinivasan who showed me a way of practising on my own. He would put an old cricket ball in a sock, and tie it with string to a washing line. Swinging it back and forth you could practise hitting the ball straight for hours. We lived three fields away from the village, on a suburban housing estate, and it was here that I put Srinivasan's advice into continual practice, until the rows of bare patches along the lawn irritated my father and he signalled enough. Thereafter, it was left to my brother Chris to provide the practice I craved. He is three years younger than I am, but even at an early age he was a decent bowler. Most days we could be found playing on the concrete strip that bisected our back lawn, the sibling rivalry characteristically intense.

When I was not in Woodhouses' scorebox on a Saturday, I went with my father, Alan, to various club grounds. I would watch intently and then at teatime or at the end of play he would teach me the rudiments of batting. He was a decent club cricketer and good enough to be able to give me a sound basic technique, but other than that, advice was thankfully thin on the ground. Once, though, in 1978 he summoned me into the lounge when England were playing Pakistan. He made me watch a young, curly-haired left-hander who was making his debut for England. 'See how still he keeps his head,' said my father. I did watch David Gower and I never forgot the lesson.

I played through the club's junior teams, making some impact. When I was fourteen years old, my father came home one Monday evening from a selection meeting.

'Congratulations,' he said. 'You've just been picked in the first team.'

'Who am I playing instead of?' I asked.

'Me,' he said. He didn't sound or look upset at all but I guess it must have niggled at him slightly because he too had been a professional sportsman and must have had a certain amount of pride.

He had been a footballer, not a cricketer, in his youth. He signed as a professional with Manchester United in the years following the Munich air disaster, when no doubt the club were on the lookout for young and talented players. In 1960 the system changed to allow apprentice professionals for the first time. As my father's surname began with A, he became the first-ever apprentice professional at Manchester United. He never played in the first team although he was a substitute on occasions (in the days when substitutes got on only through injury). He mainly played in the reserves and I keep a photograph of the 1959–60 reserve team at home. Most of the names mean nothing to me, but in the middle of the front row sits a pugnacious-looking Nobby Stiles. My father was a centre-half, and a 'decent one' according to Wilf McGuinness, the manager at the time, but he had to retire prematurely because of the same back complaint I was to suffer from later on.

My grandfather, Tommy Atherton, was also a professional sportsman. He was a boxer in and around the Manchester area in the 1930s. I like the grainy photograph I have of him at home, in boxing stance – orthodox rather than southpaw – with a crisp centre parting and heavily oiled hair slicked down on either side. His nose shows the scars of battle, and he looks every ounce the bantamweight he was. He must have been a decent fighter. I have a contract from 1936 between George Jackson of Sunderland and my grandfather's manager, W. Jones of Openshaw. The fight was for ten two-minute rounds against Tom Smith of Sunderland for 'five pounds all in'. In 1936, only decent boxers travelled outside their area, and fought ten rounds.

My mother, Wendy, and father met through sport. They were doubles partners at tennis. It must have been quite a strange partnership between my mother, naturally effusive and gregarious, with a dreadful backhand, and my father, headmasterly by nature and vocation, but ultra-competitive. Inevitably, I suppose, my character is a fusion of the two. Over the years each side has battled with the other for supremacy. Usually my father's side won out, although Scyld Berry, cricket correspondent of the *Sunday Telegraph*, noticed a change after I resigned the England captaincy in 1998. 'The boy brought up to be a Spartan is turning out an Athenian after all,' he wrote. I think he was being kind.

4

The early games for Woodhouses were an essential part of my cricketing education, for the simple fact that, aged fourteen and fifteen, I was playing against men and had to toughen up rapidly to survive. Physically unable to compete, I had to use the pace of the ball to score and, as a result, I hit the ball much squarer than is the norm. The habit never left me. At Thornham I played against Roy Gilchrist, the legendary West Indies fast bowler. I suppose he must have been in his late forties by then but he was still sharp enough and his reputation as a nasty piece of work further added to my apprehension. One of his deliveries hit me straight in the mouth (these were pre-helmet days) although that had as much to do with the spiteful pitch as any intent on his behalf. I met Gilchrist years later, shortly before his death, on our West Indies tour in 1998 and could not believe that this frail old man was the same one who had so terrified me.

As my school commitments increased, so my games for Wood-houses were restricted to the holidays. After I was capped for Lancashire in 1989, league regulations stipulated that I was not allowed to play for my club again as an amateur, and so I found myself going there less and less frequently. It seemed a ridiculous ruling to me, one that emphasised the huge and ever-widening gulf in English cricket between the professional and the amateur game. It is one of our great problems; professional players lose touch with the communities they come from and as a result give little back, while the promising amateur feels he has no chance of entering the world of professional cricket.

No other country suffers from this. In Australia there is a seam-less transition from grade (amateur) to state (professional) cricket. One time in the West Indies I took a boy from an orphan-age I have an involvement with to a practice session at the Georgetown Cricket Club. Reon King, the West Indies fast bowler, and Nicholas De Groot, a Guyanese player, were both helping out, and in the pavilion bar were any number of former first-class players, drinking and chatting. Here there was no dis-tinction between amateur and professional, top and bottom;

they mixed happily and easily. As C.L.R. James says in *Beyond A Boundary*: 'All of us knew our West Indian cricketers, when they made their first century, when they became engaged, if they drank whiskey instead of rum. A Test player with all his gifts was not a personage remote to be read about in the papers and worshipped from afar. They were all over the place, ready to play in any place, ready to talk. There was never a net at which you could not bowl to them if you kept a length . . . it was one of our greatest strengths, why we have always been able to do so much with so little.'

My involvement with amateur club cricket ended, through no fault of my own, in 1989 and I haven't played a club match since. It is a great shame. Village and club cricket of the type epitomised by Woodhouses and thousands of other clubs is the heart and soul of cricket in this country, rather than the closeted and often precious world inhabited by professionals.

My education began at Briscoe Lane County Primary School in Newton Heath, one of the roughest suburbs of North Manchester. Looking back, I suppose it could be seen as a typical school of hard knocks story, so common in successful athletes. Of course, that is not how it seemed to me then; between the ages of seven and eleven I had no idea that Briscoe Lane was a rough school, or Newton Heath an unfashionable neighbourhood. As Briscoe Lane was one of the few schools in the area with its own indoor swimming pool and as we played sport *every* afternoon, it seemed to me to be rather a good place to be. We won the Manchester Primary Schools' Cup, in cricket and soccer, for four consecutive years while I was there, and due to the passion of one teacher in particular, we were also good at chess.

But my parents knew the dangers. At that stage my father was deputy head of a large North Manchester secondary school, and he knew that Moston Brook, the secondary school for which Briscoe Lane was a feeder, was no place to send his promising young son. So every Monday I was sent for extra tuition with my form master Ted Parrett whose wife worked at the Manchester

Grammar School. She procured past exam papers for us to work through and at eleven I sat the entry exam. Surrounded by hundreds of uniformed prep school boys I felt very inferior, but I passed (just, I think) and became the first Briscoe Lane pupil ever to attend the Manchester Grammar School.

MGS was huge and daunting and, at first, an enormous struggle. Latin, for instance, was simply an unfathomable mystery to me. I also suffered from a debilitating shyness. It was compounded by the fact that 90 per cent of MGS pupils came from South Manchester, from the salubrious suburbs of Altrincham and Hale. Most came from Altrincham Prep School, and they all seemed to know each other as they gathered in their droves to catch the 709 bus home. My route took me north – the number 50 into Manchester and the 76 out, sometimes with a handful of others, often on my own.

I have an image of a rather shy, sober and solitary young boy, not entirely at ease at school, whose uniform and briefcase made him stand out once home. That, in turn, led to him being ostracised by the local kids for going to 'the posh school'. It instilled in me contentment in my own company and a self-sufficiency that has been an enduring characteristic. As a result, singular and self-sufficient, I was ready-made for batsmanship.

Eventually I began to flourish at MGS. The fact that I had not been spoon-fed into the system via Altrincham Prep helped me, and I was able to get to grips with the academic side of things at a school renowned for its academic strength. Sport helped, and even began to give me some status. I played in the football team, which went ninety-three games (over five years) before tasting defeat. I started on the left wing and, increasingly lacking in pace, ended up at left-back. In between, I marauded around in midfield, talentless but committed. I appeared in the cricket first eleven for the first time aged twelve, and stayed there, estranged from my own age group until they caught up. We lost one match in five years.

Various representative sides noticed my performances, and I

found my holidays taken up by Lancashire and England Schools' matches. At the Under 15s festival I came across Nasser Hussain for the first time. 'Go and watch him,' I was told. 'He is an absolute wizard with the ball – leg-spinners, top-spinners and googlies – a real prospect.' I went and stood by the sightscreen and watched Hussain bowl. It was immediately obvious to me that he was already afflicted by the yips, which were to finish off his bowling for good three years later. Mark Ramprakash also appeared for the south that year; he had a heavy three-pound bat, and a temper to match.

Lancashire began to take notice of, and an interest in, my performances and the head coach Peter Lever invited me to join some indoor sessions during the winter months of 1984. He had set up a 'find a fast bowler' scheme and I was to be one of the guinea-pig batsmen – guinea pig in the sense that the bowlers were raw and wild, and as none of Lancashire's professional batsmen fancied facing them, a couple of unsuspecting amateurs had to be found. The bowlers were allowed to bowl off 17 yards. They all had nicknames like the 'Royton Rocket' and were quicker than anything I had faced before, or anything I have faced since.

When we finally got to play on grass, and off 22 yards, few of them could hit the cut strip. Peter Martin was the only one to emerge from the scheme and it was seen as a failure. For me, however, it was of enormous benefit. The biggest difference between amateur and professional cricket is the pace of the ball and for the first time I had some idea of the courage and speed of reaction needed to open the batting in first-class cricket. Established Lancashire players did not feel the same way. Graeme Fowler and Neil Fairbrother came along once 'to show us how it was done'. They walked out after a couple of wild and erratic deliveries and, quite rightly, never returned.

On Saturdays, Lever dragged the whole squad to his house in the Rochdale hills. He marked out a five-mile cross-country run with sandbags and used to stand high on a vantage point that overlooked the whole area, his booming voice berating the shirkers and those who lagged behind. The finish was uphill and more gruelling than the last furlong at Cheltenham. Afterwards, Lever's long-suffering wife made us all soup and coffee. It opened my eyes for the first time to the importance of physical fitness. Lever's cricket and training sessions were the main reason why I found the transition to first-class cricket a relatively easy one.

If it sounds a rather one-dimensional childhood and upbringing, it probably was. There were no great family dramas. I wasn't interested in hanging around street corners, or in birds and booze. I had an unhealthy obsession with cricket. After Lancashire's dismal 1986 season, Lever and cricket manager, Jack Bond, were sacked but not before Bond had offered me terms for the following season. Just before that, however, I had sat and passed the Cambridge University entrance exam and it seemed too good an opportunity to pass up. It was time to expand my horizons a little – professional cricket could wait a while.

2

CAMBRIDGE BLUE

Downing College, its stark neo-classical design striking a rebellious note against the architecture of the older and grander Cambridge colleges, was the start of all good things, a chance to put life on hold for three years and drift, blissfully suspended from reality. I didn't have to go to lectures, or do any work for that matter, at least for a while. I had my own lodgings with a bedder (a cleaner, to you and me), an old lady called Vy who tidied our mess with infinite patience and no little wisdom. The college had a pub opposite (the Prince Regent, or PR) and its own bar, which seemed oblivious to the licensing laws of the land. There was even the occasional, very occasional, decent-looking girl, who would be stared at and talked about at length like a rare and precious stamp. In other words, for the first time, I had a sense of personal responsibility and freedom. And there was, of course, the chance to play first-class cricket. What more could a young man want?

At the start, however, Cambridge was a strange, strange world. It helped that John Hopkins, the admissions tutor, had put all the northern, middle-class, grammar school boys together in L Block. There was Nick Broughton from Macclesfield, Julian Pickstone from Morley, in Yorkshire, and me. At least the three of us were in it together, unsure, full of insecurities and completely lacking in self-confidence in comparison with the boys from the grander, boarding schools of the south. They seemed to have a circle of ready-made friends, and swanned around in funny coloured blazers, at ease with the world and their place in it. They had already formed an exclusive club – the ironically named Exiles – to which only those from the eleven most exclusive public schools in the land would be admitted. Needless to say, we never were.

Freshers' week came and went in an alcoholic haze. In my naïveté I would turn up to cocktail parties punctually at the appointed hour, as I had been taught to do. Usually I was first to arrive and there was little choice but to drink the sickly cocktail mixture. Usually I was also the first to leave, always the worse for wear. At the Societies' Fair, a variety of clubs, from tiddlywinks to pooh-sticks to the famous Footlights, advertised their claims. There was too much choice, and in a complete absence of adventure we mostly headed for the PR, and then the college bar. Like most students, I bought a bike on the first day, and, like most students, I had it nicked on the same day. I never replaced it, and ran everywhere after that.

There were so many new things to get your head around. What, for example, did *in statu pupillari* mean (I never did find out), or *matriculation* for that matter? Well I was soon to find that out, for matriculation dinner was the first of our formal engagements after freshers' week had ended. Soberly attired in my newly acquired gown, I made my way to the college dining rooms. Matriculation, it seemed, signalled the start of one's quest for a degree, which would end, possibly, in a graduation ceremony three years later. The Master of Downing, John Butterfield, gave a welcoming speech. He alluded to the great opportunities on offer and warned of some of the dangers, especially, he said, 'the demon drink'. The dinner turned out to be a raucous affair and by its end the Master of Downing was standing, swaying, atop a long oak table, leading the students in drunken song.

I was fortunate to have John Butterfield, later Lord Butterfield and now sadly passed away, as master of my college. He was an eminent scholar, but also president of the university cricket, tennis and rowing clubs, and a triple blue in his time as a student. In my first year I was invited to captain England Young Cricketers in Sri Lanka, which involved missing most of my second term. Initially I was refused, but when I took the matter to Butterfield he brushed the problems aside. He allowed me to go provided that I made up time in the vacations and didn't fall behind in my studies. I was true to my word and so was allowed to captain England Young Cricketers in Australia the following year, again missing the Lent term. Mine was a most unusual degree.

I had gone to Cambridge for two things: to get a history degree and to play first-class cricket. If something of life happened to come with the package, that was all very well, but mainly I was there for the cricket. I had no idea what to expect of the standard of university cricket, and after I met the captain and secretary of the club for the first time, I was still in the dark. The captain, David Price (nicknamed 'Buddy' because he was rarely seen without a bottle of Budweiser in hand) was chubby and unathletic. The secretary, Alastair Scott, was so skinny it seemed hard to believe he would be leading our attack, as claimed. They quickly dispelled any notion I might have had that I would struggle to get in the team.

We took the responsibility of first-class cricket seriously, however, and pitched up at Cambridge two weeks ahead of term for pre-season training. Graham Saville, formerly of Essex, was our coach, his gruff, cockney rhyming slang a stark contrast to the rest of us. Mostly it rained, or snowed, and we idled the time away in the Salisbury Arms. David Fell was the senior blue. He was a decent batsman and as his girlfriend Charlie was a mirage in a desert of dismal-looking girls, he was a certain pick. He terrified the freshers with tales of Wayne Daniel's searing bouncers, and Graham Gooch's vast hits into the tennis courts.

Our first match in the early summer of 1987 was against Essex. They were full to the brim with international talent. They had not just Gooch, their captain, but also Foster, Lever, Miller, the ferocious Hugh Page from Transvaal in South Africa, and wily former England captain Keith Fletcher. Fenner's could be cold and desolate in April, but the cricketing gods blessed my first-class debut with a glorious spring day, and a sizeable crowd to boot.

Sadly, we, and the crowd, saw little of Gooch – he holed out to mid-off early on off the bowling of John Davidson, a mathematician, who was also a slow and accurate dobber off a long, winding run. Mostly the stars failed to shine at Fenner's. Once, that same year, David Gower had dreamily got to 47 and was looking bored when a message came out to the middle from his captain, Peter Willey. 'Concentrate!' it said, and Gower was lbw next over offering no shot. Instead the university matches offered a chance for the lesser lights to fill their boots full of runs and wickets. After all, the *Daily Telegraph* end-of-season averages failed to discern between 100 at Fenner's against Cambridge and one at Lord's against Middlesex.

Sometimes the stars even came off second best. Phil Tufnell came to Cambridge one year, and was bowling to a Scotsman called Geoff Dyer, who stuck his backside out in his stance more than any batsman I can recall. Tufnell hopped and skipped up to bowl and, as occasionally happened, the ball slipped out of his hand and ballooned to cover. Dyer stepped out and smashed the stationary delivery for 4. Tufnell was incensed and next ball he sent down a beamer. Dyer coolly stepped aside, opened the face of his bat as if he was giving slip-catching practice, and let it run off for 4 more.

On my memorable first day, I grabbed my maiden first-class wicket – a waist-high full toss that Chris Gladwin hoisted to deep backward square. He was the first of 108 sorry souls who succumbed to my leg-spin over the years – nor was he the last to fall to the cunning waist-high full toss. After that, Foster, Lever and Page reduced our first innings to nothing. In the middle of the carnage, I scored my first first-class runs in the style of so many to come – a thick inside edge through square-leg.

At 20–7 I was desperately in need of some support and found an ally in Graham Pointer. Alastair Scott came in at 77–9. He was barely able to pick up his bat, never mind swing it, but he did stick around for a while. 'Come on, Scotty, stay with me. I think I can get a hundred here!' But I was left on 73*, and was happy that I had made a good start; good enough, in fact, for Keith Fletcher to sledge me as I walked to the crease the second time around. 'Let's get this iwitating little pwick out,' he snarled, unable to pronounce his 'r's, and I took it as a compliment from the man who was to be my England coach five years later.

Not all of our matches were first class, and the so-called 'jazz-hat' games, against the likes of the Free Foresters and the Cryptics, provided some light relief. It didn't really matter that the standard of cricket was generally poor; it was a chance to meet some weird and wonderful people. The Free Foresters, or Free Filth as we termed them, were made up of various members of the Wingfield Digby clan. There was Andrew, the vicar, whose competitiveness and sledging belied his profession, and Michael his cousin, whose prized whippets were rarely under control. After one match, Michael's whippets bounded up the stairs of the Fenner's pavilion and into the long-room itself. Once there, they proceeded to defecate all over my shoes. Michael seemed delighted. 'Colin Cowdrey last week,' he cried, 'Michael Atherton this week. A former England captain and now a future England captain. How marvellous!'

Mostly our team was made up of ordinary cricketers. There was a smattering of potential first-class players, including Stephen James (Glamorgan), Rob Turner (Somerset) and me, but we were the exception. Mostly they were student lawyers or doctors of club-cricket standard. Damien Bush, a veterinary student, opened the bowling with slow, looping left-arm seamers in my third year. If Wasim Akram had the quickest arm in world cricket, our vet certainly had the slowest. Once his bowling arm reached the vertical, only gravity helped it on the way down.

Then there was 'Pumper' Pyman, an old Harrovian and merchant banker-to-be. He pitched up to make his debut against Essex carrying an ancient, leather cricket bag that resembled a chocolate éclair. He walked out to bat wearing his father's, or grandfather's, wicker pads, and with a towel stuffed down his trousers for a thigh-pad. He creased double with pain each time Ian Pont thundered a delivery into them. But it didn't matter; we had a wonderful time and were always acutely aware of our great privilege in being able to play first-class cricket.

At Cambridge I learnt the most important lesson of all in sport – temperament as much as natural ability is the key to success. Jonathan Atkinson came to Downing at the start of my second year. He was a Millfield prodigy, hugely talented, from a wonderful sporting family. He was a contracted Somerset player, and had already represented their first team, scoring 79 on his debut at seventeen against Northants. I knew Atkinson from the various schoolboy tournaments that we had both played in, and I knew him to be far and away the most naturally gifted player of our generation. He could bowl fast and he smashed the ball a mile, and I looked forward to his arrival at Cambridge where he was sure to strengthen our team.

But at Cambridge, Atkinson rarely got any runs and usually refused to bowl. To be fair, cricket was never really high on his list of priorities and I don't think he looks back with any regret. He partied hard for most of the time, and that, of course, is fair enough. But it was also clear when he bowled that he was suffering from a debilitating case of the yips. Later I saw Ian Folley, of Lancashire, and Keith Medlycott, of Surrey, go from being England bowlers to not being able to hit the cut strip. On one pre-season tour, Folley bowled consecutive deliveries that sailed over the wicket-keeper's head. Whenever I tried to persuade Atkinson to bowl, the pain and torture on his face was such that, in the end, I gave up trying. Who knows the reasons why – pressure, expectation, your own and others', or lack of self-confidence? The results were painful, however, and affected

Atkinson's batting to the point that he looked a shadow of the cricketer we envied at fifteen. Of course, I didn't know at this stage whether I had the mental toughness to succeed at the highest level, but as I returned to Lancashire each July for the last three months of the season, I was sure to find out.

In 1987 Lancashire were about to emerge from the doldrums, from a decade of unrest and underachievement. The catalyst was the captain/coach partnership of David Hughes and Alan Ormrod, and it was helped by the introduction of a group of young and talented players such as Warren Hegg and me. Hughes was a strict disciplinarian, his fierceness a good contrast with Ormrod's more mellow approach. After Cambridge it was a shock to discover things like dress codes existed. Hughes demanded that no jeans be worn before, during or after the hours of play. It necessitated a new wardrobe for me. Middlesex also had this ruling although the suspicion among their players was that it was because their captain, Mike Gatting, could not find a pair to fit him.

After the Varsity match in 1987, I went virtually straight into the Lancashire first team. My debut was against Warwickshire at Southport. I had no means of transport so I had to prevail upon Mum to drive me there. I was so nervous and keen to get to the ground and so worried that I was going to be late that I barked at her all the way. I was the first to arrive. We won the match in two days, by ten wickets, and it sparked a run of success that ensured we finished second in the championship that year. Things struck me as only slightly different from Cambridge: the standard was a bit better, the pitches generally quicker, and with points on offer everything was taken a little more seriously, although not much. But I had to contend with the tricks of the gnarled old pros. Warwickshire's spinner was Norman Gifford, a man who had been around as long as the sands of time, and whose own debut took place before I was born. I made 53 in our first innings and faced Gifford for much of the time. His party trick was to cut short his run, and turn to bowl before you were ready. Twice he did this and twice I pulled away, and his already ruddy face turned purple in frustration.

Lancashire was another dressing room to get used to, one in which, unlike Cambridge, I had to work hard to gain the respect of my peers. At the start, it proved to be difficult. The younger players were resentful of the fact that I marched straight into the first team. Even worse, the first-team dressing room was inhabited by players I had watched while I was growing up – Hughes and Jack Simmons, the draughtsman turned cricketer still plying his trade well into his forties. There was the odd newcomer such as Gehan Mendis, the mysterious loner, who didn't buy into the team thing at all and drove Hughes to distraction.

The Lancashire players, in general, were suspicious of my university background. Most came from the leagues. The Lancashire League had a proud history and was the main source of talent and anybody with a further education was sneered at. Kevin Hayes, of Oxford and Lancashire, was given the nickname Two Heads while one Lancashire player, early on in my career, daubed the sobriquet 'FEC' on my locker. Later it was assumed to stand for Future England Captain. In fact, it stood for Fucking Educated Cunt. It was clear to me that I was going to have to work hard to earn my stripes at Old Trafford, so I played down my Cambridge education as much as I could, and emphasised my own northern and league-based roots.

Neil Fairbrother took me under his wing and warned me of all the potential pitfalls. In particular he cautioned me against the all-powerful clique of Paul Allott, Graeme Fowler and Mike Watkinson. Fowler and Allott, as the two longest serving internationals in the team, bestrode the dressing room like colossi, while Mike Watkinson's acerbic tongue was enough for him to hang on to their coat tails. Fairbrother warned me that they could make life difficult for a young player, and he told me they were likely to test me out.

The test came early on, during my first Roses match at Headingley, my third game for the club. During lunch on the second day, I had put some wet clothes in the drying machine. Paul Allott had bowled a long spell, and without saying anything he slung out my clothes and replaced them with his own damp and sweaty whites. I got up and repeated the act. He looked at me quizzically, with raised eyebrows, although nothing was said, and I assumed that would be the end of the matter.

Later that day, he and Fowler invited me to a party where, they said, lots of girls would be present. It was less of an invitation and more of an order, so I meekly got into the back of Allott's car and awaited my fate. We went to the Bradford Novotel, of all places, and after parking the car we went to the bar. We sat there for a while, drinking. Soon, Allott excused himself to go to the toilet, and shortly afterwards Fowler followed. I sat there for a while, and then suddenly realised what was happening. I had no money and no means of getting back and I sprinted out of the hotel, just in time to catch Allott's car leaving the compound. I took their message on board, and their prank in good humour. I also had a good season, becoming the first player since Paul Parker to score 1,000 runs in my debut first-class year, so I earned their respect on and off the field. Allott in fact, as vice-captain, consistently fought my corner in selection. After that there were no more problems. Playing for Lancashire was the best of times.

This idyllic mix of cricket and studies lasted for three years until my departure from Cambridge with a 2:1 in history. History was the perfect degree for me, involving as it did very few formal lectures and plenty of reading. These days, my tastes are more modern fiction than fifteenth-century English gentry. I am not sure whether my knowledge of medieval history has been of any relevance at all. I suppose my third-year paper on the Black Death stood me in good stead for Curtly Ambrose in Trinidad in 1994.

Later, some said that Cambridge had been bad for my cricket. The team, they said, was over-reliant on my batting and the pressure to score runs resulted in a risk-free approach and so I failed to develop my game fully. Captaining a team for two years that had little or no chance of winning, they said, scarred my captaincy forever with a negative and defensive outlook.

I don't agree with either sentiment. As a player you always adapt your game to the team's needs and just because we had little or no chance of winning doesn't mean that we played to lose. Indeed the Combined Universities team of 1989, under my captaincy, became the first non-county team ever to make the quarter-finals of the Benson & Hedges Cup. We would have won that, too, if Nasser Hussain, as I am fond of reminding him, had not run out of puff after scoring a brilliant 100. Besides, Cambridge was good for me in other respects. Before going there, I had, in truth, taken cricket too seriously. As a teenager, I was inconsolable every time I got out. Cambridge taught me to relax and gave me a sense of perspective, and that, above all, is the key to longevity and success in the neurotic world of professional sport.

I returned to Lancashire full time in July 1989. My graduation from university had sparked off a frenzy of garden parties and summer balls and I needed sharpening up. My first game back was against Worcestershire. Peter Marron's lightning quick pitch, the presence of Graham Dilley leading Worcester's attack and a first-innings duck jolted me out of garden-party mode. I scored a gutsy 59 second time around before I fell to a Botham outswinger. For some of the time I batted with Mike Watkinson. He later went on to play for England, but in 1989 his batting technique was rudimentary and he struggled with Graham Dilley's short ball. Each time the ball pitched, Watkinson let out a premature grunt. He knew, I knew and Dilley knew that each ball was going to hit him in the ribs and there was nothing in his technique to prevent it. It was a steep learning curve for him, and for me, as the pitches at Old Trafford were increasingly far removed from the slow, low surfaces I was used to at Fenner's.

During that match I was aware of the watchful eye of Micky Stewart, the England manager, but I had no thoughts or immediate expectation of playing for England. I was looking no further than cementing my place in the Lancashire team and pushing, maybe, for a place on the A tour that winter. However, a second rebel tour to South Africa was announced in midsummer; it reduced an already beaten England team to its bones and changed all that.

With the Ashes gone, the media clamoured for young and fresh faces. It was a wonderful thing, being 'young and promising'. Mistakes were overlooked and occasionally even turned in your favour, and 'potential' swamped reality. My actual returns for the summer were moderate but that was conveniently ignored. At Portsmouth, Neil Fairbrother scored a brilliant 100, smashing Malcolm Marshall to all parts, and yet it was my modest 37 that stole the headlines the next day. Those who said the media had no power to influence selection were entirely wrong.

At Cheltenham, Lancashire played Gloucestershire and it was to be the last match before I was selected for England. On the coach journey down, all the talk was of Courtney Walsh but after I played his first three deliveries with ease, I thought maybe my team-mates had exaggerated the danger. The next ball hit me flush on the head before I had moved and I quickly revised my opinion. He rolled us over by lunch on the first day and the game had gone.

At lunch on the second day, I took a call in the bar from Ted Dexter informing me that I had been selected for the Fifth Test at Trent Bridge and that an invitation would be sent in the post. An invitation! Was I to reply or not? I was startled and conveyed my news to the barman. 'I'm pretty surprised, too,' came the reply and he continued to pull a pint.

Afterwards, I did my first radio interview and, presaging the next ten years, it went disastrously. I called Christopher Martin-Jenkins 'Martin' throughout; he expertly dismissed my nerves as the after-effects of a Walsh bouncer.

I accepted the congratulations of my Lancashire team-mates although I suspected they felt it was a premature promotion. No matter, I did too. During the match I giggled like a naughty schoolboy when Dexter Fitton mis-fielded off Mike Watkinson's bowling. 'I bet you're not laughing like that next Thursday at Trent Bridge,' growled Paul Allott. Well, I wouldn't be, but I didn't know that then. Instead, as the team coach rolled on to the next match in Chesterfield, I drove Graham Lloyd's battered Capri back to Manchester. In anticipation of my England debut I was excited, nervous and worried – and completely unprepared.

3

ENGLAND CALLS

On 9 August 1989, the day before the Fifth Test against Australia at Trent Bridge, the England captain David Gower threw me a plastic bag with an England cap and two sweaters in it, and said nonchalantly, 'Here, you'd better have these then.' Unlike today, there was an utter lack of ceremony. Now the chairman of selectors presents a cap to a new player on the morning of the match, and the debutant gets the chance to puff out his chest and preen himself in front of a large crowd before the grim realities of Test cricket set in. Nevertheless, despite that, there was no feeling of anti-climax. I was about to realise a cherished ambition and, more than that, I was being given my cap by my boyhood hero, the man my father had told me to watch and learn from in the front room of our house eleven years earlier. I was a month out of university and nothing was more unexpected.

Prior to this, I had been to just one day's Test cricket as a spectator, during the Headingley Test of 1981. But, more recently, I had been called to the last three days of the Fourth Test at Old Trafford as twelfth man. I thought nothing of it but it was clearly a move to enable me to 'taste the atmosphere'. I knew none of the England players at that point and when I bumped into Graham Gooch he offered his hand and said, 'Hello, master.' I was thrilled as I thought the term indicated his respect for me as a young player with a certain reputation. Later

I was deflated when I heard him calling the dressing-room attendant by the same name. I thought it must be a southern phrase, used in much the same way as a northerner uses 'mate' when he hasn't got the faintest clue who you are.

I changed next to Gus Fraser in the small back room at Old Trafford. It was where my Lancashire locker was at the time so I was on familiar territory. It was a depressing Test match to watch because Australia's victory meant they reclaimed the Ashes after ten long years or more. The euphoria in the Australian dressing room far outweighed the desolation in England's, however, for this was an already beaten and demoralised England team. Some of the players had already signed for the rebel tour to South Africa, and their minds appeared to be elsewhere. I went back to Old Trafford the next day and England's dressing room was cold and bare, while Australia's bore the scars of victory – the lockers were sticky with champagne and there were discarded corks and empty beer cans everywhere.

I remember sitting with Gus on the last day, watching the television as England were batting, and suddenly the names of the rebel party were announced. Three of the rebels were playing in this match – Neil Foster, John Emburey and Tim Robinson – and nine had played in the current series. Gus watched the screen, astonished, and mumbled, 'This is unbelievable. Surely playing for your country is meant to mean more than this.' We looked at each other and shook our heads.

Earlier in the match, I listened to David Gower giving a lunchtime team-talk in his laconic way. The morning session had not gone to plan, he said. Indeed, England had leaked runs like a rusty tug. Gower stressed the need to start the next session well and he asked for maximum effort. The first ball after lunch trickled down to third man, big Gus loped around, stuck out a size 13 and the ball bobbled over his foot and went for 4. I noted Mr Gower's reaction.

Later, England's greatest all-rounder Ian Botham waltzed down the wicket to the Queensland leg-spinner Trevor Hohns, had a mighty slog, and was bowled. If he hadn't been bowled he would have been stumped by the acreage of his farm in Northumberland. Apparently, he came in and said he'd got his bat stuck in his pad. Graham Gooch looked up and asked him, 'Where was your pad Beefy, on yer fackin' head?' I was thankful not to have been around the dressing room then.

Amid the depression I had my first sighting of Ted Dexter, the chairman of selectors, who was being given a torrid time by the media that summer. The first morning I was there, he was working with Tim Curtis, the Worcestershire player who opened the batting in that Test. Dexter, dressed in a pin-striped suit and white Reebok trainers, was throwing underarm balls to Curtis from about a dozen yards away, much as you would throw a ball to a toddler. Dexter would throw Curtis sets of three balls and Curtis, bat in hand, had to leave one, defend one and attack one in that order. 'Leave, defend, attack' came the Dexter mantra. It seemed a very odd practice to me, and a strange way to treat an England opening batsman on the morning of the match. It was not the only eccentric theory Dexter had, as I came to discover later.

Preparations for Test cricket were entirely different in 1989. Now there are two, sometimes three, days of nets to prepare, a plethora of specialist coaches, and nutritional advice and video analysis is routine. Back then, you pitched up the day before the Test, had a perfunctory net and played the next day, with little thought or planning. Often players came straight from a Tuesday finish in a championship match. It was a system that could only fail to produce Test-class fast bowlers, whose need for rest is paramount. The dearth of Test-class, English fast bowlers between Willis and Gough is testimony to the inadequacy of the three-day county system during that period. How good would Graham Dilley have been with central contracts?

On the day before my debut at Trent Bridge, all that was far from my mind. I was only interested in meeting the team and settling in. Botham, especially, made me welcome. I think he had seen in the Worcester match a few weeks earlier that I had some guts if nothing else. The team for Trent Bridge was a motley crew, haphazardly put together, partly due to the rebel tour and the fact that Gooch had asked the selectors to be excluded from the Test. He had been having great problems with Terry Alderman throughout the summer, and he wanted to work on his technique away from the pressure of international cricket. Devon Malcolm was another new boy and he spearheaded as inexperienced and toothless an attack as England has ever put out.

Malcolm went on to fashion a successful international career but at this stage he looked anything but an England cricketer. He had no formal run-up. He just charged in and hurled the ball as quickly as possible, with just as little guile. At the start of his international career he was also quite the most hopeless fielder you could wish to see. Micky Stewart kept Devon for extra catching practice at the end of each session. Devon would charge around, thick-set glasses strapped to his head, his arms and hands optimistically pointed upwards, like the Madonna, usually grasping at thin air as the balls dropped unattended to the ground. He did, however, have one priceless commodity – pace.

The night before the match the traditional team dinner was held, and I was introduced to many of the pre-Test rituals. The captain gave a brief speech and then toasted the Queen. With the Ashes already gone and the team in disarray, the senior players were in no mood for a glum affair and Gower ordered the wine list. He asked me if I wanted a glass and, inexperienced as I was, I said yes. I savoured the rich tannins and in a brief, smug and self-satisfied moment, I felt I had arrived – and then Gower asked me for £50. I remembered in future to avoid drinking wine with Gower unless I was flush full of win bonus at the time.

At the end of my first day in Test cricket, Australia were 301–0, Mark Taylor and Geoff Marsh had undefeated 100s and I had cramp. I found the intensity far greater than the cricket I had experienced thus far. Even though I had done nothing on my first day, I was exhausted and that was the reason for the cramp. The second day didn't improve much but by tea I had bowled my first over in Test cricket – five leg-breaks and a googly, and a nod of approval from Mark Taylor. All were on the spot and that was as good as my bowling ever got for England.

I had to wait until after lunch on the third day for my first innings in Test cricket. I was batting at number three, but was quickly in. The first ball from Alderman flew down the leg side on a fullish length. For a medium-pace bowler Alderman had a long run-up, which gave a batsman too much time to think. At delivery he had a disconcerting grin and this combination, added to my inevitable nerves, meant I moved too soon at my second ball. It was straight and full and, as I had to play around my front pad, I missed it – I looked up to see the tall, sombre figure of Nigel Plews raise his finger and that was that. I was on my way back to the pavilion, joining the likes of Hutton and Gooch, who had also recorded ducks on their debuts.

England followed on and David Gower decided to open second time around. No doubt he wanted to lead from the front. He asked me if I wanted to drop down the order. I insisted I was fine where I was and Martyn Moxon jumped at the chance to move, which I thought strange. Despite the change, I was in during the second over after David had left a straight ball from Geoff Lawson. Lawson was a notorious sledger – his sledging had no overtones of humour or irony – but he gifted me a leg-stump half-volley which delivered me from a pair and brought my first runs in Test cricket.

I scored 47, not particularly attractive runs but 47 nonetheless. It was a start. I remember getting a weird delivery out of the front of the hand from Trevor Hohns. This is how inexperienced I was – I had never seen a flipper and didn't know what it was until that moment, and even then I only knew that it was something different. At least I could say I was watching his hand carefully. Of my debut, Ian Chappell commented that he liked the look of my leg-breaks but not my batting – hardly the impression I wanted to make. I hope the Academy which is now in place, will ensure that the next crop of Test players is not as naive and ignorant as I was.

At The Oval for the Sixth and final Test, David Gower was under constant scrutiny from the media. I felt for him because he was leading a nothing team and was clearly uncomfortable in his relationship with Micky Stewart. Only later did it emerge that Gatting had been Stewart's preferred choice for the captaincy that summer.

During the match I had my first taste of Australian sledging. They tended to pick on the youngest, or those they considered the weakest. Merv Hughes probably thought I was both young and weak and he snarled at me constantly through his ludicrous moustache. He was all bristle and bullshit and I couldn't make out what he was saying, except that every sledge ended with 'arsewipe'. I smiled and shrugged and saved my energy.

I made a point of socialising with Hughes after the match. I always feel that if there is an opponent who is trying to intimidate you, it helps to get to know him. In a way, it helps to humanise him. When I got to know Hughes I found him extremely affable, in a cuddly toy sort of way, and that helped me in our battles on the field. Afterwards I was able to laugh off his sledging. Everything else I did during the match, however, confirmed my opinion and everyone else's that I was not yet ready for Test cricket.

During the first innings, for example, as Australia and Dean Jones were piling on runs, David Gower threw me the ball before tea, without prior notice, to bowl an over of leg-breaks. I was totally unprepared and as a result bowled Jones a head-high full toss and a delivery that bounced three times. In that over I took the village green to the Test arena and the embarrassment stayed with me for a long time after that. I was never comfortable bowling for England again, despite the fact I could bowl passably for Lancashire.

All in all, my first taste of Test cricket had been an uninspiring experience. Something I had long dreamed of had been a bit of a let-down. I remember catching David Boon at slip (my first catch for England) and hearing the roar of the crowd. I turned to the rest of the slip cordon with clenched fists, ready to accept their congratulations but there was a muted response. It was both that I had done moderately and that the England team seemed to be short on pride, passion and performance, especially in comparison with Australia. One senior player said to me during that match, 'You play your first for love and the rest for money.' It summed up our attitude. I remembered that statement for a long time and I vowed never to feel like that.

I returned to Lancashire for the end of the season. At Scarborough, during the Roses match, the squads for the winter were announced. I missed the main tour to the West Indies and was selected instead for the A tour to Kenya and Zimbabwe. When the news came through, Lancashire were batting and David Bairstow, for some reason, was busy nailing Neil Fairbrother's cricket case to the wooden-slatted floor. He stopped, looked up and said to me, 'That's the best thing that could have happened to you, kid,' and continued to nail Fairbrother's bag to the floor. He was probably thinking of his own experiences in the Caribbean some years before and he was probably right.

Before the A tour, I bought a flat in Didsbury. It was my first home and I kept it for ten years. In that time it was as much a home to Lancashire's homeless and divorced as it was to me. Invariably, during any winter abroad, two or three Lancashire players would have the keys to the flat. One winter I returned to find love notes systematically placed around the flat – one in an eggcup, one under a pillow and one in the toaster all ready to pop up – but I never found out who the culprit was.

Micky Stewart had organised weekly sessions with Geoffrey

Boycott for the batsmen going to the West Indies and I was invited to join the likes of Nasser Hussain and Rob Bailey for some coaching. Graham Gooch was also there and I marvelled at the dedication and enthusiasm of this thirty-six year old who'd already played seventy-three Tests. Boycott helped him to reorganise his technique, which had been dismantled by Terry Alderman that summer. He spoke to Gooch in exactly the same fashion as he did the rest of us – disparagingly – and Gooch soaked it up. It spoke volumes for Gooch's desire to succeed, even at that age, and I think showed a lack of ego and a humility that was rare in a sportsman of his stature.

I had never met Boycott before. Initially, I was struck by how fit and strong he looked and by his strange hair implants, like a farmer's field at seeding time, layered with military precision. I was taken aback by his bluntness, or rudeness, depending on your point of view. Nor did he hold back in his criticisms. As he constantly said, 'If you want nice things said to you, go to your mother for coaching.'

Nevertheless, the sessions were crucial in giving me the chance to succeed at the highest level. I had never really thought about batting before and I knew very little. It was the first time I had heard someone with a Test pedigree talk about batting. He talked forcefully and knowledgeably about building an innings and facing fast bowlers in an intimidating atmosphere.

He got the fast bowlers to bowl short and fast off 17 yards and I worked with him on one technical change. Previously I had stood absolutely still at the crease, and on delivery, without thinking, I moved my back leg outside leg stump with the result that I was a little closed off to the bowler and didn't hit enough in the V. We worked on moving into position slightly earlier and getting my back leg more across to off stump. It may sound like a small change, but it felt a huge one. The advantage was that it gave me more time to play the ball and got me into a better position from which to play it and then play it straighter. It was hard work, but it was fun and worth every moment.

Boycott was extremely professional. He wore his England whites every day as if he was the one about to open the batting and he made sure we all had our own videos for analysis. At one session, he gathered us all around to show Nasser's batting video from the week before. The lights went out and a hush descended as we prepared to hear a sermon from the great man. He pressed the play button and on came the latest episode of 'Neighbours' (Nasser's girlfriend was a keen watcher of the Australian soap). 'Bloody university students,' Boycott muttered. He was chippy about university students.

Looking back, the only disadvantage of the sessions that I can see was that afterwards I had a tendency to think too much about batting, especially if I was out of form. Sometimes it is best just to play naturally and trust your talent. Having said that, it was probably the only time in the whole of my career when I was able to work on technical aspects of my game for a lengthy period. After that winter, I played non-stop for England until my retirement. It is one of the problems of continuous cricket – there is little opportunity to right the faults that, almost unknowingly, creep into your game.

The A team left for Kenya and Zimbabwe in early 1990 and, in the words of Derek Pringle, 'we cut a swathe of goodwill' through Africa under the captaincy of Mark Nicholas and the stewardship of Keith Fletcher. Mark was a thoughtful and enthusiastic captain and very good company although he tended towards hyperbole. On seeing a cheetah with a fresh kill in a Nairobi game park, he was heard to proclaim that it was 'the greatest day of my life!' He repeated the claim twice more before the trip was through – on seeing the Victoria Falls and on meeting Robert Mugabe. As I said, he tended to hyperbole. I was next in line to Mark when he was introduced to Zimbabwe's President. 'Will the election be close, Sir?' he asked. 'Not really,' replied Mugabe. 'It's just a matter of political buffoonery we've set up in this country.'

The Kenya leg was a non-event as half the team contracted salmonella poisoning in a Chinese restaurant and we had to cancel a one-day game in Nairobi. I roomed with Derek Pringle. I knew him vaguely from Cambridge where you would occasionally see him wandering about, wearing an exotic green poncho. I developed a strong friendship with him that remains to this day although it didn't extend to looking after me when I too contracted food poisoning. Pringle was born in Kenya and he was keen to renew old acquaintances.

In Zimbabwe the opposition were moderate and the cricket was often dull. Nevertheless, it was an important opportunity for me and I began to put my new technique into practice. I was pleased when I scored 100s in the first two international matches. In Bulawayo, two locals were clearly unimpressed by my batting. 'Hey, man, tell us when the rest day is and we can go and have some fun,' shouted one, and even I realised that I might have been scoring too slowly.

On the eve of the third international, news filtered through that Graham Gooch had broken his hand in the West Indies and they needed a replacement. My name was on the shortlist but as luck would have it I had pulled a groin muscle that morning at the Harare Sports Club. I tried to fool the physio, Dave Roberts, but he was having none of it and instead David Smith the Sussex left-hander was called up. I missed my chance and I missed the final match of the tour. It was disappointing but I had achieved what I set out to do on that tour, and I was ready for another crack at Test cricket.

I began the 1990 season in good form, helped no doubt by the TCCB's directives that reduced the seam on the balls and lowered the blades on the groundsman's mower thus providing less green pitches than the year before. This double whammy meant it was a golden summer for batsmen. I was batting at number three for Lancashire and scored 100 in the Benson & Hedges competition against Hampshire and a big 100 in the championship at The Oval. An injury to Wayne Larkins came at the right time for me and at Horsham, where we were playing Sussex, I learned that I was to open the batting for England with Graham Gooch in the first Test of the summer against New Zealand.

For the first time in a long time there were three Lancashire players in the Test team – Neil Fairbrother, Phillip DeFreitas and me. I travelled up from Horsham to Trent Bridge with Neil Fairbrother. The early omens were worrying – we bumped into the back of Micky Stewart's car in the middle of Nottingham while looking for the hotel, and when I got to my room I found a yellow rubber duck in my bathroom. That's not good if you are a superstitious cricketer. Each day I put the duck in the rubbish bin and each day on my return, the cleaner had put it back in my bathroom.

I was apprehensive about opening with Gooch for the first time. I hardly knew him and I had got the impression the summer before that he didn't really rate me – a feeling that was confirmed when I was left out of the West Indies tour party. As we walked out together at Trent Bridge, I was not to know that it would be the start of a wonderful relationship. Our partnership started badly – first ball, John Hampshire raised his hand above his head in his peculiar antipodean style, and Gooch had gone lbw to Hadlee. In the first innings of the next Test I was bowled for 0 by Danny Morrison. We had yet to register any kind of partnership in two attempts.

It was third time lucky at Edgbaston, and our opening partnership of 170 there was the best by an England opening pair for three and a half years. After that, we established a fruitful relationship; for average runs per innings, and taking 2,000 runs as a qualification, we stand fifth best on the all-time list. Good opening partnerships revolve around contrast – right- and left-handers, aggressive players and accumulators. Gooch was a powerful and aggressive player who scored mainly down the ground. I was more of a touch player, who accumulated runs and used the pace of the ball to score. We also ran extremely well together, always alert for the quick single. By the end, as with all good partnerships, there was little need for communication – just a look and a nod and we set off for a single. There was, I think, only one run-out between us.

It helped me, of course, to be batting at the other end from such a fine player. During the Boycott sessions, I was able to listen to a great Test match opening batsman, but now I was able to watch a craftsman at work, and I had the best seat in the house, 22 yards away. During the next three years, Gooch was, statistically, the best player in world cricket. At the crease he was ultra-determined. His head was always slightly bobbing and, through clenched teeth, he mumbled stock phrases in his trademark high-pitched voice: 'keep it going', 'make it count', 'don't give it away', and 'looking good'. As captain of England, Gooch always looked good, rarely gave it away and nearly always made it count, and he was a joy to bat with.

Gooch's early dismissal at Trent Bridge, therefore, was a shock, but I was in good form and felt good for a score. A succession of batsmen came and went on a slow, seaming wicket against some steady bowling, but I prospered, albeit slowly. It was pretty grim stuff, and thankfully there were few people there to witness it. Trevor Franklin dropped me in the 50s at third slip and I was determined to make him pay for the error. Throughout the nervous 90s Jack Russell was my partner. I was always fairly relaxed at the crease. Jack was not and he reminded me of the excitable canine whose name he shares – all wild eyes and panting breath. Martin Sneddon offered up the long hop that took me to my first Test century. In my eagerness, I nearly snatched at it and cut it to backward point, but I looked up to see it speeding to the cover boundary. Jack seemed far more thrilled than I was and rushed to congratulate me. Despite the grey day and the sparse crowd, it was a moment to treasure. Against an attack led by Richard Hadlee, I felt in scoring 151 I had achieved something worthwhile.

I got a duck in the next Test at Lord's, however, and it was the start of an indifferent relationship I came to have with the home of cricket. I never particularly enjoyed batting on the Lord's slope (the ground has a drop of six feet from one side to the other) – at the Nursery End I felt I was constantly reeling backwards and at the Pavilion End I thought I was going to topple forwards. Batting demands balance, and I never felt balanced at Lord's.

The rest of my first full series in England colours went in fairytale fashion although I still occasionally showed my inexperience. After doing the hard part in the second innings at Lord's I got myself out to the part-time spin of Andrew Jones, and in the Third Test at Edgbaston I really ought to have got one century and possibly two. I settled for an 80 and a 70 and it represented the start of a poor conversion rate of 50s to 100s, a problem that was to dog me throughout my Test career. At that point I think it was possibly because of limited ambition or maybe that I couldn't believe things were going so well.

The Edgbaston Test, and the series in general, established my credentials as a Test batsman and showed that I had a safe pair of hands in the slips. It was enough to get me the England man of the series award. I had played a big role in my first Test match victory for England and a big part in securing my first series win as an England player. It was marred for me only by the fact that my mate Neil Fairbrother could not transfer his county form to the Test-match arena. It was another early lesson for me that temperament is the most important quality in a Test player. Sometimes ultra-aggressive players such as Fairbrother needed to be encouraged to play their natural game and it needed patience for them to deliver.

My second stab at Test cricket had gone decidedly better than the first. More than that, I was part of a settled side that looked as if it might go places. The pride and professionalism so lacking the previous year had returned. I did not feel established in the team but I was on my way, and the second half of the summer, against India, provided the perfect opportunity to consolidate my claims.

4

INJURY AND ILLNESS

It was 10 August 1990, as beautiful a day at Old Trafford as was possible, with views clear through to the Peak District and beyond, and the 100 I had scored in front of my home crowd the day before against India ought to have been the highlight of my brief Test career to date. Instead, the pain I was feeling down my buttocks and my legs as Laurie Brown, the England physiotherapist, took us for our daily stretch, heralded the start of an altogether more troubling period.

The New Zealand series in the first half of the summer had boosted my confidence and I had gone into the Old Trafford Test match against India, the second of a three-match series, in wonderful form. The game before the Old Trafford Test had been the Roses match at Headingley. I had scored 64 and had never hit the ball better. I told all my friends who liked a flutter that I was going to get 100 in the Test, as strong a feeling as I have ever had before or since. I told them to get on the sure thing.

Besides, the Indian attack lacked the cutting edge you would expect from a Test-match team. Kapil Dev was past his best; Gooch described him as a 'lovely bowler'. His slow, swinging half-volleys arrived on to the drive of the bat with wonderful regularity, and I was in no mood to pay due deference to his reputation. He was no longer the Haryana Hurricane, more a gentle breeze that blew down from his native Chandigarh.

Manoj Prabhakar was equally ineffectual and none of the spinners, Narendra Hirwani, Anil Kumble, a gangling and bespectacled debutant, or Ravi Shastri, could get any response from a pitch that was devoid of all gremlins.

The pitch was of particular concern to Graham Gooch and Micky Stewart. They had asked for a quick and bouncy strip, the type for which Old Trafford was becoming famed. There was a suspicion that the Indian batsmen were a touch shy and they wanted to encourage our pace attack while at the same time nullifying India's spin trio. Lancashire's amiable and normally first-rate groundsman Peter Marron was usually happy to oblige, but in this instance he had forgotten which of his strips he had relaid and which he had not. Optimistically, and with all the precision of a blind man sticking the tail on the donkey, he began to roll out a centre pitch. It quickly became apparent, as the first ball of the game bounced through to the keeper twice, that he had chosen incorrectly. Gooch's shoulders sagged and he glared at me as if I, as a Lancastrian, had some control over the pitches at Old Trafford. The pitch was old and devoid of all pace and bounce.

The match descended into a run feast. There were six centuries scored in total. The biggest was from Mohammad Azharuddin but the loudest cheer was reserved for the home-boy and I became only the second Lancastrian to score a century on home turf. All were outshone, however, by the 100 from the then seventeen-year-old Sachin Tendulkar who gave an early exhibition of his precocious talent.

On the second morning of the match, Laurie Brown took the daily stretch. As we began to move sideways I felt a sudden sharp, stabbing pain in my buttocks in an area called the sacroiliac joint. I mentioned it and we thought no more of it. The pain was there sporadically for the rest of the summer but was as easily managed as India whom we beat 1–0 in a dull series.

The Australian tour the following winter was my first with the senior England team and before it we incurred the displeasure of the TCCB by playing two exhibition matches against the West Indies in New York and Toronto. New York was vast and wonderful and we had quite a time. Facing Malcolm Marshall, however, on a makeshift wicket in a stock-car racing stadium in the Bronx was nobody's idea of fun although it had to be done. I missed the match with back pain. A quack was called and he manipulated my back. The cracks I heard and felt filled me with foreboding.

The start of the Ashes tour coincided with a downturn in the team's and my fortunes. In the traditional opening match at Lilac Hill I got nought, dropped a slip catch and stepped aside for David Gower to catch a steeper. Unfortunately he did the same and the ball fell tamely to the ground between us. A bad start. I could not get a run early on and in Tasmania I reached my nadir when I succumbed to Chris Matthews, a left-arm seamer who was somewhat erratic. One Australian journalist described my efforts as having all the style 'of a tired and over-worked gravedigger'. Clearly, I was making a poor impression.

Graham Gooch was becoming increasingly infuriated with what he saw as the unwillingness of some of his squad to prac-tise, and when they did, it was without any of the enthusiasm or dedication he expected from international sportsmen. In my case, it was not so much that I didn't want to practise but that my body was unable, so stiff and sore did I feel each morning. As the tour wore on, I expressed my concerns to Laurie Brown and during a one-day international in Perth we went to see Philip Hardcastle, an eminent back specialist. Hardcastle had a lot of experience with back pain in cricketers because the concrete-like surface in Perth placed great strains on fast bowlers.

I lay on the bed and he prodded and poked at my back. I explained that the pain was in the sacroiliac joint. 'Can't be there,' he said in a gruff, no-nonsense and typically Australian manner. 'Only pregnant women get pain there. It must be referred from further up your back.' Since I was sure I was neither female nor pregnant, I took him at his word.

He took a series of scans and X-rays and pronounced himself satisfied that they showed a stress fracture at L5. He recommended that I take the scans to Jon Webb in Nottingham on my return to England. I struggled through the tour with the pain coming and going. The only time it inconvenienced me greatly was in the Fourth Test in Adelaide where I hoped for most of the game that the ball would come nowhere near me. Strangely, I played one of my better innings of the tour in a fourth-innings run chase.

I went to see Mr Webb on my return, and on the same day Angus Fraser forlornly hobbled in. He had been having trouble with his hip in the latter stages of the Ashes tour, following a marathon spell in Melbourne when he picked up six Australian wickets on the flattest of pitches – still one of the best performances I have seen from an England bowler. His hip problem was to keep him out of Test cricket for a further two years and we were a sorry sight that day in Nottingham – two young sportsmen in some degree of pain and unsure of our long-term futures.

It brought me enormous pleasure to recall Fraser to the Test scene two years later and to see him bowl England to victory over Australia. As well as having great respect for his ability, I had struck up a firm and lasting friendship with him. Some said we were made for each other, with our lugubrious features and no-nonsense attitude. His humour is sharp and dry and I thought he was great company on tour and our injuries brought us closer together, as shared experiences often do.

He was a fine bowler for England. He could give the impression of a man who didn't enjoy his work and I always think of Martin Johnson's description of him running in to bowl, as if he had a pair of braces strapped to the sightscreen. He made it look such hard work, but as he often said to me, 'You batsmen just don't understand. It is bloody hard work.' Fraser viewed batsmen with distaste. In the same way as rugby union forwards sneer at the backs, he thought batsmen were fancy-dans, quick to take the glory while the bowlers toiled away. He always seemed to be stood in the middle, hands on hips, cursing his misfortune and kicking an almighty sod out of the pitch in frustration; but he loved bowling and loved the challenge of bowling to good batsmen on good wickets, and he never shirked a contest.

I maintain, although he doesn't agree, that he was never quite the same bowler after his injury. Afterwards, his 'nip' could go missing for a while and he invariably needed something in the pitch to get his rewards. That he was still a match-winning bowler for England many times after his return from injury is testament to his quality and indicates how good he might have been but for that hip problem in 1991.

In the surgeon's room I told Mr Webb that although I was able to play I was experiencing daily stiffness and pain. We decided to see how the summer went. It went badly. In fact, it started well and I put in a match-winning performance in the first one-day international at Edgbaston against the West Indies. We whitewashed them in the one-day games and I won the England man of the series award. Moreover, just as the first ball of the West Indies innings was about to be bowled at Lord's, Graham Gooch halted proceedings, called me over, and told me I was the new vice-captain. I wasn't sure how to take the news, so I trotted back to first slip and thought no more of it. It wasn't really mentioned again, and but for one instance at The Oval, Graham never asked my advice. I didn't blame him at all although it didn't do much to dispel the 'FEC' tag.

For the rest of the summer I endured a horror trot. I wasn't the first English batsman to come unstuck against the West Indies but it was disappointing because it was my biggest challenge to date and I failed it miserably. Certainly the bowling was high-class and the pace and ferocity of the attack was an eye-opener. It was suggested at the time that I was another English batsman who couldn't stand the heat and the selectorial axe swung mercifully before the last Test of the summer against Sri Lanka.

That was my state of mind when I went to see Jon Webb again in August 1991 – no runs and plenty of pain. It is difficult to say how far the two were connected. I was sure there was some connection. So was Webb and he recommended a screw fusion to repair the stress fracture.

I went in for the operation in September at the Park Hospital in Nottingham. I felt no fear or trepidation as the risks involved were minimal. Mr Webb took a small bone graft from my hip and put a screw on top to hold the graft in place until the fracture had healed. Both scars are there to this day and the screw remains.

I awoke from the operation feeling as though my back had been nailed to the bed. When the anaesthetic and the painkillers had worn off and my mind was again my own, I had the dim awareness that the pain in the sacroiliac was still there. That evening I attempted to get up for the first time and staggered to the toilet with the help of two nurses to support me. Later one of the nurses had to administer a catheter to facilitate my natural functions that had refused to restart. While doing so, she told me that the operation had been a success and the pain would gradually subside. At that particular moment I was in no position to argue.

I spent a mildly uncomfortable week in hospital following the operation. Afterwards I adhered strictly to the three-month rehabilitation programme I had been given. The pain and the stiffness did not go away and, in fact, got much worse, and three months later I was in a terrible condition. I remember the phone ringing one evening in my flat and I could barely crawl over to answer it. If there was a low point in my career, that was it – I was in a bad way and for the first time I wondered whether I would play again.

Mechanically, the operation had been a good one, but it hadn't solved the problem. I returned to Nottingham and explained my concerns to Mr Webb. He ordered more scans, this time of the sacroiliac area. On seeing two dark and blurred lines he ordered some blood tests. I was suffering, it seemed, from a condition called ankylosing spondylitis.

It is a hereditary condition, one that I inherited from my father although I did not know at the time that he suffered from it. It is an inflammatory condition that affects the joints, primarily the spine. Typically, it expresses itself in young men in their late teens or early twenties, who complain of stiffness and pain especially in the mornings. It affects people to differing degrees so that in a mild case the person may be unaware of the condition and in a severe case complete fusion and rigidity of the spine can be the outcome. I suffer from neither of these two extremes.

I know now that I displayed some classic early signs when I was growing up. For a year at school when I was thirteen I struggled to walk down the stairs such was the pain in my knees. I must have looked a very strange sight that year descending sideways, crab-like and at a snail's pace. The next year I had a mysterious pain underneath my ankle joint. I was taken to specialists about both these problems and they were dismissed as 'growing pains'.

The problem is controlled by anti-inflammatory tablets; Voltarol, or diclofenac sodium to give its medical name, has been a constant companion for the last decade. Two tablets a day, cricket or no cricket, at a dosage of somewhere between 150g and 200g. That's a lot of tablets and a lot of damage to the stomach lining, but there is no doubt in my mind that without them I would not have been able to function as a professional athlete at all.

For much of the time throughout the early and mid 1990s the pain was perfectly manageable. The tablets and a daily stretching routine meant that between 1993 and 1998 I did not miss a Test match. Of course, I played often when I shouldn't have done but that could be said of any fast bowler throughout the decade. I mention it because the stiffness, pain and the tablets are a daily companion and have become routine for me.

After 1997, beginning with the tour to Zimbabwe, the problems became less easy to manage. Along with the usual pain and stiffness there was also a more specific and mechanical pain on the lower right side of my back that led to increasingly unmanageable spasms. I played half fit throughout the Zimbabwe tour and I missed the Sri Lanka Test in 1998, which prevented me, apparently, from breaking Alan Knott's record for the most consecutive Tests played by an Englishman.

The problems continued and got worse during the Ashes tour in 1998 and through to the World Cup in 1999, which I also missed. I was foolish to have played in that Ashes series. At Cairns the week before the First Test, I played in complete spasm. I could not bend forwards and stood at gully praying the ball would come nowhere near me. I was out first ball in the first innings, and ought to have been out first ball in the second. A week later I had four cortisone injections in my back and then played against Australia two days later.

It was a crazy thing to do. Why did I do it? I can only think that as a senior player I felt a responsibility not to let the team down, but throughout the series I ended up letting the team and myself down with my performances. It was the wrong thing to do, but it is peculiarly difficult to stand aside and watch somebody else take your place. In Australia 'don't give a sucker an even break' rules the day.

That tour ended miserably for me with a pair in Melbourne. The next match, on 2 January, was in Sydney and I was all set to put the misery of Melbourne behind me when I went into spasm during slip-catching practice on the morning of the match. I withdrew from the game despite accusing glances from my replacement Mark Butcher, whose bleary eyes beneath his sunglasses betrayed his activities of the night before. I began to realise that I was fast becoming, for the first time in my career, a fitness liability.

I had to sort the problem out. I did not play again until the following June and the six months in between were a constant misery. I was in spasm most of the time and I could not find the right cure. It was a struggle even to sit in a car and for most of the time I could not bend down sufficiently to put my shoes and socks on. Nevertheless, I had been picked for the World Cup in June and on Lancashire's pre-season trip to South Africa I desperately tried to get fit. I worked with a Pilates instructor in Cape Town and I took the advice of the South African physiotherapist who recommended long spells of swimming in the freezing oceans around that beautiful city as an alternative to ice treatment.

One morning I went to Camps Bay before breakfast. It was a cold and misty morning and the beach was deserted. I swam in the freezing ocean for about forty minutes, unable to see more than a few yards in front of me because of the fog. As I hung in the ocean, no doubt perfectly good shark meat, I reflected on this latest and rather desperate measure, and realised I was fast running out of options.

At the end of Lancashire's pre-season tour I flew to London to join up with the World Cup squad. Hours later I was on a flight to Lahore, where England had a pre-World Cup training camp. I arrived in complete spasm and within hours was on a plane back home again. It was all a bit of a shambles. The flying was agony and I was sure I was damaging myself even more.

When I arrived home, a friend with whom I had played cricket when I was thirteen rang and gave me the name of a spiritual healer he swore by. I was so desperate that I was on the verge of going but it was at the time when Glenn Hoddle and Eileen Drewery were in the news and I feared mockery. I took myself off to London and enrolled on a Pilates course instead. Pilates is a form of exercise designed to strengthen the core muscles that ultimately protect your spine. I heard the technique had helped Pat Cash recover from serious back problems and my initial experience of it in Cape Town had been positive.

Throughout this time I had no contact with the ECB and the responsibility, and cost, of getting fit was mine alone. I thought then, and I think now, that it was a disgraceful way to treat someone who had injured himself while in its employment.

With central contracts now in place that is unlikely to happen again, but it typified a less than professional and caring attitude to the players that was prevalent throughout the nineties.

Fortunately, Lancashire had a more responsible attitude and their back specialist, a man called Brad Williamson, proved to be a saviour to me. I have him to thank for prolonging my career another three years, during which time I experienced the kind of consistent success I had long yearned for with the national team. Mr Williamson recommended a series of cortisone injections into the discs that were showing damage. He injected the first and I had no reaction. When he injected the second I experienced the worst pain I have ever had and clearly the extent of my reaction showed that there had been a huge build-up of inflammation in that disc. Within a fortnight I was fit, playing again and impressing the new England coach, Duncan Fletcher, with 268* against Glamorgan at Blackpool.

After that, I managed with the help of half-yearly cortisone injections into the disc and I felt as fit in the last couple of years of my career as I had done for some time. The England management were especially understanding during that time and allowed me to cut out any training that the rest of the squad would do. It meant that I was not aerobically as fit as I would have liked to be, but I was at least fit enough to play.

My last injection was the day before we left for the tour of Pakistan. On looking at the latest scans, Mr Williamson said, 'I'm not sure I should give you another injection. There is some indication of damage to the bone around the discs.' I was on the verge of ringing Duncan Fletcher and quitting but in the end Brad thought that one more would do no harm. I spent the first week in Pakistan unable to move but since then I have not needed another injection.

Towards the end of my final series as a Test player I could gradually feel the effects of the injection wearing off. At Headingley I began to get the early indications of spasm and I got through my last two Tests with the help of bigger than usual doses of Voltarol. Immediately after my last match, with ironic timing, I seized up and spent three days in bed.

The inflammatory condition that I suffer from can affect other areas, and shortly after my operation in September 1991 I experienced my first bout of inflammation of the bowel, or ulcerative colitis. It manifests itself as a prolonged period of severe and bloody diarrhoea that leaves you feeling anaemic and pretty ill. If it is left to get out of control it can be nasty, and I was so ill in early 1992 that I needed a spell in hospital on a steroid drip.

As with the back, it is easily controlled by drugs, although I have had various flare-ups down the years. Specifically, and memorably for me, one occurred during South Africa's visit in 1998. It was the last match of the series at Headingley and both were in the balance. Instead of being on the pitch for the final day, I was in hospital having a colonic check-up. I came out of hospital and jumped into a cab. The driver was listening to 'Test Match Special' and we were a couple of miles from Headingley when Darren Gough took the last wicket to clinch the series that I had done so much to help win.

The driver presumably did not know who I was, or maybe he did, but when Gough took the last wicket he clenched his fist and said, 'I knew we'd win something now that Atherton's not in charge.' As I alighted at Headingley, conspicuous in my England tracksuit, there was not a flicker of recognition.

The colitis flared up again in South Africa in 2000. Duncan Fletcher noticed early on in the tour that I was looking pretty drained. I had been passing blood but it hadn't felt as bad as before and so I did nothing about it. In the end, I let it get out of control and during the Zimbabwe Test at Trent Bridge the following May I was anaemic and very ill and knew it was time to sort it out.

I scored 100 in the match but felt totally drained that evening and I was too ill to take the field for Zimbabwe's second innings. In our second innings I was forced to bat at number seven. Tests confirmed the colitis had flared up again and it resulted in a prolonged course of oral steroids. They are extremely powerful drugs and have the unfortunate effect of making you pile on weight. I was still on the steroids halfway through the West Indies series later that summer, and the photos of me in my one hundredth Test show a fullness in my face that betrays the effects of the drugs.

By the end of my final series as a Test player I was caught up in a vicious circle: increasing amounts of Voltarol to get through the games, which in turn were causing the colitis to flare up on a regular basis. It was a cycle I was glad to curtail.

In the end, my fitness problems have resulted in a shorter career than may have been possible. Quite how the problems affected my ability to play is difficult to say in precise terms. Clearly there were games I should not have played and certainly fielding from the late nineties onwards was less enjoyable than before. From around 1997 it also became impossible for me to do any of the fitness training that became an integral part of the game, and that I was so keen on in the early part of my career. After 1998, I was forced to change my stance, from crouched with my bat on the ground to more upright with my bat in the air. I felt less natural and more stilted as a result.

It is difficult to be more precise, and in any case I feel privileged to have played for as long as I did. The contrast is sharp when I look at two of Lancashire's young players, Richard Green and Paul Ridgway, who were forced to retire early through back problems. Cricket has been a fortunate choice for me – a sport that required rigorous fitness standards, or that involved dangerous contact, would have been much more problematic. Being a batsman, too, rather than a bowler was good. I have also been lucky to avoid other problems that sportsmen habitually suffer from; there have been no hamstring tears or shoulder or knee problems. And to open the batting for a decade against the fastest bowlers in the world and not suffer a broken bone in either hand is a remarkable piece of good fortune.

In September 1991, however, as I lay in bed recovering from

my back operation, I was, in cricketing terminology, in the corridor of uncertainty and I was not to know how long a career lay ahead. After the operation I spent some time at Lilleshall and swam religiously as I fought to regain full fitness. I have always been poor at passing time idly and I was keen to get back into action.

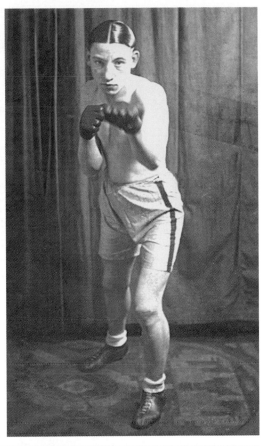

ove: Starting as I meant to go on – a stiff-looking
rward defensive.

ght: My granddad, Tommy, in boxing stance.

low: My dad (standing third from the right) with
nited. Nobby Stiles is in the front row.

On holiday in France with my mum and brother Chris.

A successful Briscoe junior school team.

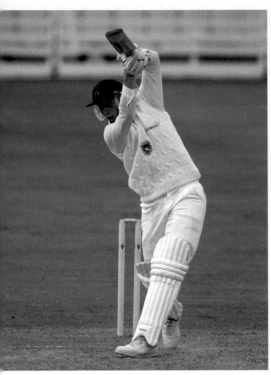

atting and bowling while at Cambridge University.

ith England Under-15s. Nasser Hussain (with a mass of dark, curly hair) is the captain; Jonathan tkinson, the talented Somerset all-rounder, is third from the right on the back row.

Collecting my degree, a 2:1 in history, from Cambridge University. My proud mother looks on.

David Hughes' captaincy was good for Lancashire. Eventually, though, his personal performances, or lack of them, took their toll.

Lancashire in 1992. Neil Fairbrother and I are in the centre of a front row that includes the clique of Graeme Fowler (*to my right*) and (*to his left*) Paul Allott and Mike Watkinson.

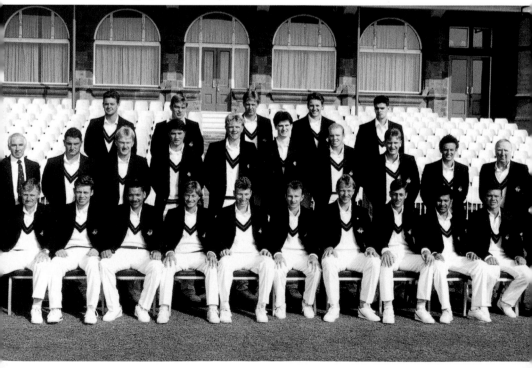

ore success with Lancashire in the 1995 Benson & Hedges final. At this stage we were happy, ccessful and united.

meone's cracked a funny. Sharing a joke with Neil Fairbrother (*left*) and Mike Watkinson during ppy times with Lancashire.

First Test hundred, against New Zealand, 1990.
Above: Getting the Man of the Match award from Geoff Boycott, the season after I benefited from his coaching.
Left: Jack Russell seems more pleased than I do.

Below: Relaxing(!) and white-water rafting in New Zeala in 1991.

raham Gooch congratulates me on a hundred against India at Old Trafford in 1990. We formed a rmidable opening partnership.

utting a swathe of goodwill through Africa' – at the Victoria Falls with the A team in 1990.

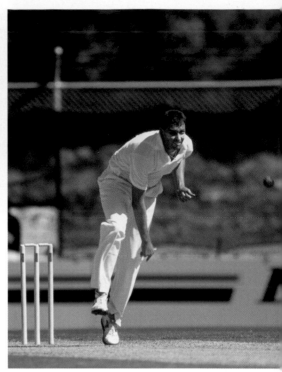

Merv Hughes preparing to unleash a bouncer, and a verbal volley.

Six wickets, and a damaged hip, for Angus Fraser in Melbourne.

Australia 1990–91 was a difficult tour for David Gower. Here, after centuries in Sydney, we celebrate in the traditional way.

5

INDIAN WILDERNESS

O ther than as team-mates, Philip Tufnell and I would be unlikely travelling companions in India. Yet, there we were, early on in the 1992–93 tour, wandering around the streets of India's most impoverished city, Calcutta. We had taken in the Hoogley River and the slums and the stench when we came across a fortune-teller, sat cross-legged on a street corner. Next to him was a cage and the luminous green of the parrot in it matched the turban on the fortune-teller's head.

He beckoned us over and said that for a small fee he would get the parrot to pick out some tarot cards and reveal our future. After some squawking the parrot performed its trick and the fortune-teller announced that our immediate outlook was bleak, but that things would pick up on 24 February. Being cricketers, Tufnell and I were highly superstitious; the last Test of the tour in Bombay was due to finish on 23 February. We looked at each other warily and hurried on.

In a way the fortune-teller was right. England, Tufnell and I were a terrible, disastrous failure in India. England lost 3–0, I played in just one Test, and Tufnell, England's best spinner, was put firmly in his place by the Indian batsmen. In another way, though, the fortune-teller was wrong. Our fortunes did not pick up on 24 February. After India we went to Sri Lanka and things got no better there.

Yet before we landed in Delhi on 29 December 1992, I was

optimistic about England's and my chances on the sub-continent. I had recovered from my back operation, forced my way back into the Test side and played reasonably well against a strong Pakistan attack.

I had been on a rehabilitation course at Lilleshall in the early months of 1992 and afterwards I went to South Africa to get fit for the new season and await Lancashire's arrival in Johannes-burg for their pre-season tour. I stayed with Steven Jack, a fiery fast bowler whom Lancashire had their eye on. England were never far from my thoughts, however, as the World Cup in Australia was in full cry. It represented South Africa's first real foray into international cricket after isolation, and Johannesburg was full of expectation when England and South Africa met in the semi-finals. Mine was the only smiling face in the room when the strange 'rain rules' of that tournament handed the match to England.

I also spent some time in Cape Town and played a couple of matches for the Green Point club. It was a time of great upheaval in South Africa and, like everyone else, I marvelled at the humil-ity and humanity of the recently released Nelson Mandela. I was in Cape Town on 17 March, the day of the all-white referendum scheduled by F.W. de Klerk. I could feel the nervousness in the city. Many people I knew were contemplating leaving if the vote had been 'no' and the relief was palpable when the 'yes' vote allowed the process of reform to continue.

I returned from South Africa with Lancashire for the start of the 1992 season. Getting back into the England team proved no easy task. They had performed well during the World Cup and Alec Stewart was flourishing as an opener. He scored a brilliant 190 in the First Test of the summer against Pakistan. I was recalled for the Third Test due to an injury to Allan Lamb, and partly no doubt because the match was to be played on my home ground at Old Trafford. Unfortunately it didn't help – I succumbed for nought to an express delivery from Wasim Akram in the Stygian gloom.

The outcome of that series revolved around the ability, or otherwise, of England's batsmen to cope with the twin threat of Wasim Akram and Waqar Younis. Because of their exploits with their respective counties, Lancashire and Surrey, neither were unknowns. But they took their bowling to new heights in 1992 and I have not seen a better or more dangerous pair of bowlers than those two that summer.

Lancashire had first seen Waqar the previous summer at Old Trafford in a Benson & Hedges match against Surrey. He had charged in from the sightscreen, literally, and his first ball was a lethal beamer to Graeme Fowler. Paul Allott was watching in the dressing room and he snorted, 'A season in county cricket will soon shorten that run-up.' Waqar continued to run in like that for the rest of the summer. He ran in like that throughout the whole of the next year and was still doing so a decade later when I last played against him. He was a magnificent competitor and there are few more glorious sights in cricket than Waqar steaming in at full tilt.

Wasim did not have such a long run-up and bustled in off no more than fifteen paces. He had an incredibly fast arm so that he lost nothing in pace in comparison with Waqar and he was probably the more difficult of the two to pick up. While Waqar tried to swing the new ball out by pitching it up, Wasim preferred to bowl short, and opening against him was always a test of courage. Indeed, after my last Test match at The Oval I was chatting to Shane Warne and he asked me if Wasim and I didn't get along. 'Jeez, mate, he's always bouncing the shit out of you.' In fact, Wasim and I were, and are, great mates but, for some reason, he always bounced the shit out of me.

Both of them were more dangerous with the old ball. It was the first time the phenomenon of reverse swing came to obvious prominence in England. Time and again, Wasim and Waqar would undo the good work of the top order and blow away the middle and tailend. At Lord's, England were 197–3 and 255 all out, and at Headingley we were 270–1 and 320 all out. Batting in the middle order was a dangerous proposition against Pakistan that summer.

I remember one delivery in particular, which castled a bemused Derek Pringle. It appeared to swing both ways in the air, turning Pringle first this way and then that before knocking his stumps flat. Many years later, I asked Pringle about the delivery and he confirmed that it was the best he ever received and is adamant that neither he, nor anyone, could have kept it out. The point is, I think, that a new batsman to the crease had little or no chance; only if you had been in a while did your chances of survival increase.

Waqar's signature ball was the inswinging yorker. He would set a batsman up by bowling outside the off stump and then produce a ball of maximum effort which zeroed in, with unerring accuracy, on a batsman's toes or the base of his stumps. Wasim was less predictable and could reverse the ball both ways. He excelled at coming around the wicket, angling it in to the right-hander and then swinging it away. He had a slight change in action for his yorker. As he approached the crease, he would swing his bowling arm back in an arc high above his head before he got into his action. The problem was that he also did this for his bouncer and it was a hazardous business to predict which one was coming.

We had numerous team meetings about how to cope with these twin threats. 'Reinforce your toe-caps,' said Robin Smith. 'Don't play the big cover drive to Waqar's inswinger,' said Gooch. 'Bat deep inside your crease,' said another and, 'Keep your feet out of the way and bat inside the line of the ball,' offered someone else. All were good suggestions but in the end each batsman had to sort it out for himself. I decided to keep a low back-lift when the ball was reversing so that I could keep out the yorkers, play the ball as late as possible, and use the pace of the ball to score. I kept my footwork to a minimum and tried not to get my front foot in the way of the inswinger. It was almost like playing French cricket.

I had as much success as anybody and scored good half centuries at Headingley and The Oval. But, like everyone else, I succumbed occasionally. In the second innings at The Oval, Waqar got me cheaply and bowled the quickest spell, through the air, that I have ever faced. I was in good company. He also dismissed David Gower that day with a wonderful inswinger that David mis-picked and left, only to see it cannon into his stumps. It was his final innings for England.

In the end, we had to admit that Wasim and Waqar had proved to be too good. It was no disgrace to lose and we hadn't lost badly. I was reasonably happy with how the summer had gone – I had scored 1,600 runs at over 50 and was back opening for England. I felt it was a foregone conclusion that I would be going to India and I was confident of doing well.

India proved to be anything but a foregone conclusion. Keith Fletcher, the new England coach, had gone on a scouting mission to South Africa to watch India play and returned saying that we had little to worry about. For the dusty turners of India we prepared on the rock-hard surfaces of Lilleshall. We knew we would be facing a phalanx of spinners so we left out our best player of spin, David Gower. In Calcutta the pitch looked dry and cracked so we played four seamers. We knew that the food could be dodgy so we ate prawns in Madras and got food poisoning. It was that kind of trip.

At Lilleshall, before the tour, we talked ourselves up. With memories of the run feast against India in 1990 fresh in my mind, I remember asking Neil Fairbrother, 'Who is going to get Goochy out?' He replied, 'I hope they prepare turners. Embers and Tuffers will spin 'em out.' Those of us who had never been to India before, and had only seen them play abroad, were guilty of naïveté. But if the senior players knew any better, they were not saying.

The most experienced player in Indian conditions would have

been David Gower but he had been controversially omitted in favour of Mike Gatting. Gatting's ban for his participation in the 1989–90 rebel tour had been rescinded now that South Africa were back in the international fold. Yet Gower was a better player than Gatting, he had been more loyal and had been a winning captain on the sub-continent. His omission was a mistake and was based around a personality clash with Gooch, something that Gooch, I think, now regrets.

During our preparation week in Delhi there was no sign of the troubles to come. We trained like dervishes. Graeme Hick's knees were constantly in shreds from diving on the hard, bare practice ground. Only John Emburey was unfit to train; he had an eye infection and took tea most of the time. At the end of the first week, Gooch managed to persuade Emburey to give him batting practice. Afterwards Emburey complained of blisters. 'On his arse?' scoffed Gatting.

That first week was portentous for the Middlesex off-spinner. The second match of the tour was at Lucknow, and a very dull game it was, too. The match was petering out into a draw and both captains had the option to end the game early but Gooch decided our bowlers needed more time in the middle and opted to play out the game. Navjot Singh Sidhu, a hard-hitting opening batsman who wore a turban and had a turbo of a bat, welcomed the extra time and made his intentions clear. He smashed Emburey to all parts of the ground.

This continued throughout the tour. The next match was in Delhi and again Sidhu went on the attack. By this stage, he had hit Emburey for twelve mighty sixes in three innings. He treated England's other spinners – Salisbury, Tufnell and even Hick – with utmost respect but each time Emburey came on a kind of red mist descended and Sidhu would leap out of his crease and smash him out of the park. He rarely missed. The onslaught had a profound effect on Emburey who talked himself out of the First Test and endured a fruitless tour. Even now, a decade later, Emburey has a nervous twitch at the mention of Sidhu's name – he is the Pink Panther to Emburey's Herbert Lom.

Logistically, the tour was proving to be a difficult one. There was violence in Bombay and killings and curfews in Ahmedabad. A plane crash in Delhi forced the Minister of Aviation to resign and all internal flights were grounded. We had to travel every-where by train.

Some of the players were struggling to come to terms with this and with touring India and all its attendant problems. Fundamen-tally, a touring team has to get used to a scale of humanity that is difficult to comprehend, and other than in the hotel room there is rarely much privacy to be had. I went wandering through the streets of Chandigarh and was followed by literally hundreds of street urchins, constantly tugging at my clothes, fingers and thumbs bunched together touching their lips in supplication.

Before the World Cup in 1996, 100,000 people turned up at Eden Gardens just to see the opening ceremony and each team do a gentle lap of honour. After that, every time we emerged from our hotel to get on the team bus there were thousands of people trying to get the slightest glimpse.

The constant scrutiny of prying eyes through the dressing-room windows can be wearying. Then, of course, there is the poverty. Any cricketer struggling to come to terms with it would do well to remember the words of Mark Tully, at the time the BBC's India correspondent, who when asked how he coped with it said, 'I don't have to, they do.'

If a team can come to terms with the massive culture shock, there is no better place to be playing cricket than India. The people have a love of the game that is unequalled, except per-haps in the West Indies. On that 1992–93 tour, every Test was played to a full house, and everywhere we went we were treated like heroes.

Despite the fact that I had a reasonably enlightened attitude to touring and was keen to get about to see what India had to offer, little would go right for me on the cricket field. I was all set to play at Lucknow but felt nauseous on the morning of the match. I threw up in the changing rooms and spent three days in bed with food poisoning. After that, I was assured that I would play in one of the next two one-day games in Delhi. Yet, without explanation, I was omitted from both and with the one-day internationals around the corner, it was unlikely that I would be playing for another fortnight. It left me just one match, against the Indian Under 25s at Cuttack, to find some form before the First Test.

In the end, I missed the First Test as well due to a flu virus that was doing the rounds. I was immensely frustrated to miss the game. Each morning a dense smog sat over Eden Gardens and although the players could hear 100,000 people in the ground, they could see nothing. Miraculously, each morning the smog would lift just in time for the start to reveal the huge crowd. It was a wonderful atmosphere and a thrilling sight.

We were well beaten and the media went on the attack. Our selections and performance came under severe scrutiny, quite rightly, but as was so often the case in defeat they also criticised our dress and appearance. It was the type of criticism that really galled me and had little to do with our performance in the Test match. Moreover, the criticism was totally out of place. It is true that we arrived in Calcutta looking fairly dishevelled in our tracksuits, but we had travelled twelve hours by train from Cuttack and arrived at 5.30 in the morning. Besides, twelve hours in a railway carriage with Dermot Reeve and his guitar is enough to make anyone feel utterly dishevelled. In response, Ted Dexter commissioned a report into the effects of pollution in India's major cities and promised those concerned that the grave issue of 'facial hair' would be looked into.

In between Tests we travelled to Vishakhapatnam to play the Rest of India. If the early part of the tour had been tough for our senior spinner John Emburey, it was here in the south of India that Phil Tufnell gave notice of the frustrations that had been building up inside him. Tufnell and Emburey were England's first-choice spinners and the selectors hoped that they would have the same kind of success they enjoyed in combination at Middlesex. For the first week of the tour, however, Sussex's leg-spinner Ian Salisbury had been asked along as a net bowler. He had looked our most dangerous bowler in practice and he was not only asked to stay on but leapfrogged ahead of Emburey and Tufnell to play in the First Test.

Tufnell had kept his counsel but was privately fuming. At Vishakhapatnam his frustrations boiled over when Richard Blakey missed a straightforward stumping off Sachin Tendulkar in his first over. At the end of the over, Tufnell snatched his cap from the umpire and kicked it all the way to square-leg where he was fielding. The management took a dim view and an inevitable hearing followed. It was, by all accounts, an ill-tempered affair and shouts, screams and even the sound of broken bottles could be heard down the corridor. The Reverend Andrew Wingfield Digby was on tour and he was called to calm Tufnell down and offer some pastoral support. The £500 fine would not have done much to improve the left-arm spinner's mood.

Tufnell's reaction was out of order but it was the Salisbury situation more than the missed stumping that was eating away at him, and the tour management had to shoulder some responsibility. Salisbury ought to have been selected for the full party or left at home. Furthermore, to pick someone solely on net form was pure folly and it was to affect Tufnell, and to a lesser extent Emburey, throughout the tour. It seemed a simple case of poor man-management; both players were pivotal to England's chances of success on tour and yet both had been undermined from an early stage.

As we sat down for the team meeting prior to the next Test in Madras, I had no inkling of the shock that was in store for me. None of the batsmen had scored heavily in Calcutta and so I had convinced myself that I would play in Madras, especially as I had heard nothing to the contrary. Gooch read out the team and my name was missing. I was numb. I offered some words in the meeting but I am sure that the trembling in my voice must have betrayed my feelings. I collared Gooch immediately afterwards and told him that I was staggered by the selection. I was right to feel aggrieved and I was right to confront Gooch face to face. When I was captain, I much preferred the approach of players who were honest and straightforward, even if I didn't always like what they were saying.

What was unacceptable was my reaction in the days following. Once I had got the grievance off my chest that ought to have been the end of it. Instead, I descended into an almighty sulk. I completely withdrew into myself and spoke to no one for days. I couldn't even bring myself to say well played to my great mate Neil Fairbrother who scored 83 in the first innings of the Test. It was a totally immature reaction and not one that I am proud to recall.

I was a hopeless twelfth man. Occasionally I came across cricketers who secretly liked the role, the feeling of involvement without the pressure of performing. I was the other way around; I needed to feel at first-hand the emotions of the game, the pleasure of victory and the pain in defeat. Otherwise, what was the point of playing at all?

I began to feel more and more excluded from events. Graham Gooch succumbed to the flu bug on the morning of the Second Test and even though I was the only other specialist opening batsman in the squad, I was omitted in favour of Dick Blakey. Even I, however, could appreciate that it would have been impossible for Alec Stewart to captain the side, keep wicket and open the batting. Besides, I was rooming with Dick and was genuinely pleased for him on his debut.

On the eve of that match some of us had eaten prawns in the Chinese restaurant at the hotel. Robin Smith and Mike Gatting in particular were ill the next day and in no fit state to field. All our non-playing substitutes were used to replace them on the field from time to time, all except me – and I was by no means the worst fielder of the four. It added to my feelings of exclusion.

I had plenty of time on my hands. I had been a voracious

reader ever since childhood and on every England tour my bags were filled with more books than clothes. On this tour I soon ran out of reading matter so I played marathon chess matches against John Emburey, my attacking style the complete antithesis of my batting. I also tried to get around and experience what India's vast land had to offer. The eight-hour round trip from Delhi to Agra to see the Taj Mahal was clearly a well-worn tourist route, judging by the distasteful displays of chained elephants and bears at the side of the road. Occasionally I found the road less travelled. With Derek Pringle and Peter Roebuck I visited the studio of the famous Indian film maker Satyajit Ray, and we marvelled at the primitive technology that could produce such masterful films. Looking back, I am glad I made the most of my time off. Due to a quirk of the fixture list, other than a brief stay during the World Cup, I never toured India again. Cricket and my exclusion, though, were never far from my thoughts. As we wandered around Ray's studio in Calcutta, I complained bitterly to Peter Roebuck about my enforced absence. 'I feel I have so much more to offer,' I told him. 'I just hope I can find a way of releasing it.'

I got my chance when I played my only Test of the tour in Bombay, Neil Fairbrother having become the latest victim of the flu bug. My presence made little difference to the outcome. We were well beaten and I made 37 and 11. My efforts were not without incident. During the first innings, Alec Stewart and I were involved in a farcical run-out. He pushed the ball to the off side and called for a quick single. I immediately refused but Stewart was tracking the line of the ball and failed to hear my call. We both ended up at the non-striker's end and the enduring photograph is of Alec glaring at me while I had half turned my back on him awaiting the umpire's verdict.

The media had already done their best to place Alec and me at opposite ends of the spectrum – southerner against northerner, comprehensive school against public school, the 'oik' against the 'toff' and both potential rivals for the captain's job in due course. The run-out fuelled their arguments and was written up as my attempt to stake my claims and regain the ground I had lost in the last year. In truth, the run-out was a simple cock-up. Of course we blamed each other – I thought he was ball watching and he thought I was slow to react. Beyond that, however, there were no feelings of antagonism. If I was standing my ground or staking my claim, it was entirely subconscious.

Vinod Kambli, a cocky young left-hander from Bombay, was another to travel the well-worn centurions' path against us in his home-town. We had seen him earlier in the tour and although he had got runs, he had looked vulnerable outside off stump. Chris Lewis had been dismissive. 'I reckon I can get this guy out any time I want to,' he had said. As Kambli passed his double century and India neared 600 I mentioned to Lewis that now might be quite a good time. I got a withering look.

The defeat in Bombay completed our rout. After the match, the Indian authorities presented every player with a mountain bike. It seemed an odd choice of gift – even odder was to see some of the England squad trying out their new toys in a crass lap of honour around the Wankhede Stadium. It showed a lack of concern about our performances and opened us up for more justifiable criticism.

For the most part, I had stood on the sidelines and watched our annihilation. I achieved little and yet I felt I had learnt a lot. The experience of being a bit-part player was a new one and although I should have handled it better, it gave me an insight into the problems faced by players on the sidelines and the need for constant communication with them. More importantly, I watched in admiration as the Indian batsmen gave us a master-class in the art of playing spin. I had learnt the previous summer against Pakistan about how to play reverse swing, and watching Tendulkar and Azharuddin play our spinners took my batting education one step nearer completion.

The tour was a personal triumph for the Indian captain, Mohammad Azharuddin. Before the First Test in Calcutta he was a batsman and captain under extreme pressure. He scored 182 in that first innings and he never looked back. Other than Brian Lara, I thought that Azharuddin was the only player of my generation who possessed a touch of genius. I picked up his bat after the Calcutta match and it was wafer thin, the lightest bat in the game. Despite his light frame, his forearms were strong and wiry and his hands faster than a Chinese masseuse. He propelled the blade through the ball quicker than any modern batsman save Steve Waugh, and when he was on the go, there was no finer sight in the game.

Tendulkar had a fine series, too. His 165 in the Second Test at Madras sealed our defeat. In time, he has proved himself to be the greatest player of my generation but back then his was a more understandable talent to me. He played in an entirely orthodox manner. Unlike Azharuddin, his bat was among the heaviest around and the swing of his blade was pendulum like – slower and straighter than Azharuddin's but just as effective.

Despite their differing styles, they had two things in common: they played aggressively and they were both keen to use their feet to the spinners. I had always considered myself a good player of spin. Instinctively, I judged length well and because of my upbringing on the soft wickets of northern England I played late and with soft hands. These were key ingredients in playing spin. But throughout my cricketing education I had been taught little about the value of coming down the wicket to the spinner to upset his length. Watching the Indian masters made me realise that I was a good defensive player of spin but that I needed to learn to expand my repertoire and have more aggressive intent.

On that tour, England's batsmen were shown to be poor players of spin in comparison with India's. Richard Blakey's approach against Anil Kumble summed up our problems. He was stuck on the crease, with minimal foot movement, like a rabbit in the headlights, an lbw or pad/bat catch waiting to happen. In contrast, our spinners enjoyed a fruitless tour. When the Indian batsmen were not attacking, they defended close to the ball, almost smothering it, and against the off-spin they used the pad as a second line of defence. The Indian umpires refused to entertain the idea of giving anybody out on the front foot and that drove as experienced and good a bowler as John Emburey to distraction. 'I just don't know how I'm going to get another fackin' wicket,' he complained. He wasn't the only one – Phillip DeFreitas failed to get a first-class wicket all tour, and India scored at will against most of our bowlers.

On 26 February, two days after the fortune-teller had predicted an upturn in our fortunes, Phil Tufnell and I sat in the gardens of our hotel in Bangalore, taking tea. It was during the one-day internationals and the team had chartered a private plane to Jamshedpur for the next match. There were only fourteen seats available and Tufnell and I were considered the least likely to play so we had been left behind. Bangalore is a cool, green city with good restaurants and a wonderful turf race-track so there were worse places to be, and we passed the time idly, reflecting on a tour that was not going to plan. 'This place is like a toilet, Athers,' Tufnell complained. 'I've done the elephants and I've done the poverty – it's time to go home.'

That day we were not to know that things would continue in the same vein for another month in Sri Lanka. Graham Gooch would return home and Alec Stewart would lead the team, although little would change. We would be badly beaten in Colombo, as we had been in Calcutta, Madras and Bombay. As we sat sipping tea that day, Tufnell and I, we were two disaffected souls, feeling forever on the fringe of things.

6

CAPTAIN OF ENGLAND

W ithin five months I had been made captain of England. It was 28 July 1993 and England had been heavily beaten days before by Australia at Headingley. Graham Gooch had resigned as captain, and I had gone to the Lake District for a short break with my girlfriend of the time, Susie Carman, a doctor I had met at Cambridge. Within ten minutes of checking in at our hotel, the phone rang and Ted Dexter said, 'We'd very much like you to captain England in the next Test match at Edgbaston.' I accepted immediately and we travelled home to Manchester. I had moved at a stroke from the fringe to the very centre of decision-making and attention.

On the way south, my head was filled with a thousand thoughts. Was I too young? Was I up to the job? Was it an impossible job? And how the hell was I going to try to turn around an apparently hopeless situation? England had lost eight out of their last nine Test matches and Australia were already three up with only two matches of the summer left. I stopped at my flat in Didsbury and then drove straight to Neil Fairbrother's house in Hale. I tapped on the window, let myself in, opened a bottle of champagne and announced, 'I've just been given some good news.' I was twenty-five years old, blissfully naïve, and totally unaware of the roller-coaster ride to come.

As my name had long been bandied around as 'captaincy material', my appointment was seen by some as the fulfilment of a cricketing destiny. At the beginning of 1993, however, I genuinely didn't go along with the notion. I saw myself as a young player still trying to establish himself at Test level, despite the fact that Graham Gooch had appointed me his vice-captain two years before. Since then my stock had fallen. I knew I had the ability and temperament to succeed. I had three Test centuries to my name, but I had performed fitfully in India and was by no means a certain starter against Australia that summer. Captaincy could not have been further from my thoughts.

Indeed, my performance in the First Test at Old Trafford merely confirmed my precarious existence in the team. I made 19 and 25 and I was once again a verbal target for Merv Hughes. I had not played against him for two years and had missed his kind and gentle countenance. As I nicked his first ball for 4 through third man the moustache hissed at me, 'Jesus Christ, you've not got any better in two fucking years!' And then, as I ran past him, he added 'arsewipe' for good measure, just in case I had forgotten his calling card.

I knew the next match at Lord's was the critical one for me. If I did well, there was the possibility of a bright and challenging future ahead. If not, I was sure I would be dropped and remembered as just another promising player who had failed to make an impact on the only stage that matters. Whatever luck was going certainly ran with me for that week. The pitch was a belter and offered only some slow turn; Craig McDermott, Australia's most potent new-ball bowler, had a twisted bowel and missed the match; I cut uppishly early on in the first innings and was dropped at gully; and I was the recipient of an umpiring reprieve early on in my first innings off Tim May. It may be a cliché, but it is a fine line that separates success and failure.

I was freakishly dismissed for 80 in the first innings when I drove a ball from Warne on to my boot only to see it roll backwards on to the stumps. In the second innings I was on 97, and on song, when I turned a ball from Allan Border to the midwicket boundary. Mike Gatting, who was batting with me, was jogging the runs but I knew I had not timed the flick perfectly. 'You'll have to run hard, Gatt,' I hissed as we crossed. As Merv Hughes gathered the ball under the grandstand Gatting called me for the third run that would have brought up my 100, and then he sent me back. I was batting in half rubbers and slipped on the lush green grass next to the cut strip. I tried to make my ground and slipped again and was still grovelling yards short when Ian Healy gathered in the throw and broke the stumps. Run out on 99, England v. Australia at Lord's – a nightmare.

I stormed off and smashed my bat against the dressing-room door. The glass in it had been repaired just a few weeks earlier after a tantrum by Gatting himself which had left him needing stitches in his arm. I was inconsolable – I was desperate for another Test century, desperate to get on the honours board at Lord's and desperate to help England save a Test match. Mercifully, I didn't know then that it was the closest I would ever come to scoring a Test 100 at Lord's.

Despite that disappointment, my performance at Lord's confirmed my rehabilitation as a Test player and saved me from the selectors' axe. Others were not so fortunate. Phillip DeFreitas had already been dropped after the First Test. In between Tests, Lancashire played Essex and on the Sunday DeFreitas vented his frustration on the way down the dressing-room stairs – he issued a loud cry, like a warrior going into battle, and smashed a window in the Essex dressing room.

By this stage, all the players knew that Graham Gooch was nearing the end of the road as captain. India had gone poorly, his form and health had suffered and he had left Alec Stewart in charge for the Sri Lankan leg of the tour. He had made it clear to the team that if the performances did not improve during the early Ashes Tests, he would step down. If we were keen for him to stay, it was not apparent in our efforts. Two feeble performances at Old Trafford and Lord's had left us 2–0 down and Gooch despondent. After the Lord's match I saw Gooch in animated conversation with Keith Fletcher and Ted Dexter. I am sure he wanted to step down then but was dissuaded. In the showers after that match I stood next to Mike Gatting. 'I think we'll have a new captain next game,' he said. I think he had his eyes on the prize.

After Lord's, Hick, Lewis, Foster and Tufnell were all dropped. Gatting disappeared, too, effectively ending his captaincy ambitions. In came Thorpe, Hussain, Lathwell, Igglesden, McCague, Bicknell and Ilott. The selectorial merry-go-round reminded me of 1989. Many of the new guys did not know each other and it necessitated a 'meet the players' cocktail party for the players themselves before the next Test at Trent Bridge.

Gooch remained as captain for two more games until the Ashes had been lost at Headingley. As we travelled back to the hotel together on the second evening of that match, he told me that he had decided to resign. For the next three days he was demob happy and we spent many hours in the Fox and Hounds in Bramhope sampling the local ales. It was an emotional time for him. He had given the captaincy his all and it was easy to see the strain he was under. It was an indication also that the responsibilities had begun to weigh too heavily on him.

As I left Headingley, I knew that I would be a front-runner for the job. Lancashire's match before the Headingley Test had been at Old Trafford against Glamorgan and Keith Fletcher had driven up specifically to have dinner with me. I had known Fletcher since my A tour days in Zimbabwe and we got on well. Over dinner we discussed various issues surrounding the team – it was as near an interview for the job as could be. So when Dexter's call came I was not totally surprised and I had already thought my answer through. Nevertheless, it was quite some turn around from five months before when I was constantly on the sidelines in India. Was any man more unprepared for a top job? I doubt it.

*　　*　　*

I did have some attractive qualities for those entrusted with selecting the new captain. I had a good cricket brain, a good instinct for people and was intelligent enough to know that I had plenty to learn. I had read Mike Brearley's fascinating book *The Art of Captaincy* countless times as a teenager and had tried to put that knowledge into practice in the various representative teams I had captained. Moreover, I was young, fresh-faced, quick to smile (in those days), worth my place in the team and was seen as central to England's future.

I was as convinced then as I am now that the captain of a modern Test team must be worth his place in the team and that the captain must be selected from the best eleven. Even fine players such as Mark Taylor have found the pressure of captaincy almost intolerable when the runs have dried up, as they did for him during 1996. Media scrutiny and pressure combine to make the stay of a captain not worth his place in the team a brief one. Mike Brearley disagrees; the captain, in his opinion, is an all-rounder. That is all very well, but my definition of an all-rounder is someone who is worth his place in the team in both disciplines.

Other than that, I had little to recommend me. I had captained various schoolboy representative teams, usually on the back of being the best player, but I had no experience of captaining Lancashire full time. I had no media or management training and I had not spoken to anybody from the TCCB, even after accepting the job, and therefore had no idea of the extent and nature of the England captain's responsibilities.

Since I had been given the job, I assumed that the selectors – Fletcher, Amiss and Dexter – were all in favour. Micky Stewart still had some influence and understandably he spoke up for Alec, but I was somewhat taken aback when Ted Dexter openly revealed this during my first press conference. 'Dad had plenty to say,' Dexter announced, 'and he was loyal to the boy, as we would expect him to be.' Micky felt I was too young and had yet to mature fully as a Test batsman. Both were fair points.

Apart from my own captaincy experience, I had played under a handful of other captains, albeit briefly, and I had observed their strengths and weaknesses carefully. Nasser Hussain captained England Under 15s in 1983 against the might of Scotland and Wales. With a mass of curly dark hair, he scarcely resembled the man I was to play under for the senior team fifteen years later although, even then, he had a fiery temper and was rarely out. His captaincy at that time did not show any of the tactical nous he was to display later – against Scotland in Glasgow he bowled us both for hours on end, leg-spinners in tandem, and seemed oblivious to the need for change.

David Price was a popular cricketer for the Cambridge side of 1987. When he wasn't studying at Homerton College, drinking in the Salisbury Arms, or recording songs for his band Ideal Dave and the Supremes, he had the unenviable task of leading a team of students against full-time professionals. Clearly, victories were unexpected and, in this instance, it would be unfair to base an assessment of captaincy on results. It is possible to be a good captain of a bad side by making a bad side better. Nevertheless, as a captain he often fretted at first slip with a worried expression on his face and could dither over field placings, chasing the ball and trying to plug gaps in the field. Later as a captain, I learnt that everyone worries at some point and occasionally a captain can feel absolutely powerless, but it was good not to let the rest of the team know.

David Hughes took over the captaincy of Lancashire when the club was in the doldrums in 1987. He was unable to lead by example as his best playing days were long behind him, and he batted at number six, with little success, rarely bowled and fielded at short-leg. He led Lancashire impressively, however, and the club experienced an immediate upturn of fortunes under his captaincy, finishing second in the championship in 1987 and going on to dominate the domestic one-day scene in the 1990s. There was a big age gap between Hughes and the rest of the team and this enabled him to distance himself easily and enforce strict discipline. The younger players, myself included, were visibly wary of Hughes and any lapse in concentration or focus would result in a severe tongue lashing.

This leadership by force of personality rather than example was exactly what Lancashire needed at the time, as the dressing room had become fractious and cliquey. Even so, his demise after four successful years in charge highlighted the problems for a captain whose form did not warrant a place in the team. Things came to a head during a NatWest tie against Hampshire, the day before the Benson & Hedges final of 1991. Paul Allott told Hughes in no uncertain terms that he was wasting a place in the team; the rest of the side agreed with Allott's sentiments but headed rapidly to the showers as the showdown ensued. The result was that Hughes left himself out of the final against Worcestershire and retired at the end of the season.

Neil Fairbrother replaced him for a couple of difficult seasons. Fairbrother was tactically sound, a fine player and widely respected within the Lancashire dressing room. However, he was the classic example of a good player whose form dipped upon being given the responsibility of captaincy. He was a natural worrier. He cared passionately about the job and the players in his charge, and not only was his form affected but the stress caused a series of debilitating hamstring injuries. Scarcely a month went by without someone captaining in his stead and the team missed the stability an injury-free captain provided.

I played under David Gower during my first two Tests in 1989. It would be unfair to offer a full assessment of his captaincy then because the team was at the fag end of a disastrous campaign, the South African rebels had deserted and Gower was clearly ill at ease with the coach Micky Stewart. I had heard from other players that Gower had led England impressively in India in 1984, and against Australia in 1985, but at the end of 1989 he had little to offer the team. There were no team meetings, he failed to turn up for practice before The Oval, and during that match he was severely distracted by the media pressure. At one point he called on the twelfth man to go to the press box and find out whom they thought he ought to bowl next. When the message came back, Gower laughed uproariously and continued to let Nick Cook get merrily milked. It was all in good humour, and it was to his credit that he could maintain his sense of humour at that time, yet it did little to help a struggling team.

Graham Gooch led England firmly by example between 1990 and 1993. I thought he was a much better captain than he has since been given credit for and he was much admired and respected by his team. Under him, the team performed creditably, save during the India tour and the early part of 1993 when he knew his time was up. He demanded a strict work ethic. He was a near obsessive trainer himself and he could often be seen going for a lengthy run after he had been dismissed. I remember seeing him running with weights up and down the many flights of stairs of our hotel in Delhi, just a few hours after we landed. He pushed himself to levels of fitness that few could match and he carried others with him – even John Morris was seen doing a sit-up or two during the Australia tour of 1991.

Most of all, he led by example at the crease and the team had enormous respect for him as a player. His match-winning 100 against the West Indies at Headingley in 1991 was the ultimate captain's knock. Even throughout the matches against Australia in 1993 when he knew his time was up, he still smashed 100s at Old Trafford and Trent Bridge. They were brave, bold and aggressive centuries.

His weaknesses as captain were that although he was tactically sound he could be predictable, and occasionally he found idiosyncratic characters difficult to handle. Essex's success in the county championship under his captaincy was based around a rigid plan of bowling 'in the channel' outside off stump. Of course, this was the line to trouble most players but it failed to encourage bowlers to think for themselves and they became almost automatons.

Gooch was ill at ease with players who failed to share his outlook on the game, in particular his enthusiasm for practice and training. His problem with David Gower on that Australian tour was the clearest example. Unlike the obsessive Gooch, Gower rarely trained. His idea of a punishing morning was a gentle stroll down to the Swann River to take in Perth's fresh morning air, before settling down to lunch with a couple of bottles of decent wine. Nor did he ever exert himself in the nets. On any given morning during our two-week preparatory stay in Perth, you would see Robin Smith in one net facing Devon Malcolm off 19 yards, emerging black and blue with a masochistic smile on his face, and in the other, Gower would be hitting a few gentle throw downs. He liked to check only that his timing was in order, and he took that feel-good factor to the crease with him.

Gower's methods worked on that tour despite Gooch's reservations. He scored a century in Melbourne, and in Sydney his was the most brilliant, attacking 100 I had seen from an England player until Mark Butcher superseded it at Headingley a decade later. I was at the other end for most of Gower's innings in Sydney – I was 70 odd when he came to the crease and he nearly beat me to three figures. He dismantled the Australian attack and was savage on Terry Alderman, and in the process it looked as though an ugly shot would have been an impossibility. He had a beautiful high back-lift, but his occasional lack of footwork meant he was essentially a good-wicket player. It would have been interesting to see how he would have coped with the poor Test wickets that characterised the second half of my England career.

It was in Sydney that the rumblings between Gooch and Gower erupted into the open. We had bowled and fielded terribly on the first day and Gooch's team-talk in the middle of the Sydney oval before the second day reminded us of our shortcomings. Gower ventured that we ought to be thinking more positively at which point Gooch rebuffed him pretty smartly. 'I'm the captain here, so shut up and listen.' The unease between them simmered on.

After Sydney, we travelled to Albury and then to Carrara, on Queensland's Gold Coast, for our warm-up game before the Adelaide Test. Gower heard that there was an airfield and a couple of 1939 vintage Tiger Moths sitting idly by. He thought that 'buzzing' the ground would be the perfect way to have some fun and give the team a lift. He asked me to join him but, thankfully, I sniffed out the potential danger and scurried off to the nets to practise my flipper. John Morris took my place.

The Tiger Moths, with Gower and Morris to the fore, flew in low between the floodlights and the match was halted momentarily. Even the tour manager, Peter Lush, was briefly amused until, that is, he found out who was in the plane. Gower had prepared some water-bomb balloons which he resisted releasing, otherwise the ensuing £1,000 fine might have been much steeper. The incident did little to ease the tension between the captain and the senior player.

It was exacerbated during the next match, the Fourth Test at Adelaide. At the fall of the third wicket, Gower walked out to bat to the tune of 'Those Magnificent Men in their Flying Machines'. That would have been fine except that the last ball before lunch was deliberately bowled down the leg side to a leg trap. Gower flicked idly and found one of two men positioned at fine-leg. Gooch was at the other end and as he walked off his face was thunderous. I think it was the last straw for him, and Gower played only intermittently for England after that.

Gooch and Gower are classic examples of the fact that the road to success can be travelled in entirely different ways. In the age of professionalism, work ethic and ever-increasing amounts of training, in many ways Gower's was the road less travelled. Because of that, I thought he was above all a brave player. Not physically brave, although he was that too, but brave in the sense that he resisted the pressure to change both his method and style. As a captain, Gooch could not come to terms with that and he felt that, as a senior player, Gower ought to have offered more to the team. It was a shame that two fine England players, and two fundamentally decent people, should have finished with their relationship soured.

I learnt from all the captains I played under – what to do, what not to do, what worked and what didn't. I had to marry that to my own natural instincts, which I think were sound, and my own character. As a captain it is impossible to escape your natural character, and it would be foolish to attempt to do so. I was quiet and thoughtful, not table-thumping, but still demanding. I spoke only when necessary so that those words carried weight.

There was no chance for forward planning in 1993 because I had been appointed for two Test matches only. I just hoped to get through those matches, to show that I was not out of my depth and thus to be appointed for the West Indies tour that winter.

My first Test in charge was at Edgbaston. Before that I had to attend my first selection meeting with Ted Dexter, Keith Fletcher and Dennis Amiss. Dexter's comments were scarce but nevertheless perceptive. His first question to me concerned the fate of Graham Gooch. I had little doubt that Gooch would be supportive of me and, since he was still our best player, I wanted him to play.

My main concern surrounded our strategy. Australia's fast-bowling resources were stretched to the limit. Craig McDermott had returned home injured with a twisted bowel and Merv Hughes was struggling badly with a knee injury. Australia's main threat centred around their spinners, Tim May and Shane Warne, and all summer we had been playing into their hands on flat and dry pitches. I was keen to take our chance on a pacy pitch that offered some lateral movement for the quicks. We sent word of our wishes, via Dennis Amiss, to Edgbaston and we filled our team with seam bowlers – Devon Malcolm, Steve Watkin, Martin Bicknell and Mark Ilott – and only one spinner, Peter Such.

I believe that Test matches should, as far as possible, be played on good, true surfaces that offer enough pace and bounce for the bowlers. Therefore, I rarely got involved in debates about pitch preparation during my time as captain. Before most Tests, however, groundsmen would invariably ask the selectors how much grass we wanted left on, and we were happy to guide them. In this instance, I hoped some grass would produce enough pace and lateral movement to justify our selections.

I arrived at Edgbaston and was astonished to find a pitch that was white, grassless and snuff-dry. We had no option but to call for another spinner. Phil Tufnell and John Emburey were the choices. Tufnell had had little success against Australia in the first two Tests of the summer, and since Emburey could also bat and was a better fielder, we went for a second off-spinner despite the fact that it gave an unbalanced look to the team.

I remember being remarkably relaxed the night before the match started. Some friends from Cambridge had come up for the game. We went out for a few drinks and since they had nowhere to sleep that evening they all bunked down on my floor. I can't believe I was so laid-back. I won the toss, batted and made 72 before being bowled by a Paul Reiffel grubber.

I was at the non-striker's end when Tim May bowled his first delivery of the match. It spun like a top and he turned to me, wide-eyed, and said, 'Jeez, mate, this is better than playing in India.' May was a big spinner of the ball, so much so that he had a huge gash on his spinning finger (which was, unusually for an off-spinner, his middle finger). Faced with such a friendly pitch, I am sure he didn't feel the pain. Both May and Warne revelled in the conditions and were the chief architects of a fairly comfortable Australian victory.

I had never expected an overnight miracle and as I left Edgbaston my optimism was undimmed. I remember that, as I was loading my kit into my car, Bob Dylan's 'The times they are a changin'' was playing on the radio. 'They certainly are,' said one spectator as I signed her autograph book. I believed they were, too.

We got the pacy pitch I craved at The Oval and the miracle happened. The architects of our victory were Devon Malcolm and Angus Fraser. Malcolm had developed as a Test cricketer since his debut in 1989; he was still liable to blow hot and cold, however, and, like the girl with the curl, when he was good he was very, very good and when he was bad he was horrid. In this match, as he was so often at The Oval, he was on target. In the first innings, he hit Mark Taylor under the heart and Taylor wheezed and groaned like a giant walrus. On the fourth evening, before we came off for bad light, Malcolm bowled like the wind.

Fraser's recall was entirely down to Ted Dexter, who had seen him take seven wickets in Middlesex's previous championship game but one. 'His snap has returned,' Dexter announced, and indeed it had. I needed little persuading because I admired Fraser's ability and attitude immensely. He was the perfect foil for Malcolm and my new-ball pairing began to take shape in my mind.

Graeme Hick had also been recalled. Hick was a player I had faith in but earlier in the year he had been found wanting against the bouncers and verbals of Merv Hughes. As we walked over to the nets on one of the practice days, I told him it was a problem that he had to confront head on, that I believed he could do it and that he would be batting at number three throughout the match.

Hick made runs and for the first time in the series our batting was positive and uninhibited. Neither May nor Warne were the same threat on The Oval's glassy surface and Australia could not match our firepower. I was hit on the head by Hughes early on and decided to play some shots afterwards. I scored a 50 and a 40 only but, more importantly, I felt the manner of my batting had given an aggressive lead to the team. We scored at a rate that gave us enough time to bowl Australia out twice.

On the final morning, Australia needed 390 more and we needed ten wickets. Devon Malcolm arrived at the ground lathered in sweat, like an over-excited racehorse. It was not at the prospect of bowling – his car had broken down on Vauxhall Bridge and he had had no option but to run to the ground. I gave a short team-talk to the effect that I felt we could win the match if we believed in ourselves, bowled aggressively and held our catches.

We were the fortunate recipients of a couple of umpiring decisions early on that set us on our way. After that, I had a good day tactically. I posted Ramprakash on the hook for Mark Waugh, who duly obliged. Later, I moved Steve Watkin very precisely into precisely nowhere on the leg side and this time Merv Hughes swiped across the line and picked him out. I moved easily between attack and defence, using Malcolm in attacking short bursts, and Fraser as my pressure bowler.

When Fraser trapped Warne lbw to win the match, my second as captain, we ended a dismal sequence of ten Tests and thirteen months without a victory, and it was the first time we had beaten Australia for seven years. It was a golden moment, of the type The Oval seems to have had in endless supply down the years – a sunny day, a full house, Australia vanquished and a young and vibrant England team rushing from the field as the spectators swarmed on.

Earlier that day, after my morning team-talk, Ted Dexter had wandered into the dressing room. He had vaguely wished everyone well, including the physiotherapist whom he mistook for a player, and, in his last act as chairman of selectors, announced that I had been appointed for the winter tour to the West Indies. Now I felt I could do some serious thinking and plan ahead with some purpose.

7

HONEYMOON PERIOD

What type of England team did I want to lead? That was the question that occupied my thoughts in the weeks that separated The Oval Test and the selection meeting for the West Indies tour. Prior to that I was in no position to think long-term. Initially, I had been appointed for two matches only and my overriding concern was to stop the horrendous run of defeats, so short-termism was very much the order of the day.

Even now, I had been appointed just for the duration of the winter. Throughout the period of my captaincy, I was only ever appointed on a short-term basis – a couple of matches here or a series there – as were England captains before me. The unfortunate consequence was that the issue of the captaincy seemed to be forever hanging in the air, or in the media at least. At the end of my tenure, I argued strongly to David Graveney that the captain should be appointed until he is sacked or he resigns, however long or short a period that may be. Happily, that is now the case.

Despite the ephemeral nature of my appointment, I felt in a strong position. I had made a good early impression, scoring runs, leading the side well and securing a victory that was as unexpected as it was stunning. Ted Dexter had resigned and had yet to be replaced as chairman of selectors, and I felt confident that Keith Fletcher and I would be the dominant voices in selection. As it turned out, I had almost complete control over the selection of the squad – far more influence than I was ever to exert again.

I was firmly of the opinion that it was time to plan for the future. We should draw a line under what had gone before, put an end to the selectorial merry-go-round and pick a group of young players with attitude, in whom we had faith, and move boldly forward. Keith Fletcher needed little persuading. Instinctively he was of a more conservative persuasion than me – for example, when Graham Thorpe broke his thumb on the morning of The Oval match, Fletcher was keen on Gatting not Ramprakash – but I think he had seen something at The Oval that excited him.

Graham Gooch had already announced that he had no intention of touring. I could not see the point of going back to Mike Gatting or Allan Lamb – Gatting's return in India had been unproductive and Lamb, despite his fine record against the West Indies, had not played internationally for fifteen months. David Gower was more of a problem. He was still a wonderful player, as I had seen at first-hand when Lancashire were at the wrong end of a typically serene 100 in mid August. He had been poorly treated in the last twelve months and his selection would be sure to get the public on our side. If we had taken a senior player, he would have been the one, but after much soul-searching I decided that he, too, would have been a backward step and it was time to bring the era of the three Gs to an end. It was time to move on.

Clearly, this was a precarious policy. The West Indies were still the dominant force in world cricket and were regarded as unbeatable at home. In touring with a bunch of near rookies, I was risking a period of defeat and disappointment before we turned the corner, and therefore I was putting my position in jeopardy. But I genuinely felt I had as much chance of success with youth as with the older players – they had been beaten by the West Indies time and again and there was bound to be some mental scarring. It was much better to go with players who knew neither fear nor defeat.

Throughout the 1980s the England team had the reputation of being a closed shop and there was a suspicion that young players were invariably picked too late, especially in comparison with other countries. In 1993 I overheard a crusty MCC member ask Ian Chappell how it was Australia managed to find so many good young players. 'That's easy,' he replied. 'We pick 'em.' Certainly in the late 1980s and early 1990s, England's selectors were guilty of failing to plan for the future. All the experienced players came to the end of their careers at the same time, leaving a huge hole to fill. In that sense, I had no option but to go with youth. Since then, England have picked their best young players more readily, and with the likes of Chris Read and Chris Schofield, it could be argued too readily.

At the beginning of my captaincy, I felt it was vital to have a dream to follow and a journey to undertake. My vision was of a group of young, athletic and talented players with the dedication to work hard together and grow together, taking a few knocks along the way but coming through on the other side. It was a vision inspired by the Australian team of the mid 1980s. In that period, Australian cricket was in the doldrums and Bobby Simpson and Allan Border had made the difficult decisions I was now contemplating. They had rid themselves of the cynics and gone with young, talented and tough players including Steve Waugh and David Boon. They had taken some knocks but the World Cup victory in 1987 and the Ashes victories in 1989, 1990–91 and 1993 had proved the wisdom of their patience and far-sightedness. Australia and Allan Border were my role models and very much in my thoughts as I drove through the Grace Gates on 14 September to select *my* team to tour the West Indies.

In fact, Keith Fletcher, Dennis Amiss and I had already met in Tino's, a restaurant in St John's Wood, on 10 September, during the Lancashire/Middlesex match, to thrash out our policy. On the fourteenth we merely expected our choices to be ratified by the other members of the board who were present –

Tim Lamb, M.J.K. Smith (the new tour manager) and A.C. Smith, the chief executive of the board.

We met in a dark and musty room along one of the numerous hidden corridors at Lord's. I felt the ghosts of many England captains watching over me and I prepared to approach proceedings with due solemnity. Then, just as we sat down, A.C. Smith got on his hands and knees and started crawling around the room peering under the tables and chairs. I looked at him quizzically. 'Bugs, old boy. I'm looking for listening devices. You can't be too careful, you know.' We ascertained that we were talking in privacy and carried on.

I began by emphasising the need to break with the past and to move forward with a youthful team, and handed over to Keith Fletcher, who went through the names of the bowlers we fancied. 'Fwaser.' Nods all round. 'Malcolm.' General murmurings of assent. 'Watkin.' Silent acquiescence. 'McCaddick.' We all looked up. 'Who?' 'Martin McCaddick,' said Fletcher, nonplussed.

We all started to giggle. It was not that the England coach had started to lose his mind but that he had a well-known (in cricketing circles) propensity for getting names horribly confused. On the India tour of 1992 he had introduced Paul Allott to a local dignitary as John Arlott. And once when Derek Pringle had invited Fletcher to a rock concert where Eric Clapton was playing he declined, saying he didn't 'much like Ernie Clapham anyway'.

In this instance it wasn't clear whether he wanted Andrew Caddick or Martin McCague. He had confused the names – a fusion of their bowling combining McCague's pace with Caddick's bounce would have been very handy indeed – but as Caddick had played for most of the summer and was the better prospect, we assumed Fletcher meant him. I hope he did anyway.

I got exactly the tour party I wanted and left the meeting extremely happy. We had decided against an older, more experienced batsman, but I felt that in Hick, Smith, Stewart and myself, I had four 'bankers'. I was sure that one or two of Hussain,

Thorpe, Ramprakash and Maynard would emerge. All were talented players and, especially in the case of the first three, I liked their attitude. I saw them as street-fighters with plenty of spunk and I hoped they would thrive on the extra pressure and responsibility. All were good fielders and I wanted to lead an athletic team that would be the equal of other teams in the field. We had lagged behind in this area in recent years.

Devon Malcolm and Angus Fraser were my spearheads, backed up by Alan Igglesden, Steve Watkin and Andrew Caddick with Chris Lewis to provide the balance as the all-rounder. Like every other captain in the last decade, I fancied my chances of getting the best out of the enigmatic Lewis, and like every other captain I failed. In the end, you can only lead a player to the well; you can't drink the water for him.

There were two glaring errors in selection, for which I must take the blame. We omitted Peter Such who had been our best spinner throughout the summer against Australia. My thinking was fine – I viewed spin as an attacking option and felt Tufnell and Salisbury would have a better chance of winning matches. But I did not envisage the phalanx of left-handers who would play against us and I soon regretted Such's omission. Secondly, we took seventeen players, at least one too many. It became impossible to keep everyone happy and with the limited cricket outside the one-day internationals, sixteen would have been more than enough.

Other than that, I look back with some pride at our policy and selections. Even now I feel we did exactly what was required and our judgement on the young players was sound. Thorpe, Hussain, Ramprakash, Stewart, Caddick and I were all central to England's plans eight years later against Australia but back then we had just a handful of caps between us.

After selecting the team, we retired to Tino's once more for dinner. It was my first chance to get to know M.J.K. Smith, the former England captain, and I sat to his left with Micky Stewart to his right. Halfway through the dinner M.J.K. gesticulated grandly with his right arm and knocked a glass of red wine all over Micky. M.J.K. didn't seem in the least bit bothered. He announced that white wine was the only way to neutralise the red and prevent a permanent stain, and proceeded, in full view of the whole restaurant, to pour half a bottle of Chardonnay all over an astonished Micky Stewart. Apart from wasting some decent wine, M.J.K. seemed like my kind of manager and I was sure we would get on well.

There was a four-month hiatus between the selection of the touring party and our departure in mid January. We had some sessions at Lilleshall and a week in Portugal at the Barrington Club. I was delighted with the squad's attitude to fitness and training, and for that I had to thank my predecessor Graham Gooch. Because of his example there now seemed to be an in-built culture of hard work, which augured well for the coming months.

In the intervening period I had to decide how my captaincy was to differ from Gooch's and how I might impose my character on the team. I wanted to be less domineering. Obviously, I needed to give clear direction on the field but off it I wanted more of a cooperative approach, to encourage the players to think for themselves. I also wanted to draw them into the decision-making process. I was sure that the more the players felt that they were masters of their own destiny, the easier it would be to carry them along. More team meetings were required. We needed to talk more about cricket and give every player the opportunity to have his say.

I also thought it important to give the players more time off than had been the case under Gooch. My own philosophy was that, in anything, freshness is vital and I was keen for the team to work hard at the ground but to have plenty of time to relax and get away from the game. To that end, it was good that the early games were in Antigua, St Kitts and Barbados, three islands renowned for their beach resorts. We needed a Mars-bar attitude to the tour – work, rest and play in equal measure.

Looking through the tour party, Phil Tufnell was the only one whom I felt had the potential to cause me some grief. I am certainly not against difficult individuals; I believe it is the captain's job to get the best out of the various characters found in every team. Also, despite the fact that it is generally pace bowlers who win Tests in the West Indies, Tufnell was a skilful flight bowler, who didn't necessarily need a turning pitch to take wickets, and was therefore central to our plans. He required some careful thought and tender handling. I decided that his greatest strength was his ability to bowl well regardless of what was going on in his turbulent life off the field. To that end, I was happy to allow him plenty of slack. Of course, I did not tell Tufnell that. It would have been akin to giving Billy Bunter not just the keys to, but the lease for, the tuck-shop.

The policy was well intentioned but, in the end, I probably gave him too much leeway. He partied hard for most of the trip, so much so that other members of the squad often complained. I wasn't too worried about that but when Tufnell failed to turn up to give support during one of the matches he wasn't involved in, I had to read him the riot act.

As far as the press were concerned, I could do little wrong in the early weeks of the tour and there was no doubt I was in my honeymoon period. The runs were flowing – I scored 100s against an Antiguan eleven and Barbados – and the team were unbeaten prior to the first international, winning two of the four warm-up matches.

I was enjoying the occasional eccentricities of West Indies cricket. The second match of the tour was in St Kitts and their captain greeted me at the toss; he flipped the coin and I called correctly. The coin landed on the pitch but then rolled off it. He demanded a re-toss. 'The coin got to stay on the pitch, man,' he said. Their manager, dressed in full white tie ensemble as if he was about to sit his finals at Oxford, was strolling nearby, a touch self-importantly, and so I called him over. Between us we managed to persuade the captain that there was little in the laws of the game that would back up his claims. Nice try, though.

At the Recreation Ground in Antigua we got our first taste of cricket Caribbean style. The Leeward Islands' bowlers were keen to test out England's young guns in the traditional Caribbean way and Chickie's disco, in full earshot of the dressing room, throbbed its approval. Chickie at least chose his music well – Jack Russell went out to bat to the Dambusters' march and returned 56 runs later, after a fearful bombardment, to 'Land of Hope and Glory'.

I was happy with our preparations and delighted with the relationship I was developing with Keith Fletcher. Fletcher had a slightly hunched bearing and constantly worried expression and had been regarded by some as an overly cautious England captain in the early 1980s. He was not everybody's idea of an England coach, but I found him to be both tough and shrewd. He could speak falteringly when faced by a big audience but worked brilliantly one-to-one with players. He cared deeply about the cricketers in his charge but was not afraid to bawl them out either.

Chris Lewis in particular exasperated Fletcher early on in the tour. Lewis had shaved his head, got sunstroke and missed one of the early matches. 'He's gone and had a cue-ball, the pwat,' muttered Fletcher. Later, on the second day of the First Test in Jamaica, Lewis bowled at medium pace for much of the day until, in the last over, he unleashed a bouncer at Keith Arthurton that was as quick as anything that had been bowled in the match. Fletcher was livid and was quick to let Lewis know.

Fletcher coached England until the end of the 1995 Ashes series. I don't think he ever recovered from a disastrous start to his tenure in India and against Australia when the team lost eight out of his first nine matches in charge. He was always playing catch-up after that. Nevertheless, I found him to be absolutely loyal during the time we worked together. He was one of the very few people – I could count them on one hand – whom I could trust completely.

We surprised our hosts and the partisan crowd by winning the first one-day international in Barbados. I scored 86, won the man of the match award and captained with a sure touch. Nevertheless, I knew our victory was based as much on the disarray in the West Indies camp as anything else. They were in the middle of a pay dispute and the Antiguan players had not even bothered to turn up for practice before the game. Unfortunately for us, the dispute was settled shortly afterwards.

Once the West Indies had settled their problems they swiftly put us in our place, winning the one-day series 3–2. It was a steep and harsh learning curve for my team and for me, and I was acutely aware that I had made a couple of glaring mistakes. In the second one-day international in Jamaica, I was too slow to react to cut off the leg-side boundaries during Jimmy Adams' late surge to victory, and in the next match at St Vincent I made an error of judgement at the toss, putting the West Indies in. We went down to a then record defeat for England in one-day internationals.

The day before that game I had been, literally, sitting on the dock of the bay watching the time go by, and pondering the team for the next day. A Rastafarian smoking a huge spliff came by and we got chatting. 'Man,' he said, 'you always got to bat first in St Vincent and then bowl second when the tide comes in.' The pitch the next day looked mottled and uneven and I looked at it uncertainly. Geoff Boycott was also on the wicket and I asked his opinion. 'I think you've got to bowl first,' he said, 'just to see how bad it is before you bat.' In fact, it was very good and the West Indies plundered 313, and then, when the tide came in, it was very bad and we were skittled for 148. I learnt my lesson. When it came to pitches you had never seen before, local knowledge, rather than the Great Yorkshireman's, was eminently preferable.

These errors of judgement were largely overlooked. I would

have been crucified for them five years later but in this instance the press were prepared to give me and my young team time, and they were well aware that we were up against it. It helped that my form continued to be good and I showed in the first two Tests in Jamaica and Guyana that I had put the memories of my nightmare against the West Indies in 1991 firmly behind me, and that I had the courage and technique to succeed against the most formidable pace attack of them all.

The Test series got under way at Sabina Park in Jamaica and by the time the second innings came around we were facing defeat. We had failed to capitalise on a century partnership in the first innings between Alec Stewart and me and had allowed the West Indies to get 407 after being 23–3. It had long been the policy of the West Indies, since Clive Lloyd in the 1980s, to target the opposition captain – 'cut off the head and the rest will fall'. So it was that, as Alec Stewart and I set out to reduce a first-innings deficit of 173, Courtney Walsh decided to test out England's young captain with some 'chin music'.

The pitch was hard and fast. It had been spun-rolled, as was the custom at Sabina Park, and the result was a shimmering, almost glassy, strip of concrete. As you took guard on the first morning, you could almost see your reflection in it. Walsh was the local hero and as he lengthened his run the crowd whipped itself into a frenzy. Sabina Park has the most hostile atmosphere in the region, and there was a definite whiff of ganja in the air at the popular end behind where Walsh was fielding.

Walsh bowled ferociously for just under two hours, for about a dozen overs on the trot. Midway through he began to tease the crowd by pretending to take his sweater from the umpire at the end of each over, signalling the end of his spell. The crowd roared its disapproval, urging him to keep going, and in that way Walsh used the crowd to keep his energy high and his juices flowing.

It was among the fastest spells that I ever faced and, until Allan Donald's famous spell at Trent Bridge in 1998, it was the most intense period of cricket I had experienced. I felt Walsh was too quick to hook that day and there was nothing to do other than duck and weave and hope to survive. At one point, Walsh hit me on the arm with a bouncer. 'You wanker,' I muttered to myself, annoyed that I had taken my eye off the ball. 'You swearing at me?' said Walsh, who promptly stepped up another gear and sat me on my backside next ball. I quietly put him right.

I nearly survived the onslaught but just as Walsh was tiring, I took my eye off another bouncer and punched it to Jimmy Adams at short-leg. Jimmy took the catch and set off running, holding the ball triumphantly in the air. His team-mates caught up with him at about deep extra-cover while I turned quietly and walked the other way. Despite the fact that I had failed to survive the spell and scored just 28, it was a vital innings for me – it was the first time I had really been targeted and I felt I had stood my ground. After I was out I watched from the sidelines and only then did I realise how quickly Walsh was bowling. It did wonders for my confidence. I thought that if I could withstand that, I could withstand anything.

That confidence spurred me on to 144 in the next Test in Guyana. It was my best innings to date for England. I thought about the Jamaica bombardment carefully and decided that, on Bourda's slower pitch, if Walsh reverted to the same tactics I would take him on. I also thought about my technique and decided to open up my stance more to prevent the kind of blind spot that had brought my downfall in Jamaica. Halfway through the first day Walsh came around the wicket and I hooked him hard. Earlier on that morning we had been in terrible trouble at 2–2 and the 100 I scored showed that I was beginning to excel when we were under the most severe pressure.

The West Indies wrapped up the five-match series in Trinidad, and that match and its aftermath presented my biggest challenge to date as England captain. We had played some of our best Test cricket of the series during the first three days and by the rest day we were contemplating victory. The West Indies at that stage were effectively 67–5 in their second innings with only Shivnarine Chanderpaul, the last of the recognised batsmen, standing in our way. On the fourth morning, Graeme Hick dropped Chanderpaul twice and after tea the West Indies were able to set us 194 for victory with an hour and a day to go.

In that hour the series was lost and our dream was shattered by an astonishing spell of fast bowling by Curtly Ambrose. It was entirely different in its intent from Walsh's spell in Jamaica. Walsh's main aim was to intimidate while Ambrose, sensing a match to win and a wearing pitch to exploit, was only interested in wickets. Of course, there was the occasional bouncer – I remember with one, Graham Thorpe had no choice but to withdraw his left hand from the bat and catch the ball in front of his nose – but Ambrose's general length was full and the effect was dramatic.

He nipped the first ball of the innings back to trap me lbw and after that I could only watch the destruction from the dressing room. Soon after, Mark Ramprakash called for a suicidal second run that betrayed his nerves under pressure. I retired to the shower and when I emerged we were six wickets down, our innings in tatters and the series effectively over. Ambrose completed our humiliation the next day and our 46 all out was the second lowest score in England's history. Ambrose soaked up the adulation, a calypso was penned in his honour and the West Indies danced to its beat throughout the rest of the tour.

It was a testing time for me. At the post-match presentations I completely lost my cool with Gary Franses, a television producer (and ironically now my producer at Channel 4), who was trying to get the teams in order. I recovered my composure in time for the press conference. I often found that I was at my best in press conferences when the team had performed badly. In this case, I looked at the match objectively; I felt we had played well for much of the game and all we needed to do next time was finish off the job.

Privately, however, I was beginning to have my doubts. In a sense, the results were not the most important aspect of the tour – I was just as interested in the level of performance and I hoped to see a general improvement over time, a graph curving upwards with only the occasional blip. As Geoffrey Boycott often said to me, 'You're going to take one step forwards and two steps backwards, so be patient.' Defeats like the one in Trinidad, however, could cause a rapid loss of confidence and have damaging and long-lasting consequences, and I began to worry about the younger members of the team.

It was vital that we recovered quickly and, to that end, I erred in sitting out the next match in Grenada – the last before back-to-back Tests in Barbados and Antigua. My motives were laudable – we had to consider batting changes after Trinidad and both Hussain and Maynard needed some cricket. The error in taking seventeen players came home to me and in order to keep them both happy, I had no option but to leave myself out. It was a mistake because, above all, the team needed clear direction and leadership. We lost to a moderate team and Raul Lewis embarrassed us with nine wickets.

As we arrived in Barbados for the next match, we read that Roland Holder, the Barbados captain, had predicted a 'blackwash'. There is no doubt that we were at a low ebb. Given this and the fact that the West Indies had not lost in Bridgetown since 1935, what happened over the next five days must go down as one of the great sporting upsets.

I would like to claim great credit for inspiring the victory but that would be to ignore the many fine performances from some England players in the match – Alec Stewart's twin 100s for example, and five-wicket hauls for Angus Fraser and Andrew Caddick. In the previous Test, I had dropped a catch off Fraser's bowling that cost him another 'five for' against the West Indies. He was livid. On each tour we ran a wager between us based on who would get most centuries or 'five fors'. Fraser's haul in Barbados probably meant I would be paying up, but it was a bet I was happy to lose.

What I did do between Grenada and Barbados was keep calm and maintain a sense of perspective. I tried to impress upon the players the good things that had come out of the Trinidad game and, most importantly, I argued strongly with my fellow selectors for an unchanged team. Both M.J.K. and Fletcher felt it was time to change the batting line-up but I felt it was the perfect opportunity to show that we were going to get away from the chop and change mentality that had afflicted our cricket in recent years. Nasser Hussain had reasonably expected to play in Barbados and was incensed after I announced the team. 'It's an absolute disgrace,' he said to me. I had been in his position a year earlier in India so I could understand his frustration.

As he had done all tour, Richie Richardson did the opposite of what I would have done on winning the toss. He decided to bowl first, probably to see if the scars remained after Trinidad. Alec Stewart and I walked out to an enormous ovation from the 6,000 or so visiting English supporters. There was some ironic applause when we passed 46 but we were not separated until we had posted 171 for the first wicket. It was a vital partnership, both in its timing and manner, and must have reassured a dressing room that would have been understandably nervous at the start. I nicked Kenny Benjamin 15 short of 100 but I had proved my worth as an opener – and as a captain who was prepared to lead from the front in a tough situation.

The next five days were as joyous as the climax in Trinidad had been disastrous. It was exactly what I had been yearning to see – a young, dynamic England team playing with skill and passion. As we closed on victory, the normally animated Bajan crowd grew silent and a lone bugler in the popular stand played 'We Shall Overcome'. Nobody seemed to believe him. After the doubts in Trinidad, Barbados reaffirmed my confidence in what we were trying to do. If we could win here, and against this team, what was there to stop us?

There was little time to reflect upon our victory, and no time at all to celebrate. We were flying out of Barbados that evening to prepare for the final Test three days later in Antigua. I had played the whole match with tonsillitis and fell asleep exhausted on the floor of the Grantley Adams airport.

Desmond Haynes and Richie Richardson were injured for the final Test and it was the West Indies who were now uncertain of their team. When we had them 12–2 early on in the first session, the pendulum had certainly swung in our favour, and we were confident of building upon our success in Barbados. Those early wickets served only to bring Brian Lara to the crease and over the next two and a half days he played a wonderful, chanceless innings of 375, breaking Garry Sobers' record in the process.

Lara had been in good form all tour, scoring 83 and 167 in the first two Tests. He had looked a brilliant player at times, with a touch of genius, but he had always looked the type of player to give a chance. In Antigua, on the flattest of pitches, it was almost as though he realised from the start that a giant score was in the offing. He played faultlessly; I can't remember him giving one chance. On 291 I took first slip out for the first time and he nicked Andrew Caddick's next ball through the gaping hole. He could quite conceivably have been taking the mickey. I wouldn't know because the scale of his talent was way outside my understanding. Throughout his innings, quick feet and a high back-lift combined to produce such timing as a Swiss watch-maker would be proud of.

On the third morning, he approached Sobers' record. I had known Lara since the Youth World Cup in Australia in 1988. We were quite friendly and as the series was meandering to a close it was tempting to sit back and admire his play. I didn't want to make things easy for him, however, and we tried to prevent him taking the singles and dominating the strike. For the first time, he began to look nervous. 'Come on, Athers, you're making it hard for me,' he complained. On about 340, Angus Fraser made him play and miss. 'Arsey bastard,' said Fraser with an ironic, if exhausted, smile on his face.

Shortly before lunch on the third day, Lara pulled Chris Lewis to the square-leg boundary for 4 to break Sobers' record. Pandemonium ensued. The crowd rushed on and Sobers limped out to congratulate Lara who triumphantly went down on both knees, pope-like, to kiss his field of dreams. We stood back and watched history in the making. Darrell Hair, the Australian umpire, was flapping because the crowd were running all over the pitch. He grabbed the spectator nearest to him by the scruff of the neck and gave him a roasting. It was George the groundsman, who was also trying to prevent further damage to his pride and joy. The chaos lasted for ten minutes and at least it spared us from having to bat before lunch.

Lara's run of form continued into the English season when he scored 501 for Warwickshire against Durham. Later in his career, in 1999, he played perhaps the greatest innings I have seen when he single-handedly took the West Indies to victory over Australia in Bridgetown. I would not class him above Tendulkar or Steve Waugh but he was capable of playing innings that those two could not have played. He was certainly the most thrilling player of my generation.

Since his golden period in the mid 1990s, Lara's star has waned a little. In a way it is understandable – after 375, 501 and the brilliance in Barbados in 1999, what else can he achieve? Perhaps the only way forward is to dedicate himself to the team and set himself the challenge of helping the West Indies back to the top of the tree. It is said in the Caribbean that he has too much of an ego for that. That, too, is understandable. I was holidaying in Trinidad the week after his 375 and 'Laramania' was in full swing. There seemed to be a party, parade or dinner in his honour every minute of the day, and it would take a strong man indeed not to have his head turned by such adulation.

My homecoming was naturally more understated. I didn't go

straight home with the team, but spent a week in Trinidad and Tobago with Isabelle de Caires, a girl I had met in Guyana while she was visiting her parents. My holiday did not go unnoticed, and the Lancashire players were quick to plaster photos that a freelance photographer had snapped of us in Tobago, all around the Old Trafford dressing room.

I was happy with my efforts on my first tour as England captain, and my batting had flourished. I had scored 500 runs at over 50 an innings with two centuries, a good return for an opener in the Caribbean. The team was beginning to take shape in my mind. To the core batsmen I could add Graham Thorpe, while Fraser, Malcolm, Caddick and Tufnell were the basis around whom an attack could be built. John Crawley and Darren Gough had caught the eye on the A tour of South Africa and would push hard for a place in the coming months. New Zealand were soon to arrive in England and I felt sure it was the perfect opportunity to achieve some long overdue success.

8

SELECTION DILEMMAS

After the end of the Ashes tour in 1995 I spent a couple of fruitful hours in the Perth dressing room chatting to Mark Taylor, the Australian captain, whom I liked and admired in equal measure. We got through a crate of beer and I asked him about their forthcoming tour of the West Indies and his input on selection. 'Mate, I don't officially sit in on selection, but by and large they'll let me take who I want.' I listened enviously. He seemed at ease with the Australian system and his place in it, as I had been eighteen months previously, before our tour of the West Indies. After that tour, following the appointment of Raymond Illingworth as chairman of selectors, I grew increasingly disillusioned with my role in selection. By the time I talked with Mark, I was in almost the opposite position to him. Officially I sat in on selection, and therefore was damned by association, but my influence on it had been severely reduced.

As we neared the end of the West Indies tour, the TCCB were looking for a successor to Ted Dexter as chairman of selectors and the choice, it seemed, was between Raymond Illingworth and M.J.K. Smith, two former England captains with very different backgrounds between whom there was little love lost. Possibly, following Dexter, Smith's Oxbridge background counted against him. The working party recommended Illingworth and his appointment was ratified at the board's spring meeting. Illingworth agreed to take on the job with the proviso that he had the ultimate say in selection. 'I asked for and got an assurance that I would have the final say,' were his words at the time. While all this was going on, I was kept in the dark.

I knew Illingworth only as someone who had a moderate record as a Test player, but who was highly regarded as an England captain. He had the reputation of being both tough and shrewd and was probably the type of captain I would have liked to play alongside. I remember asking Alan Knott about Illingworth and he said that, in a tight situation, Illingworth was the best captain he had played under. No less a judge than Ian Chappell thought Illingworth the best captain he played against.

I had met Illingworth occasionally, usually in the sponsor's tent at the end of a day's play, although we had rarely chatted. Our first meeting after his appointment was on 1 May during a one-day friendly between Lancashire and Yorkshire. Illingworth arrived in sunglasses and a brown leather jacket that had seen better days. He was tanned from his winter in Spain and the combination gave him the look of a second-hand car salesman. Initially, we viewed each other a little suspiciously. Perhaps he looked upon me as a privileged kid from a private school and Oxbridge background who, at the tender age of twenty-five, had been given the ultimate toy to play with. He probably thought I was a little too sure of myself and had a little too much to say. I, on the other hand, had been unimpressed by his remarks about my team-mates. Illingworth's opening comments as chairman had come in the middle of the Antigua Test and he had been less than complimentary about Fraser, Hick, Lewis, Ramprakash and Russell. Obviously, as captain I felt a primary loyalty to them.

There were no niceties, no well done or bad luck, nor even any kind of review of the tour. He merely said, 'Right lad, let's get down to business,' and produced a list of around sixty players whom he was keen to look at before the first international of the summer. Sixty players! I was doubtful if there were two dozen county players with enough class to be successful in Test cricket. It was clear to me from the start that whatever vision I had had, and whatever plans I had made, would be cast aside. Illingworth's selection policies appeared to be completely ad hoc, based around picking in-form players for each match with no easily discernible long-term view or regard to class or stability.

This was all very well in the era in which Illingworth had played. In the 1960s and 1970s, English county cricket was probably the strongest domestic competition in the world, and any player selected for England would be likely to be well prepared and able to flourish. My view was that times had changed and there was a widening gulf between county and Test cricket. Consequently, there were fewer players likely to succeed and those who were selected needed time to come to terms with the higher standards required. My idea that the England team should be a constant entity, almost a nineteenth county, was anathema to Illingworth. Other than general policy, however, we were not poles apart in our views of most players.

Over time, the initial frostiness between us thawed and on a purely personal level we got along fine and came to have, I think, a grudging respect for each other. It was fortunate that I was happy to talk about the past because that was a frequent topic of conversation. I went along with it and baited Illingworth along the way. 'Just see if you can get Dover into the conversation next time,' Alan Knott said. I duly did and Illy was off – 'I got fourteen wickets and a hundred in the match once there, you know . . .'

I would never describe relations between us as warm, in the way that they were between David Lloyd and me, or Nasser Hussain and Duncan Fletcher years later. Illingworth's public pronouncements prevented it. David Lloyd and Duncan Fletcher were careful never to contradict the captain in public, whatever their views in private, and they were always publicly supportive of the players. It is difficult to say the same about Illingworth.

While we were in Australia in 1995, he criticised me at a press lunch in London for failing to ring him about selection prior to the First Test in Brisbane, despite the fact that tour selection was traditionally the captain's sole domain. Before we left for South Africa in 1995, he did a series of articles with Geoff Boycott in the *Sun* that were intensely critical of both my character and my captaincy.

Initially, I could not work out whether he was being naïve or whether he was using the press to keep me in my place. Later, I came to the conclusion that his comments were not designed deliberately to hurt me although he must have been extraordinarily insensitive to think that they did not. The press pack he faced as chairman of selectors was an entirely different animal from the one he had known as captain of England in the 1970s, so I gave him the benefit of the doubt.

Later, Illingworth's responsibilities were widened to take in both a managerial and selection role – a kind of supremo, as he liked to think of himself. But at the start of 1994, as the Kiwis arrived for a three-match series, his powers were limited to the selection of the team and it was my role within the selection process that concerned me most.

Since the turn of the last century, the England captain had been coopted on to the selection panel for home series. As Mike Brearley says in *The Art of Captaincy*, 'The principle of co-option embodies a compromise. The captain is not in sole charge; but nor is he excluded from the process. How much say he then has depends on the respective persuasiveness of him and the selectors.' Obviously, since Illingworth had been guaranteed the final say, the influence I had exerted on the selection of the West Indies tour party would be diminished. I wasn't unduly worried about that, but I was keen that my views should be heard. Illingworth had not directly appointed his fellow selectors but he had starred his preference for Brian Bolus and Fred Titmus. Both were duly voted on to the panel, which was completed by Keith Fletcher and me.

In time, I came to have little respect for either Bolus or Titmus as selectors. Titmus had little to offer and it was rare to hear him give an opinion or judgement on a player. Even in matters of spin bowling, in which Titmus was expert, it was difficult to drag him off his perch. In 1995, Illingworth sent Titmus to look at the Edgbaston pitch prior to our match with the West Indies. Titmus reported back and didn't seem too alarmed. His judgement on the uneven, mottled surface was seriously awry.

Titmus was virtually deaf in one ear and if you happened to be sitting on his deaf side, you had to shout to make yourself heard. To his credit, he was happy enough to poke fun at himself about this. On one occasion he brought a wooden horn to the meeting. He would stick one end in his deaf ear while you bellowed down the other end. 'Not Cork, Fred, Thorpe!'

Although Titmus had little to offer, he was harmless. This was not the case with Bolus, a man to whom I took a fairly immediate and visceral dislike. At least you could never accuse Bolus of sitting on the fence; he was always ready to give a forthright opinion. I got the immediate impression that he didn't think I ought to be England captain. Indeed, during the selection meeting after the First Test against New Zealand, which we won by an innings and in which I got 100, he told me as much. I think that Mike Gatting would have been his preferred choice from the start.

He generally had too much to say. Like children, selectors should be seen and not heard and above all, whatever their views in private, the notion of collective responsibility demanded, in public at least, a united front. Bolus was always a loose cannon. Later, after he was replaced on the selection committee, he went on to chair the England Management Advisory Committee and so he remained at the heart of decision-making within the English game. His influence over selection continued, and he, among others, persuaded Nasser Hussain and Duncan Fletcher to take an untried team to South Africa after we had been beaten by New Zealand in 1999. It left Hussain with a team that had very little chance of winning.

In 1994, New Zealand arrived with a moderate team and we won an uneventful one-day series. After the first one-day international, both Illingworth and I were put before the press. I was mildly miffed as the post-match press conference was usually the captain's domain. No doubt the journalists felt they had more chance of extracting some juice from the chairman than the captain. I was asked about the team for the First Test and I blandly said that I didn't think there would be too many changes. Afterwards Illingworth pulled me up and told me to leave matters of selection to the selectors. He served notice that when it came to selection, they were very much in charge.

It was all slightly confusing for me. Before the announcement of the West Indies touring party, I had been told by the TCCB that I would be the one to announce the team to the press because they were keen to restore the natural authority of the captain. Now I was being told I could not even comment on it. Yet in between this apparent volte-face nobody from Lord's had bothered to speak to me.

The selection meeting for the First Test was held at the Copthorne Hotel in Manchester on 28 May. Naturally, I argued strongly for the players who had been in the Caribbean. There were a couple of changes that were unavoidable – Caddick was suffering from shin splints and was unavailable, and Tufnell's tumultuous private life meant that he was not even playing for Middlesex in the early months of the season. This was the only time in my experience of selection that a player was not selected for purely non-cricketing reasons. I took offence later on when Illingworth suggested in print that my friendship with Angus Fraser, and the fact that I had 'history' with Phillip DeFreitas, had an undue bearing on selection.

At the start of the series, Illingworth, Bolus and Titmus were committed specifically to two things – having an all-rounder at number six to enable us to play five bowlers, and trying to get two spinners in the team or at least in the squad. I thought both arguments were fundamentally flawed. In principle, I was in favour of the balance that an all-rounder would provide as long as we had somebody good enough to fill the role. Other than giving Stewart the gloves, which because of his outstanding form as an opener in the Caribbean I was not in favour of, I could not see that we had a good enough all-rounder. Besides, every other country was going in with six batsmen, a wicket-keeper and four bowlers – Test match sessions consisted of only thirty overs and, in cool, bowler-friendly English conditions, four bowlers were usually enough.

The two spinners theory failed to take into account the changing nature of pitches in England since the period when Bolus, Titmus and Illingworth had played. Then, uncovered and natural soil pitches had provided perfect conditions in which finger spinners could thrive. More recently, the pitches had been re-laid to a Surrey and Ongar loam specification. These pitches were harder and more likely to crack and become uneven than break up in the traditional way. Even on a wearing surface, pace bowlers could do more damage than finger spinners. To prove the point, in the last couple of years, other than at Old Trafford and The Oval, we have hardly considered playing one, never mind two, spinners.

Despite my reservations, these were arguments I was destined to lose. Illingworth had been impressed by the young Yorkshire all-rounder Craig White at the start of the season. 'Honestly, Mike, when he bats he gets a bigger stride in than anybody in England and he bowls pretty quick too,' was his glowing reference. I had not seen White but was happy to go along with Illingworth's assessment. The downside was that there was no room for Graham Thorpe, and of the West Indies party, there were only six survivors.

We trounced New Zealand by an innings at Trent Bridge and so the meeting prior to the Second Test was shorter and less contentious. Even so, I was taken aback when Bolus suggested that, tactically, I had not had a good game. I thought an innings victory and scoring my third Test century in five games represented fair form. Bolus clearly thought otherwise.

For the Second Test, at Lord's, the selectors were unsure about Devon Malcolm, who had bowled moderately at Nottingham. I felt that dropping Malcolm after one indifferent match would send the wrong signals and would return us to the days of chopping and changing. I strongly believed that the team should be changed only if it could be made stronger. I was outvoted and Malcolm was released on the Wednesday, the day before the Test, so that he could play for his county the next day. He was understandably aggrieved; I felt no less upset having to convey the bad news to someone I felt should be in the team. On top of that, the selectors grandly told me on the morning of the game that the final choice, between Richard Stemp and Paul Taylor, was down to me. Given that my strike bowler was a hundred miles away, it was a futile gesture.

As captain, I always felt it was important to tell players personally if they were omitted. It was less important to tell them of their inclusion because this was easier news to accept. If they had been dropped from the squad, I would ring them on the Sunday morning after selection. I came to dread Sunday mornings. Sometimes there was no logical reason why a player had been left out and there wasn't much to say. Most players accepted it was a tricky call to make and I can't remember an instance of a player making life too awkward. Over time, it became more difficult to make the calls if I did not agree with the decision. Nevertheless, collective responsibility was important and I could hardly say, '*I* wanted you in but . . .'

However preferable it was to tell players personally of their exclusion, it was not always possible. We didn't finish selecting the 1995 Ashes tour party until well after midnight and Angus Fraser learnt of his omission early next morning on Sky news. Naturally he was livid with me. Again it was not a decision I agreed with but I still wanted to speak to him personally. As Mike Brearley says, if an oversight happens rarely, 'the captain will be forgiven: if common, it is a sign of insensitivity, and hints at unsuitability for the job.'

Manchester was again the venue for the selection meeting prior to the Third Test. Lancashire were playing Glamorgan at Colwyn Bay and it was normal practice for the selectors to travel to where the captain was playing. In this instance, I had to do the travelling and it necessitated me missing the last hour of play on the Saturday and a drive of two hours that evening, and two hours back on Sunday morning. That unnecessary hassle was not the only reason why the meeting was the most difficult so far. The fate of Robin Smith, England's number four and senior player, was under scrutiny.

After a wonderful start to his Test career, it had been a difficult twelve months for Smith. He had struggled in India and against Tim May and Shane Warne in the '93 Ashes series and had been dropped for the first time in his career for the final Test at The Oval. I had been staying with Smith that weekend, but friendship could never interfere with difficult decisions. Nevertheless, I looked upon him as my absolute 'banker' in the West Indies and I pencilled him in for the pivotal number four position and put him down for 400 runs plus.

The start of the tour did not go well for him and he struggled for form. He was certainly partying hard – he had signalled his intentions to enjoy himself on the flight over and had staggered off the plane much the worse for wear. I was not too concerned. Smith was always last to leave the bar but he was always first in the nets and last to leave the training pitch. He was definitely from the 'work hard, play hard' school.

However, during the warm-up games, Smith overslept twice and was fifty-seven minutes late for the Leeward Islands match. We had to send Doug Insole, a board official, to wake him up and when he did, Smith seemed oblivious to the fact that he ought to have been at the ground and invited Doug in for a cup of tea. Clearly, I needed to do something, but what precisely? A fine seemed irrelevant, dropping him would hurt us more and so I decided a dressing down in front of the team was the answer. Normally I abided by the 'praise in public, bollock in private' rule but in this instance I made him apologise to the team, hoping the embarrassment would shake him out of his lethargy and remind him of his responsibilities.

I had played in the England team with Robin since 1990. I was good friends with him and thought I knew him well. Before every Test match in England we would go out for a pasta lunch to wish each other well for the match to come. But in many ways I had misread him. In inking down Smith in the number four position, I looked upon him not only as a strong player but also as a strong character and a leader for my young team.

Most players, I would say, bat in a manner that reflects their character – in Gatting you can see the bulldog; in Stewart, the pride; in Border, the battler; in Lara, the flawed genius; and in Russell, the eccentricity. In my case, my batting was a perfect reflection of my obdurate and stubborn nature. Smith is one of the few players I can think of whose batting is quite the inverse of his character. At the crease he is a strong, chest-thumping, no-nonsense player whose enormous forearms smash the ball unforgivingly through point at the first sign of any width. His two innings against the West Indies at Edgbaston in 1995, on a shocking wicket, were the bravest I have seen.

Off the field, however, he proved to be a follower not a leader, and a man who often seemed to be lacking in self-confidence, full of uncertainties, insecurities and doubts. Smith recovered to score 175 in the last Test in Antigua but I think he still felt under pressure although, in this case, it was a false intuition. Maybe I was at fault for failing to persuade him of my faith in him. He batted nervously in the opening Tests of the summer against New Zealand, more like a novice than a man with fifty Tests to his name. Because of that, the selectors were keen to discuss his position.

In the event, I managed to save him for one more game but after another moderate performance in the Third Test he was dropped for the forthcoming South Africa series. Smith returned for the West Indies series in 1995 and for the South African tour of 1995–96 but didn't play again after that. It could be argued that a man with such a fine Test record should have played more than he did, but difficult decisions have to be made and they are made in good faith and for the right reasons. In 1996 Smith was thirty-two years old and his average had dropped from the low 50s to the low 40s and we decided to move on. Who can say whether it was the right thing to do? But I was keen to follow the example of other Test-playing countries that seemed to realise, before it was too late, when a player was past his best. In England we rarely did.

The only other name up for debate before the Third Test was Peter Such. Illingworth felt Such was too one-dimensional and was keen to look at Ian Salisbury on Old Trafford's granite-like surface. In the event, Bolus sided against Illingworth and the chairman went along with the majority verdict. Throughout the Test, however, Illingworth made no secret of the fact that he had wanted the leg-spinner to play. Regardless of the rights or wrongs of selection, there seemed to be no notion of collective responsibility and information about selection regularly appeared in the press. It presented a problem for both captain and players. In this instance, how did Such feel knowing that Illingworth did not want him to play, and by simple deduction how did Salisbury feel knowing that I did not want *him* to play?

Two days of rain enabled New Zealand to escape with a draw and the series was won 1–0. My fourth Test 100 in seven Tests confirmed my growing reputation as a Test-match opener. Looking back, however, the New Zealand series was interesting for the wrong reasons, for the political goings-on behind the not-so-closed doors of the selection meetings. That series highlighted the problem of selection that was to be a constant source of aggravation throughout the next couple of years.

Slowly, my influence over selection declined. For instance, before the Ashes tour of 1994–95, I had Martin McCague foisted upon me instead of Angus Fraser, and Mike Gatting instead of any number of young batsmen who would have improved our athleticism in the field. Over time, selectors came and went. David Graveney, Graham Gooch and Mike Gatting were all, at various times, selectors when I was captain. Graveney eventually replaced Illingworth as chairman. I think he felt his lack of Test experience was a handicap and he looked for far more consensus than Illingworth. By 1997, the wheel had turned full circle and I asked not to sit in officially on selection, with the proviso that my views would occasionally be heard.

Looking back, having full control over selection, as I did at the beginning, and washing my hands of it, as I did at the end, were the times when I felt most comfortable. I was happy to have the responsibility and to be judged on results, and happy also for the selectors to give me the team. Where I was less happy was the middle ground between 1994 and 1996, when I was perceived to be influencing things yet in reality had little say. That was a kind of halfway house and I felt it made my relationships with the rest of the team more difficult. With the ethos of collective responsibility absent, and leaks aplenty, a player could not always be sure whether a captain was with him or not. When Nasser Hussain became captain, I passed on my experiences of selection to him and told him he would find it one of the most frustrating parts of the job. I think he has.

Before the era of central contracts when the England captain and coach were fully involved with domestic cricket, I thought the solution was to abandon the traditional selection committee. I felt it was time for the England coach to be given sole responsibility for picking the team in the same way that the England football and rugby coaches do. He would have his informants around the county scene and would select the team in close consultation with the captain. I know that David Lloyd would have loved the chance to select *his* team.

At least it would have put an end to selectorial squabbling. It would have done away with selectors who are one-eyed about their counties, and players being frowned on for having a certain reputation, and a voting system that was no way to determine a player's career. The public would have known precisely where the buck stopped.

Now, with the advent of central contracts, and an increased amount of international cricket, the captain and coach are virtually divorced from the domestic scene. They see so little county cricket that the role of the selectors is more vital than before. The process must be clear-cut and transparent. The public, and the players for that matter, must know where the ultimate responsibility for selection lies in order to prevent the kind of confused muddle that often characterised selection before, during and after my time as captain.

At the fag end of the New Zealand series, the South Africans arrived for a three Test match tour that was to conclude the second half of the summer. It was South Africa's first tour of England for twenty-nine years and it was keenly anticipated. In Allan Donald and Hansie Cronje they had star names and the cricket promised to be more riveting and competitive than against New Zealand. After the events of the First Test against South Africa, however, I would be fervently praying for a return to calmer waters.

9

COLD AND TIMID
SOULS

Saturday, 23 July 1994

Hot and humid day. Mid-afternoon Gough bowls from the Nursery
End. He is getting some reverse swing and he tells Sals [Ian Salis-
bury] and me [mid-on and mid-off] to make sure that we keep
our sweaty hands off the rough side of the ball. [Reverse swing
occurs only when one side of the ball is dry and abrasive.] He says
dust from the footholds would be a good idea. Sals rubs his hand
in the footholds of an old pitch on the grandstand side and I put
some dust in my pocket from a used pitch on the Tavern side. I
use the dust to keep my hands and the ball dry three or four times.

During Gough's spell, the umpires are in constant communication with Merv Kitchen, the third umpire. They ask to see the
ball at the end of each over. Dickie Bird checks it and throws it
back to me and nothing is said.

Four overs before tea I get a message from the dressing room,
via Graham Gooch, that I have to go straight to the dressing room
at tea because there is a ball-tampering row. He laughs and says
to me, 'It must be their ball because ours is doing fuck all.'

At tea I go straight to the dressing room. Both Fletcher and
Illingworth are waiting for me. They tell me of the TV pictures and
ask for an explanation. I tell them exactly what happened and turn
out my right-hand trouser pocket for Illy. He seems satisfied.

At the end of play I am told to hang around because the match
referee, Peter Burge, wants to see me. At 7.45 p.m. he calls me in
to a meeting with Keith Fletcher. I take my whites in with me. Also

in there are Bird, Randell and Kitchen, the umpires, and Alan Curtis, the public-address announcer, who works the video. He apologises to me for his presence and seems a little embarrassed.

Burge shows the TV pictures to me and asks the umpires whether the condition of the ball has been changed. They say no and are asked to leave. Burge rambles on about how he has seen an increase in ball tampering in recent years, and that the usual practice on the sub-continent is to use resin in the quarter seam to make one side of the ball heavier. He asks me three questions: 'Have you an explanation for your actions?' 'Did you have resin in your pocket?' 'Did you have any other artificial substance in your pocket?' To the first I say that I was drying my sweaty hands, to the second and third I reply, 'No.'

He sends me out, and shortly afterwards calls me back in to tell me that no further action will be taken. I leave Lord's with Fletcher. Mark Baldwin of the Press Association is at the Grace Gates and he asks me if everything is OK. 'I think so, Stanley,' I replied. I go back to the Marriott Hotel and consider going into the bar, which is by the lifts, but the presence of a number of Sunday journos convinces me otherwise. Watch the pictures in bed on the nightly news. Ouch!

I was keeping a reasonably full diary at the time – and certainly did for the next two weeks – and that is my entry for that fateful day at Lord's. As such it is my immediate view of what took place, albeit in very bland terms. The consequences of that day threw me into a media spotlight that I could not imagine being so harsh and unforgiving. I was to learn that the England cricket captain was expected to act with greater moral probity than the highest officers in the land, and it was to push me to the brink of resignation from a job I had held for only a year.

Looking back, it all seems to me to have been a storm in a teacup although that is, of course, for others to judge. I suppose the first thing to say is that ball tampering was *the* issue of the day. Being caught doing something to the ball in 1994 was akin to, in today's terms, being seen in Ladbroke's in your whites in the middle of a Test match, pen behind your ear and a betting slip in hand. The media had focused on the issue of ball tampering during the Pakistan tour of 1992 and it had resolutely remained their battleground ever since. Perhaps it is less of a cause célèbre now. When Sachin Tendulkar was accused of ball tampering in 2001, for example, it was the match referee, Mike Denness, who had to explain his actions. Tendulkar suffered none of the opprobrium heaped on me.

And 'doing something' to the ball is undoubtedly what TV pictures showed me doing on that fateful Lord's afternoon. I was not altering the condition of the ball, however; I was trying to *maintain* its dry and rough condition. That fundamentally was the crux of the issue as I saw it at the time. It was not the first time I had done it – as a bowler I had often dried my hands with dust in my pockets.

Why then did I not come entirely clean with Peter Burge on Saturday evening as I had with Illingworth and Fletcher at teatime? That, of course, is the issue I most regretted then; and although the passage of time has blurred the images of that meeting and I look back at events now with a wry humour I would not have contemplated then, that is the thing I most regret now. In a sense, you can be judged by how you react in the most difficult times and I failed myself then.

I had never met Peter Burge before. His reputation had been as a ferocious hitter of the cricket ball and he looked fearsome, stern and headmasterly in his office that evening. In short, I panicked. I sensed that he felt I was guilty and I was not about to incriminate myself. So I convinced myself that dust was not an illegal or artificial substance, told him as much, and assured him that no resin, iron filings, bottle-tops or any other instruments had been used. That was why I took my trousers to the meeting with me.

Later Burge admitted that had he known about the dust he would have suspended me and I would, in all probability, have lost the captaincy. I would, I think, have had no option but to take the matter to a court of law. While the loss of the captaincy would have been painful, to have been labelled a cheat permanently would have been much more damaging. After all, both umpires had said the condition of the ball had not been altered in any way.

As I went to bed that Saturday evening, I was well aware that the story would follow the next day. I had no idea, however, of the ferocity of the argument that was to haunt me for the next ten days. In any case, I was more worried about the fact that South Africa were closing in on victory. Here are extracts from my diary for the next, crucial, few days.

Sunday, 24 July

Lost the game by 356 runs – totally outplayed. During our innings, I call Goochy into the toilets at the back and ask him if he thinks it is a resigning issue. He looks horrified and tells me definitely not.

The story builds momentum throughout the day and it is clear it is not going to go away. I talk to Richard Little [the TCCB's media relations officer] about the day before and the need to issue some sort of statement and clear the matter up. He prepares a statement but it is unacceptable to Burge who is livid. He says had he known about the dust he would have suspended me for two games. A statement is found which is finally acceptable to him on the grounds that I get a heavy fine. I find some of the statement objectionable, especially the apology to South Africa.

Illy is under pressure to fine me so that he can cover his back and so I can keep my job and play in the next Test. Fines me on two counts – lying to Burge, and actions with the ball, although he reiterates to me that he thinks I have done nothing wrong. I am sorry I put him in this position.

Press conference: complete shambles. Fed to the lions. I had no idea before I went in that it would be live. It was unbelievably hot and humid and Agnew was constantly climbing all over me to interview Illy, who kept mopping his brow, looking hot and flustered. Definitely a major story.

Monday, 25 July

Both teams have a photo-call at 11 a.m. to commemorate South Africa's return to Lord's. None of the South African players say a word to me.

On the way home with Isabelle, Mendo [Gehan Mendis] rings to tell me not to go home because the press pack is outside my house. Ring Mum and Dad – they are worried. Ring Paul Clayton at Mottram Hall and he books me in for the evening. Go to Old Trafford to see some of the lads who are having a barbecue. Some piss-take although not as much as might have expected. I really am in the shit! Eat with Issy at the Whitehouse in Prestbury – accusing eyes everywhere. Paranoia?

Tuesday, 26 July

Decide to go to the Lake District. Pissing down. Growing calls for me to resign: Boycott and Agnew especially. Boycott rings me on my mobile to tell me to resign (!) on the grounds that it would make my life a misery and it would be impossible to continue to captain the side. Why's he so interested all of a sudden? Lunch at the Cavendish in Cartmel and stay in Grange over Sands. A conference is going on with lots of Lancashire businessmen – they wish me good luck.

Wednesday, 27 July

Good weather. Go to Coniston, then go rowing on Grasmere. On to Ambleside and then to Cartmel. Bump into Bumble [David Lloyd] and have a beer with him in the King's Arms. Dinner with him in the Cavendish at 8.15. Speak to Bob Bennett (very supportive). Speak to Jon Holmes [agent] who tells me to make sure the press conference on Friday is better organised. Phone Illy and ask him if he wants me to continue as captain. He says he does. Speak to Bumpy Rhodes [England player Steven Rhodes] to get the feeling of the team – he says they are behind me.

Thursday, 28 July

Obviously someone has shopped me. There is a blue Vauxhall (reg. ending MGC) with two reporters waiting in it outside our hotel. One has a camera. Drove out and they followed. James Bond-like manoeuvre up a country lane and watched them drive by – managed to lose them.

Go back to Cheshire and get the keys to Mendo's flat and stay there for a couple of nights. Meet BB [Bennett], John Brewer and Eddie Slinger [all are Lancashire committee men] in Great Eccleston at 7.30 p.m. to discuss my statement and press conference tomorrow. Get home 1.30 a.m.

Friday, 29 July

Press conference at Old Trafford 1.30 p.m. Snappers are waiting for me at the gates. Fifteen minutes before the start I call Agnew into another room and tell him that I am disappointed in what he has been saying, but that I respect his opinion and I would not bear any grudges.

Take my dirty whites to Spriggo [Ron Spriggs, dressing-room attendant at Old Trafford] to be washed. He tells me Harv [Neil Fairbrother] has left instructions not to wash THE pair as he wants to auction them in his benefit year. Issue statement and get through as best I can. They don't seem convinced. Go to watch a film at the Cornerhouse with Issy and eat that evening with Walt [Paul Allott], Pam and Del Boy [Derek Pringle].

Saturday, 30 July

Ring Paul Getty's secretary as I am playing in a game at Wormsley on Sunday. I explain my concerns to her about possible press intrusion. She appreciates the call and says they will not be allowed in.

Selection meeting in Leeds. Despite Illy's reassurance, I am not sure the other selectors want me as captain. They think I am too inexperienced and they don't like my manner at selection (too much to say). BB [Bennett] who has heard it from other county chairmen confirms this to me.

pening the batting against Wasim Akram was always a test of courage. Here he delivers the usual
eatment.

aqar responding in kind to Robin Smith. Wasim and Waqar were the best pair of opening bowlers I
ve seen.

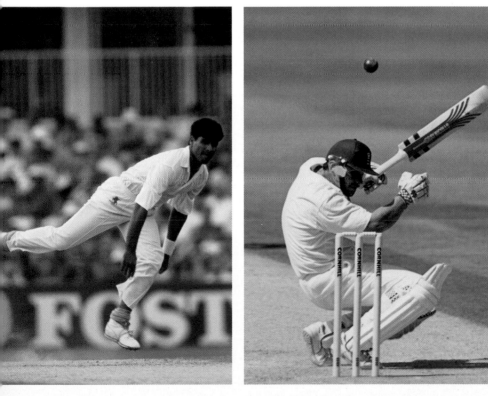

Above: Hit on the head by Merv Hughes at The Oval 1993. I'm not sure Geoffrey Boycott would like the position I've got myself into.

Left: Plenty of time for reading in India 1992–93.

Below: Alec Stewart stares disbelievingly as we end up at the same end in Bombay 1993.

nother run but this time I had to go, one ort of a Test hundred at Lord's v. Australia in '93.

'Young, naïve and blissfully unaware of the roller-coaster to come' – my first press conference as England captain, 1993.

ngus Fraser traps Shane Warne lbw to cap a fine comeback for him and stop a horrendous run of defeats r us. It meant victory in my second game as captain.

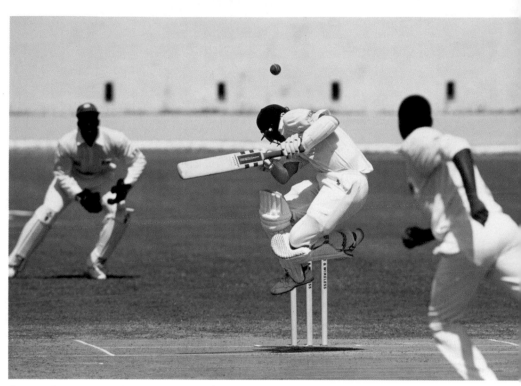

Getting the treatment from Courtney Walsh at Sabina Park in 1994.

With a pensive Phil Tufnell – notice the slightly defensive look, arms folded.

had a difficult relationship with Brian Bolus, whom I felt was an unsupportive selector in 1994.

Ray Illingworth failed to deal effectively with Devon Malcolm in South Africa in 1995–96.

Garry Sobers congratulates Brian Lara on his record-breaking score against us in Antigua in 1994.

Opposite above: Under pressure after ball-tampering allegations at Lord's in 1994.

Opposite below: Trying, unsuccessfully, to clear the air in my Old Trafford press conference, days later.

Right: The moment that sparked off the controversy and media frenzy.

Below: A Lancastrian's nightmare! Plenty of advice from Yorkshire's finest, Boycott and Illingworth.

Above: The greatest prize of them all – The Ashe[...]
Sadly, they eluded me throughout my career.

Left: Oops! Graeme Hick wasn't happy when I
declared on him in Sydney when he was 98
not out.

Below: A sweet-looking drive, during a century
against New Zealand in 1994.

White is injured and so we are back to six batsmen again. Tufnell and Thorpe return, which is good news. Apart from that, it is a very awkward meeting. There is an embarrassed silence about my problems of the week before, and after thanking Illy for his support nothing more is said. The silence weighs heavily around us.

Sunday, 31 July

Play for the Quidnuncs [a Cambridge Old Boys team] against Paul Getty's XI. Takes on a little added significance since this will be my only knock between Tests. Don't get many. Clive Rice is there. He has hardly been supportive of me but now warmly shakes my hand and says he hopes I am coping with the attention. I shake his hand but say nothing else.

The diary is a faithful record of my movements in the week following the Lord's Test. Mostly it is a bald statement of fact, but in between those facts it is possible to reconstruct some of my mood that week. It shows the extent to which I felt pursued – I didn't go home between Tests; the reporters in the Lake District; the prying eyes in the restaurant and ringing Getty's secretary to warn of potential problems.

Only a small percentage of people in the country will know what it feels like to have the full force of the press pack bearing down – the odd politician caught with his hands in the till, or some other place they shouldn't have been; a sportsman such as Lawrence Dallaglio who fell foul of a *News of the World* sting; and, I suppose, a number of today's footballers, the Beckhams and Gerrards, who seem to be fair game wherever they go. It is not a pleasant feeling. Mostly sportsmen play for the back-page headlines. In general, I could barely bring myself to read the good stories on the back page that were about me, never mind the bad. A week of being front-page news was exactly my kind of hell. I developed a strong sense of self-consciousness; walking the streets in Cartmel I would constantly look behind to see if people were staring at me. They invariably were.

And, boy, did the great and good speak out. I was the lead item on the news, front page of tabloids and broadsheets alike. There was consternation expressed at the Headmasters' Conference, and the moral high ground was being claimed by characters as diverse as Jonathan Agnew and Jimmy Tarbuck. This *Times* leader was typical of the week: 'If the captain of England's cricket team fails to uphold the values of his society – or the values to which his society aspires – he is unworthy of that uncommon honour which the captaincy represents.' The implication of the editorial was that the England cricket captain has a greater obligation than the common man to uphold society's values. I don't agree – a captain has an obligation, above all, to the game and then to his team. That is enough responsibility for any man.

I did consider resigning and I told Neil Fairbrother as much on the Monday evening barbecue at Old Trafford. Other than a brief phone call with Ray Illingworth, I spoke to no one from the TCCB and had no idea of their wishes. My chief source of support was Lancashire and my family, as they were so often in times of need. My father urged me to resign only if I felt I had done something wrong while the unexpected arrival of David Lloyd, the Lancashire coach, in Cartmel spoke volumes for the attention he gave to those under his care. As the week dragged on I became more inclined to stay, for the reason that I did not think I had done anything wrong on the field, although I had been foolish to allow myself to get caught up in it all, and had reacted badly afterwards.

I made one other call, and in a sense it was the most important one. I had to speak to someone in the team to gauge its reaction. It needed to be someone who had no axe to grind and who was likely to give me an honest answer. I chose the straight-talking Steven Rhodes and he said the team supported me fully. That, along with Illingworth's support, persuaded me to stay.

Down the years many people have said to me that the best

course of action would have been to resign immediately and, when people realised that I had been a fool rather than a cheat, I would have been reinstated with all my authority intact. Maybe that would have been better, but it assumes that you are thinking logically and clearly. I was twenty-six years old and it was my first experience (and thankfully my last) of the full, icy blast of the media. I simply wasn't thinking logically; I probably wasn't thinking very much at all. Like the swan swimming gracefully on the surface, but whose legs are kicking madly beneath, I may have given the impression of being cool and calm but that was far from the reality.

Having decided to stay, the question remained – could I cope with the focus and attention that would be on me during the next Test at Headingley? Had my authority been fatally undermined and could I help, both as captain and opener, turn around the catastrophic defeat that South Africa had inflicted upon us at Lord's? I was the only one who could answer those questions, and if I was to rehabilitate myself in the eyes of the public, I simply had to do it.

When I arrived at Headingley it was only the second time since the Lord's match that I had been seen in public. There is always more focus on the captain than other players but in this case it was magnified many times over. Television cameras and snappers were under my nose at every turn, recording my every movement. I had expected it and prepared myself for it but it didn't make it any easier to cope with.

Before the match I had two meetings to attend. The first was with Alan Smith, the chief executive of the TCCB. In public, Smith's reputation was that of a typical establishment figure with little to say. 'No comment, but don't quote me on that,' was his stock phrase. In private, I found Smith would rarely let a meeting go by without his natural good humour emerging. Here he was serious without being stern. He said that I had just started out in the job I had been appointed to do and that I had the board's full support. It would have been nice to have heard it midweek and I left the meeting feeling like a football manager who has just had the chairman's 'full backing' – a little nervous.

The second meeting was with Peter Burge. In the years following this episode we got along famously and never failed to have a chuckle over it. Sadly, Burge passed away in 2001. In this meeting, however, it was clear Burge had not forgotten the events at Lord's and I certainly didn't have *his* full support. 'Michael,' (I always knew a lecture was coming when somebody called me Michael) 'the eyes of the world will be on you. More than that, my eyes will be on you and if you so much as sneeze at eleven o'clock you will catch double pneumonia by six.' I thought it would be wise to stay out of the headmaster's study this game.

That I cannot remember a single thing about the two days' preparation for the match is an indication of how unfocused I was. Normally, I can remember the nets, fielding practices and team-talks with great clarity. The only images that come to my mind about the preparations for this game are the television cameras, the snappers and the ferocious visage of Peter Burge, looming over me like the giant eyes of Doctor T.J. Eckleburg in Scott Fitzgerald's *The Great Gatsby*.

The morning of the match dawned overcast and humid (I had a towel ready should the ball have needed drying). At the toss I looked at the wicket uncertainly – there was plenty of moisture there. At Headingley I had the habit of feeling the pitch with both hands, palms downwards, and if the pitch felt cold it was a good indication of dampness. That, along with the overhead conditions, meant that it would be a tough morning for batting. There were also some early indications of cracking and I was always loath to bat last at Headingley when the cracks would invariably lead to an uneven surface.

I won the toss and was faced with an awkward decision. With my heart in my mouth I told Kepler Wessels we would bat. It is always easier to bat against the ball that moves sideways rather than up and down. At least you can back your skill against lateral movement. On an uneven surface later in the game, luck, rather than skill, is the only ally. Whichever way you look at it, given my personal circumstances, it was a brave call to make.

As I walked to the wicket I listened carefully to the crowd's reaction. Usually I didn't bother about what kind of reception I got. Away from home, I often revelled in a hostile welcome. In this instance, however, some kind of public support was very important to me. I need not have worried. The Yorkshire crowd gave me a rousing reception and I walked to the crease to await my fate feeling not quite so alone.

At the crease was the best place for me to be. With Allan Donald bearing down, new ball in hand, that might sound a strange thing to say but at least out there I was in control. Philip Tufnell once said to me that when things were going wrong in his private life, bowling in the middle was the best antidote because nobody could get to him out there. That day, I knew how he felt.

Trying to rank various innings is a difficult and tedious business but, in the circumstances, that day I played what I consider to be, mentally, my toughest innings. I had not played a serious match since Lord's and as my preparations had been so unfocused, effectively I had not picked up a bat for ten days. The wicket offered plenty to South Africa's all-pace attack, which with Allan Donald, Fanie De Villiers, Craig Matthews and Brian McMillan, was among the most testing and disciplined around.

It was certainly not my prettiest innings. I scored just 19 in the pre-lunch session and my technique was all over the place. I knew that if I tried to play more aggressively I would get out and so I concentrated on staying in until my touch returned. I did what I always tried to do when I was out of sorts: blank my mind and watch the ball, more specifically the seam on the ball, intently. When you are out of form, it is too easy to start thinking of all the things that could be wrong – feet, head, hands, back-lift – and then you forget to do the most fundamental thing of all which is to watch the ball and hit it. I probably watched the ball more carefully that day than during any other innings I have played.

There was one other thing that helped me through. Sports psychologists would call the technique 'self-talk' although I did not know that then. I kept saying to myself through gritted teeth, 'This bloke is not going to get me out today.' I said it before every delivery, repeated it like a mantra, and by doing so made it happen.

The catalyst for my scoring runs, rather than just surviving, was the arrival of Graham Thorpe at the crease. We had missed his left-handedness and his aggression against the quicker bowlers and that combination upset South Africa's bowlers for the first time in the series. In fact, that was the moment the series began to swing in our favour. Gradually, with Thorpe's help, my touch and timing returned. I began to get a few of my favourite leg-side shots away as the bowlers lost their line and I scored freely between lunch and tea. Just before tea I hit a cover drive off Donald. There was no movement of the feet but the balance and timing were perfect and I fancied myself to get a big score.

As I closed in on a century, I tightened up and lost focus for the first time that day. I nearly edged a bouncer off the shoulder of the bat straight back to Donald and then I snatched at a good-length ball from McMillan in my eagerness to get to 100. I hit it well, but early and uppishly, to McMillan's right hand. McMillan had huge hands and was agile for a big man. He was a wonderful slip fielder (I don't remember ever seeing him drop a catch) and he made no mistake off his own bowling this time. I walked off for 99, for the second time in my Test career, to a rousing reception.

I was dismissed forty minutes before the end of play, and barely had the chance to shower, change and relax before

Richard Little asked me to do the evening press conference. It would, he said, be a good opportunity to mend some damaged relationships. It probably would have been had I been in the right frame of mind to do it. Instead my emotions were highly charged and running wild. I had just been dismissed for 99 after batting for a draining five and a half hours and I was still hurting from the week I had just gone through. In those circumstances, I ought to have said no, but then I would have been criticised for snubbing the media. The only way to do the press conference would have been to give nothing away, poker-faced, and not show any emotion. But that would have required a maturity that, at twenty-six, I didn't possess.

So I armed myself with Theodore Roosevelt's words, which I had carried around in my wallet since about the time of my England debut:

> It is not the critic who counts, not the one who points out how the strong man stumbled or how the doer of deeds might have done them better. The credit belongs to the man who is in the arena; whose face is marred with sweat and dust and blood; who strives valiantly; who errs and comes short again and again; who knows the great enthusiasms, the great devotions and spends himself in a worthy cause and who, if he fails, at least fails while bearing greatly so that his place shall never be with those cold and timid souls who know neither victory or defeat.

It may seem a bit melodramatic to have taken those words into the press conference with me, but it is a clue to my feelings at that moment, to my antagonistic attitude towards the press in general, and, what the hell, it made me feel better.

Inevitably I let myself down in the press conference by referring twice to the 'gutter' press and showing that the wounds of the previous week were still there. It wasn't a particularly clever thing to do as it reopened old rifts at a time when I should have been trying to heal them. I swiftly learnt that it was fair game for the press to criticise me, but not the other way around. The next day's papers focused as much on my stupid remarks as my courageous batting. It wasn't my most intelligent hour, however understandable.

Throughout my career, I have had the reputation of being someone who has had a turbulent relationship with the media. I am not sure that is entirely accurate. There were times when we were at loggerheads. I was upset when the *Sun* printed pictures of me getting undressed in the Old Trafford changing room the day after our defeat against the West Indies at Edgbaston in 1995. In Zimbabwe, relations between the team and the press were at a low ebb and I didn't take kindly to a reporter suggesting that I was in need of psychiatric help.

But I don't have too many complaints. Generally, I feel that I have been given a reasonably fair deal over the years. I bear few grudges and count one or two in the press box as genuinely good friends. There are also some outstanding journalists for whom I have great respect. Whenever John Woodcock writes an article, which is all too rare these days, I make sure I read it. He possesses a wisdom and perspective on the game that few can match.

My private life has remained just that although it has helped that I have never been interested in playing the fame game. Of course, there have been some unfair criticisms of my captaincy and character, but as a sportsman you have to accept that you will win in the media only if you win on the field. Overall, I have had a few too many dog days, and I wouldn't expect to escape the criticism that inevitably follows.

In return, I don't feel that I was too unhelpful. I was always available for one-on-one interviews. I was happier in that environment because I was in control of whom I agreed to speak to (there were only one or two on my blacklist) and what I could say. In the more general pre- and post-match conferences I was less helpful. I was wary of talking too much for fear of what I said being twisted, and I restricted myself to blandness. Often I tried to see how little I could give away. In any case, what was the point of discussing the game properly when mostly all that was needed were soundbites?

I had some simple ground rules – I never criticised my team-mates or the opposition, and I tried never to hide behind excuses, such as injuries or umpiring decisions. Unless there was a compelling reason not to be, I always tried to be honest. Occasionally I wanted to discuss an issue of the day, but mindful of how things can be taken out of context I usually bit my lip. And, on the advice of Sir Alex Ferguson, I stopped reading my press, good or bad. It hurt losing, so why hurt yourself all over again reading about it? It is a stronger person than I am who says he is totally unaffected by what he reads about himself.

As captain, handling the media was one of my failings. I didn't attach much importance to it and rarely gave it any thought. I certainly did not use the media to my best advantage, as other captains have done. On the Ashes tour in 2001, the Australians showed how it could be done – extracts from team-talks would mysteriously appear under a journalist's door and the Australian press were compliant in allowing questions to be planted that the Australian management wanted to discuss. In the end, I don't think I was devious enough for that. Ultimately, my attitude to the media as captain was characterised by obstinacy and it didn't do me, or my team, any favours at all. Spin and PR were anathema to me. As a player, I just didn't feel the press were important – like a Sunday morning visit to the mother-in-law, I saw a press conference as something of a chore to be endured and survived. Perhaps it was my way of coping with the criticism.

Given that attitude, some may see my move across the line into the media as a hypocritical one, but I think the two roles are completely divorced from each other. Although I am now part of the media, I still don't see why there should be a cosy relationship between players and the press. It is equally danger-ous for journalists whose need for impartiality is paramount. The players are there to play and the media is there to act as a conduit, in a colourful and interesting way, between that play and the paying and watching public. It is an important role, but it is no more and no less than that.

On a pitch that failed to deteriorate as much as expected, we got the better of a draw at Headingley. In the second innings, despite the slowness of the pitch, several South African batsmen, especially Hansie Cronje, looked uncomfortable against Darren Gough. Previously we had felt that spin would be South Africa's Achilles heel but now we looked forward to a quick pitch at The Oval and we were keen to recall Devon Malcolm to his favourite hunting ground.

That Test match will be remembered as Malcolm's match and indeed his 9–57 did more than anything to win the game and square the series. Before all that, however, I had another run-in with Mr Burge. In our first innings I faced Fanie De Villiers and his first ball to me was fast and straight. I moved a fraction early, got too far to the off side of the ball and inside-nicked it on to my pads. I looked up to see Ken Palmer's raised finger and trudged off, shaking my head as always and looking at the inside edge of my bat as I made my way to the pavilion.

Halfway through the afternoon, Illingworth came to me and said, 'The match referee's not happy again.' 'Really? Who does he want to see this time?' I asked, innocently. I was astonished when Illingworth indicated it was me. I went with the vice-captain, Alec Stewart, at the end of play to the match referee's room. At first he could not work out how to operate the video, and when he did it showed little of the dissent he said he had seen. Neither umpire, Palmer nor Dunne, felt there was any show of dissent although, to my surprise, Alan Whitehead, the third umpire, thought there was. Burge sent me out and when he called me back he said that despite the fact there was no video evidence he was going to fine me on the strength of what he had seen with his own eyes. He fined me 50 per cent of my match fee. I looked at Alec; we laughed and took our leave.

I had learnt my lesson from Headingley and I was determined not to comment on the incident to the press. Firstly, though, I had to avoid them and they were all well aware that I was scheduled to go to the annual *Wisden Cricket Monthly* dinner at Green's in Piccadilly that evening. I was determined not to pull out. Towards the end of the dinner the editor, David Frith, told me that there was a gaggle of journalists waiting outside. I left through the kitchens at the back of the restaurant, climbed the fire-escape and a couple of rooftops and descended into the middle of Piccadilly's bright lights two blocks away, feeling pleased with myself – not perhaps the most orthodox route back from dinner for an England captain in the middle of a Test match in the capital, but effective nevertheless.

By keeping my counsel on Burge's decision I hoped that the majority of fair-minded journalists would see that Burge had acted with retribution in mind. Even if he genuinely felt there had been dissent, he was acting inconsistently because he had ignored a far more obvious show of 'disappointment' from Jonty Rhodes at Headingley. The tactic worked, and although I got my share of pounding the next day from the press, generally the public were on my side, but £2,500 was an expensive return to favour.

The inconsistency of match referees has been a blight on the system since their inception in the early 1990s. The sentences have been totally unpredictable and the players have no recourse to appeal. Hence the problems in the wake of the Mike Denness affair in South Africa in 2001, when he fined and reprimanded more than half the Indian team. Throughout my career I had little faith in either the presence or the judgement of ICC referees.

What I most needed now was a victory. There was no doubt that the team rallied behind me. The morning after Burge's fine, Keith Fletcher called me in to the coach's room for a chat. It was pre-arranged and gave Graham Gooch the chance to call the team together, without my knowledge, and tell them I was obviously going through a difficult period and that I would need their full support. It was a grand gesture from a man who knew the pressures of captaining England.

Devon Malcolm held the keys to victory, but in the first innings I had been less than impressed by his failure to bounce South Africa's tailenders. It was an agreed part of our game plan but he simply didn't comply. Graham Gooch had often said to me, not always in jest, that the only way to captain Malcolm was to tell him to do the exact opposite of what you wanted him to do. In this instance, I merely gave Malcolm a private roasting.

The story goes, of course, that the motivation for Malcolm's performance came after he had been hit on the head, while batting, by Fanie De Villiers. After the stuffing from his helmet had stopped swirling around his dazed head, Malcolm had reputedly and prophetically said, 'You guys are history!' Darren Gough was at the other end and later confirmed this to be an apocryphal story.

Neither this unexpected blow to the head nor my strong words probably had any effect on Malcolm at all. It was just as likely to be one of those days when everything clicked for him. The pitch was fast and his follow-through was straight and long. His follow-through was usually a clear indication of his form – when he was falling away, he used only his shoulders and as a result he lost most of his pace. That day, Daryll Cullinan excepted, South Africa showed little stomach for the fight and Malcolm's three short spells were devastating. Most cricketers have one performance for which they will be remembered and that will surely be his.

The batsmen were spurred on by Malcolm's performance. We knocked off the 204 needed in thirty-five overs of aggressive and stirring batting, and levelled the series 1–1 on a glorious sunny Sunday afternoon. Raymond Illingworth, about as likely to give undue praise as the Pope is to condone abortion, thought it was the most positive display of cricket he had seen from an England team in thirty years. If only it had been a five-match series and not a three. The only downside for me was the sight of Graham Gooch, dewy-eyed, in the hotel that evening – he had dropped a simple skier at fine-leg earlier in the game and this, along with his moderate form, had persuaded him it was time to call it a day. He was clearly emotional and so I told him to think it over and not to make a rash decision. The Ashes were coming up and if he felt like one more go at the Australians, he would have my full support.

The one-day series that completed the summer passed successfully and, just as importantly for me, without incident. I did have a slight altercation with Kepler Wessels at Old Trafford. I didn't take it too far, not because of the presence of Burge, but because Wessels was a noted boxer in his younger days in South Africa and had a flattened and disjointed nose to prove it. And so an incident-packed summer ended. I went into it a young, carefree captain with an unblemished reputation as both a cricketer and a person and I emerged, older and wiser, with question marks over both.

In cricketing terms, the summer had gone well. We were victorious in three series with one drawn, and throughout the traumas my batting form had withstood the pressure. But it was not the cricket that had occupied my thoughts or dominated the headlines. My role in selection had been fundamentally altered and I felt a deep sense of unease about two of the new selectors. Moreover, the events at Lord's had catapulted me into the limelight for all the wrong reasons.

The events of the second half of the summer had some immediate consequences. My relationship with the media was damaged and probably never fully recovered although the grudges have long since disappeared on my part. What was certain was that my honeymoon period was emphatically over and I knew that every mistake would be magnified thereafter. Perhaps it changed me a little as a person. Possibly I became more cynical and distrustful as a result, and less quick to see the good side in people at the expense of the bad. Maybe Captain Grumpy emerged from the dust at the home of cricket. Maybe.

Whether the incident affected my captaincy is hard to say. Possibly for a short while I became more cautious and more afraid of making mistakes. If so, it was only for a short period. But as our Ashes hopes were turning to dust before New Year on Australia's parched and blood-red soil, there was no doubt about where the finger of blame was pointing.

10
THE ASHES

W e came off the field exhausted and facing defeat on the
fourth evening of the final Test of the 1994–95 series in
Perth. I prepared to face a torrid hour from Australia's opening
bowlers, but before doing so I needed to find a nightwatchman,
should the situation arise. I looked around the room. Lewis and
DeFreitas were too valuable to lose and Malcolm was a walking
wicket. Angus Fraser, dripping with sweat, saw me looking at
him. Without a word, but with a disgusted look on his face, he
wearily removed his heavy bowling boots and replaced them
with lighter batting shoes, as befitted a nimble-footed tailender
with some misplaced pretensions.

During that hour, Australia's best bowler Craig McDermott
finished off the Test careers of Mike Gatting and Graham Gooch,
and inevitably Fraser was called upon. I met him halfway. 'Oh
shit,' he said, feeling his groin, 'I've forgotten my protector.' We
looked at each other and laughed, and, like naughty schoolboys,
proceeded to change over the protector in the middle of the
WACA. We did that in the middle of the pitch for the next few
overs, each time the strike was rotated. It was a fitting, farcical
and amateurish end to a tour that had decidedly not gone to
plan. Six months after routing South Africa at The Oval I felt we
were no nearer to the kind of steady and obvious progression
that I wanted to see.

The start of the tour was the most difficult in my experience, but the seeds of destruction had been sown in Manchester on 1 September when the touring side was announced. I had serious reservations about two players, Martin McCague and Mike Gatting. I had seen McCague's A team tour report from a year earlier and it indicated that he was likely to be a major injury risk. I had nothing against Gatting, except that I felt his time was past. We had gone down that particular road a year earlier and I felt there was no reason to turn back now. In my diary, against Gatting's name, I had this entry: 'Too old, liability in the field, recent Test record not good, another left-hander needed to counter Warne.'

Generally, I had worries about the athleticism of the squad we had chosen. My only previous Ashes tour in 1990–91 had convinced me of the need to have a mobile fielding unit in Australia. Then, the Australian media and spectators alike had revelled in our shoddy fielding displays. Australia has the biggest grounds in the world, Test match conditions can be as trying as anywhere and it is no place for the physically frail. Australia were sure to put out a good catching unit and an athletic team and we could not afford to give them a head start in the field.

Australia's good weather and outdoor lifestyle resulted in most of their cricketers being athletic and dynamic in the field. On our tour to Australia with England Young Cricketers in 1988, I was immediately struck by how much more physically developed they were than us. Fielding skills have generally improved worldwide in the last twenty years although some of our selectors seemed oblivious to it.

My fears were confirmed in our early tour matches. The most athletic fielders in the team – Hick, Thorpe and Stewart – were also the safest catchers and I could not risk weakening our slip cordon. At Perth against Western Australia it left me with the veterans Gooch and Gatting at mid-on and mid-off and Joey Benjamin at cover. I knew then that it was going to be a long, long tour.

There was no doubting our commitment or desire to improve, but no amount of hard work could make up for the fact that, fundamentally, we were not an athletic team. The second one-day international against Australia A in Sydney was our nadir. Before the game the public address announcer, no doubt tittering at our geriatric fielding drills, decided that the only fitting musical accompaniment to the practice was the theme tune to 'The Muppet Show'. By the end of the match Kermit the Frog would have done a better job as captain, for my head was spinning with the need to hide at least six players in the field. Mike Gatting ended up at short extra-cover but Australia's young bucks were still able to saunter a single.

Graham Thorpe summed up our appalling fielding in the last Test in Perth. We went into the match with a chance to level the series and might well have done so but for a glut of spurned chances. Thorpe was the last offender when he dropped Steve Waugh off Devon Malcolm. As Malcolm looked skywards and I sat on my haunches, head in hands, Thorpe booted the ball into the covers in disgust. Thorpe was a noted schoolboy footballer and his touch had not deserted him. The ball sped through the astonished cover cordon and the Australian batsmen scampered through for two. The need for a good, athletic fielding team had been the central plank of my selection policy for the West Indies and here I was, a year later, captaining an outfit that was a laughing stock in that very department.

In 1991 Philip Tufnell's fielding had been the subject of much derision, but in the early weeks of this tour it was not his fielding but his state of mind that concerned me most. We had selected him halfway through the South African series in England when it was clear that his private life was back on an even keel and he was bowling well for Middlesex. However, during the opening match in Perth it was obvious that something was amiss at home and we sent him back to the hotel to try to sort the problem out.

When Alec Stewart and I went to see him in his room at the close of play we could not believe our eyes. His room had been completely trashed and Tufnell was sitting on the end of his bed in a tearful state, wearing nothing but a towel. I confess I am not at my best in such situations and all I could think of, while trying to comfort him, was that the ash on the end of his fag was getting longer and about to fall in his lap. We called for Dave Roberts, the physio, who in turn called a Perth psychiatrist. Tufnell was taken to hospital and left there in the hands of the specialist who recommended a sedative and a couple of days' rest. As we left the psychiatric unit, M.J.K. Smith, our manager, turned to Roberts and said, 'He's fucked then, isn't he?' It summed up the situation nicely.

We returned to the manager's suite and decided that we would need to call Lord's for a replacement. After an hour or so there was a knock on the door. I got up, opened it, and to my eternal astonishment there stood Tufnell, beer in hand, fag in mouth. He walked in aggressively and proceeded to do a kind of Michael Barrymore impression: 'Awright? You awright? I'm awright!' On and on he went. He had discharged himself from hospital and put us in an invidious position.

Despite his outwardly aggressive attitude and image, Tufnell was low on self-confidence and needed constant reassurance about his cricket and life in general. On the pitch, in the dressing room, and even in the bar, he would constantly sidle up to his team-mates to ask, 'How's it comin' out? Spinnin' it, am I?' Mostly he needed reassuring that the opposition fast bowler wasn't too quick. With Malcolm and Tufnell in the same team, it was a toss-up who should bat at number ten but whenever I asked Tufnell if he fancied a promotion he screwed up his face. 'Nah, mate, I don't really like walking back to the pavy alone.' At number eleven he was guaranteed some company. Usually we had to assure him that Walsh/Donald/Ambrose was bowling 'gnat's pace' that day. Once, just once, during a spell from Donald, we told him it was seriously quick. The anguished look on his face made the deception worthwhile.

I liked Tufnell, and felt that his bowling and match-winning potential was worth the extra aggravation. In this instance, however, I was adamant that he should be sent home. I felt he needed proper, professional guidance of a type we were ill-equipped to provide. M.J.K. Smith was sure that legally we had no grounds to do so and that a letter of warning had to be our first course of action.

We left for Adelaide the next day, with Tufnell officially on his final warning. I could not see him lasting the trip but, remarkably, after that there were few problems with him and Tufnell proceeded to play a full part in the tour. Not for the first time, cricket and bowling proved to be his saviour.

Meanwhile, our problems were exacerbated by an injury list that was growing ever longer. Before we had played a game, Stewart and Shaun Udal had broken fingers. Stewart was to break his index finger three times all told on the tour, and the final time in Melbourne was enough to finish his winter. Devon Malcolm missed the First Test with chicken pox and Joey Benjamin was diagnosed with shingles. Craig White's tour ended with a side strain around Christmas, and Gough (fractured foot) and Hick (prolapsed disc) joined him on the plane home. In all, six players – Fraser, Lewis, Russell, Ramprakash, Ilott and Fairbrother – were called up as replacements. The situation reached farcical proportions in Bendigo when Dave Roberts, who was a keen amateur cricketer, was called upon to do some emergency fielding. So as not to embarrass us (not much chance of that) he diligently did some fielding practice to prepare and, inevitably, he broke his index finger. Consequently, he could neither field nor treat the injured.

If all this was not enough to keep my mind occupied, my running battle with the selectors continued. Three days before the First Test, Raymond Illingworth spoke at a sponsors' lunch in London, and although he claimed his comments were misrepresented what was published seemed to me to be extraordinarily ill timed and tactless. His main gripe seemed to be my failure to ring him during the first month of the tour – although I'm not quite sure how he could have performed the oracle 12,000 miles away in Pudsey.

Inevitably, a faxed copy of his comments was slipped under my door and the media awaited my response with interest. I was learning fast how to avoid the media trap and I said nothing. A month later, however, in an interview I suggested that the selectors were too old and out of touch with the modern game. This didn't go down too well, not in England anyway. The Australians loved it. 'Are you in trouble?' Ian Chappell asked me in Melbourne. 'Probably,' I replied. 'Well, you shouldn't get your knuckles rapped for telling the truth.' Chappell was fiercely iconoclastic and loved a row with the establishment.

Given the background, it was hardly surprising that we were soundly beaten in the first two Tests at Brisbane and Melbourne. Shane Warne was the star of the show, taking 8–71 in the second innings of the First Test when Mark Taylor's decision not to enforce the follow-on briefly looked like backfiring. Warne then dismantled our second innings in Melbourne with the first Ashes hat-trick for ninety-one years.

There are times as a captain when you feel, like Canute, totally overwhelmed and powerless. Brisbane was one of those occasions. Michael Slater gorged himself on a feast of leg-stump half-volleys and wide long-hops from Martin McCague on his way to a first innings 176. I was sensitive to the fact that it was a difficult time for McCague. As an Australian-born Englishman he had copped some fearful abuse in the early games and I had often talked to him about it. In the end, however, only he could show the necessary resilience to come through and in Brisbane he looked totally overawed by the occasion. In reply we were bowled out for a paltry 167 to set the scene for Warne's second-innings magic.

In Melbourne I was less happy about my performance as captain. Our first-innings deficit was only 67 yet I gave Devon Malcolm just two slips when we went out to bowl. My usual thinking for Malcolm was to ignore the bad balls and the fact that he could be expensive, and try to get fielders in catching positions for his good balls. In this instance I failed to do that and my tactics were too negative. We ought to have been trying to get early wickets to put Australia on the defensive, yet my field placings gave out overly cautious signals.

Why? Perhaps the early problems on the tour had a depressing impact on me; perhaps I had not fully recovered from the traumas of the summer. Whatever the reason, Ian Chappell was right when he suggested that I seemed to have lost faith in my bowlers and that I was setting fields for bad balls. In other words, I was thinking about saving runs rather than taking wickets – never a good mindset for a captain. After our resounding defeat in Melbourne, I thought long and hard about what Chappell had said and about my general performance as captain in that game.

Before the Fourth Test in Adelaide, I invited Chappell out to dinner. When he asked why I said it was because I respected his comments, which were always forthright and honest, and that I felt I had a lot to learn. 'Well, I'm not in the business of helping the Poms, but I'll certainly come and have dinner.' On the subject of captaincy that night, I thought Chappell was fascinating and since then, whenever I have had the opportunity, I have gone out of my way to talk to him. More recently, he has been enlisted to help our Academy (helping the Poms?) and that can only be good news.

We dominated the Third Test in Sydney and may have won but for the bad light, which prevented me from bowling my quicker bowlers at Australia's tailenders. We then won a remarkable victory in Adelaide against the odds with the only eleven fit players we had remaining. There were many reasons for our upturn in fortunes – I captained more aggressively; Angus Fraser proved the folly of his original omission; and a young lad from Barnsley called Darren Gough made the cricketing world sit up and take notice.

We had first selected Gough the previous summer against New Zealand and his impact on the field had been immediate. His aggressive batting in partnership with Phillip DeFreitas in the Third Test against New Zealand and in The Oval Test against

South Africa had helped turn both matches in our favour. I liked his bowling, too; his pace and reverse swing gave us an extra dimension.

More than that, he had impressed me with the way he had immediately and naturally taken to the big stage and a foreign environment. During his first Test he was changing with Craig White in the smaller of the two dressing rooms at Old Trafford. Gough brashly slapped a 'Yorkshire only' notice on the door and told those in the know that the password for entry was 'Brian Close'. The episode was indicative of his self-confidence.

At the start of the Ashes tour his bowling had been one of the few bright spots, and in Sydney he took his performance to a new level. Before he went in to bat in our first innings he told the dressing room to 'strap on your seatbelts', and he proceeded to smash 51 off 56 balls. Gough made me giggle when he batted. His follow-through, which was so expansive that it often slapped him on the behind, was the complete antithesis of my more measured approach. But in the early days, before he knew any fear of failure, and before the quicker bowlers had shaken him up, he was fantastic to watch. Then, with the ball, he reduced Australia to the point of following on with 6–49, including Mark Taylor with an outrageous slower-ball googly.

Gough's tour ended prematurely shortly afterwards when he collapsed during a one-day international in Melbourne with a fractured foot. His performance in Sydney, however, catapulted him into the nation's consciousness, and the media, in their desperate search for a hero, not for the first time or the last, hailed a 'new Botham'. This overreaction from the media and his rapid rise to fame made for a difficult period after that for Gough, as it did for many young cricketers over the years – Dominic Cork, Andrew Flintoff and Ben Hollioake, for instance, each of whom was also labelled the 'new Botham'. Adulation can be a difficult thing to cope with, especially when you are young and lacking in guidance. In this period before central contracts, there was nothing in place to help them, and if their

counties were not supportive, they were left to fend for themselves. In a way, they became personalities and caricatures before
their natural character had been allowed to develop fully. They
were victims of what the media wanted them to be rather than
what they were. Gough became the only cricketer of my generation fully to embrace the cult of celebrity; he still managed to
concentrate on his cricket, but I hope the inevitable come down
at the end of his career will not be too difficult to handle.

Gough endured a couple of moderate seasons after the Ashes
tour, struggling with injury and loss of form as he strived to
recapture the glories of Sydney. Since then, he has coped better
than the other pretenders to Botham's crown and I am full of
admiration for the way he has knuckled down to lead England's
bowling attack with dedication and consistency. Gough's persistently upbeat and bubbly character is perceived to have been
the heartbeat of the England team. A dressing room is full of
different characters, of course, and too many Goughs would
spoil the broth, but you need his type to keep a light touch
around a place that is often fraught with nerves and tension.

His character has always been reflected in his bowling – up
front, honest and full of spunk. If body language counts for
anything in sport, Gough is a world-beater, for no matter what
the situation he strides back to his mark with his chest puffed
out and his head filled with self-belief. Because of his attitude
and the fact that he usually saved his best for Ashes contests,
the Australians took him to their hearts in that 1995 series as
one of their own – as true a blue, fair-dinkum cricketer as ever
came out of the old country. Indeed, in 1998 when Mark Taylor
was asked which Englishman he would have in his team, he
said, 'None, but I'd take Gough as twelfth man to be around the
dressing room.'

But it was Angus Fraser, an altogether more traditional English
cricketer both in character and style, who took us to the brink
of victory in Sydney with five Australian wickets in the second
innings. The fact that it was a typical English day, dank, drizzly

and overcast, was perfect for Fraser, and he exploited the pitch, which had soaked up the moisture, by doing what he did best – putting the ball in the right place, often.

Fraser had been called up as a replacement and he got his chance in Sydney because of a hamstring injury to Phillip DeFreitas. After his original omission, can ever a man have been more motivated? In our first innings he batted stubbornly for over an hour, and then on the last day he bowled most of the middle session until he was exhausted. At the end of his spell, he had to chase a ball to the third-man boundary, and he seized up with cramp. Still he chased the ball, limping and hobbling, until he could run no more and had to be substituted. I chastened him for being 'a soft-cock' but I knew it was a performance of heart and substance – it put McCague's bowling in the First Test to shame and made Illingworth's pre-tour assessment of them both look foolish.

The Sydney Test was notable also for my declaration when Graeme Hick was 98* in our second innings. At the time we were almost 450 runs on, and tea was approaching. I sent word that I wanted to have two goes with the new ball, one before the break and one after, and so I needed to declare at least half an hour before the interval. Hick was becalmed in the 90s, Thorpe seemed to be monopolising the strike and we were dawdling.

That, along with the fact that after Melbourne I was determined to be more decisive, persuaded me to declare, leaving Hick short of his 100. In purely cricketing terms the move was entirely justified. However, it had a disheartening effect on the team precisely at a time when we ought to have been itching to get at Australia. For that reason, it is not a decision I would have taken again.

Hick took it badly. He didn't speak to me for the rest of the day, nor would he even throw the ball to me in the field. That evening I went round to his room to try to smooth things out face to face. His wife Jackie opened the door and welcomed me in but the hurt on Hick's face was plain to see and he refused to allow me to heal the rift. He barely spoke to me for the rest of his tour, until a prolapsed disc forced his premature withdrawal.

It was a rare blip in my relationship with Hick. I liked and respected him and felt I got on well with him. Since I had taken over as captain, he had enjoyed his best period in Test cricket. I had shown confidence in him and we had reaped the benefits of that. At that stage, Hick was an automatic pick and averaged in the high 40s between 1993 and 1996.

There were still those who felt that Hick under-performed at the highest level. My own feelings were that he suffered from the kind of lofty expectations visited upon very few. His wonderful record in county cricket for Worcestershire counted against him. When he made his debut for England against the West Indies in 1991, the expectation was immense.

That year, during the traditional opening fixture, MCC v. the county champions, Neil Fairbrother said to me, after watching Hick bat, 'Athers, I've just seen a genius at work.' But I never felt that about Hick. I always thought he was good, but not in the Lara or Tendulkar class. At the start of his Test career, I felt he was too stiff-legged and, with his upright stance and high back-lift, he looked too mechanical and rigid. There seemed to be little give in his hands and no touch in his shots.

Hick had a difficult time at first in Test cricket because of these technical flaws. He wasn't the first batsman to struggle against the West Indies but it did show that, despite his achievements in county cricket, his game was some way short of where it needed to be. He made adjustments to his technique and by 1995 he had come to terms with the demands of facing the world's best bowlers. He had lowered his stance, flexed his knees and now lifted his bat rhythmically from the floor. He looked to me altogether more fluid and natural, and he had fewer problems evading the short ball. His performances in the mid 1990s were testimony to that.

The selectors had no option but to drop Hick after a disastrous run of form in 1996, and after that he played intermittently for

England, although sixty odd Tests is more than enough opportunity. In the end, the general perception is that Hick failed to do justice to his talent at Test level, that he often failed to produce at critical moments and shied away from the personal confrontations between batsmen and bowlers that are the lifeblood of Test cricket.

If so, it must have been down to a vital missing ingredient in his mental make-up. Interestingly, the only time I can remember Hick sledging on the field was when he came on as substitute in the Colombo Test during our tour of Sri Lanka in 2000–01. I thought that illuminating, not because I am in favour of sledging but because there was no chance of him being sledged back at the crease. I wondered briefly at that moment whether the episode highlighted a problem, one that stretched back to 1993 when he wilted in the face of Merv Hughes' verbal attack, and one which possibly made him reluctant to confront me in his room in Sydney the evening I declared on him.

Sydney had thrown up three fine performances from three very different England players. If Hick had more of Gough's bravado, or more of Fraser's sheer bloodymindedness, who knows, he might well have fulfilled the unfair level of expectation that was placed upon him back in 1991.

Our upturn in fortunes continued in the next Test in Adelaide. With only eleven fit players, and five fit batsmen, it ranks as the most extraordinary victory in my time as captain. On the last day, an aggressive innings from DeFreitas, an early burst from Malcolm and later some reverse swing from Lewis completed the victory. Before that though, the scene had been set by Mike Gatting's first Test century for seven and a half years.

Regardless of whether or not Gatting should have been on the tour, it was a brave performance from him. He had endured a poor trot in the first three Tests, and before he went out to bat in Adelaide he sat motionless in his seat for an age, with his eyes closed, completely calm. He was composing his performance in his mind – his penultimate one as an England player.

Most of all, I felt pleased for Keith Fletcher. During a state game in Toowoomba a fortnight after the First Test, the *Sun* had printed our hotel fax number and encouraged its readers to send their thoughts to Fletcher. That week Fletcher was vilified more than any other England official or player that I can recall. I worried for him, but he kept his cool and his dignity. 'Don't fwet, Michael,' he said. 'I'm stwonger than all of them.'

Indeed he was. But the Adelaide victory was to be the last that Fletcher enjoyed as an England coach. On our return he was to pay the price for the team's 3–1 defeat on that tour, and modest results generally under his tenure. Meanwhile, Raymond Illingworth was sitting at home watching developments with interest, and the TCCB was about to grant him the absolute control for which he yearned.

11

A QUESTION OF LEADERSHIP

I was golfing in Florida when I heard of Keith Fletcher's demise. I had developed a good relationship with Fletcher and was sorry to see him go although I could understand the reasons – a coach, like a captain, can be in charge of a losing team for only so long. Shortly afterwards, Raymond Illingworth was offered an extension to his responsibilities; he was now in charge not only of selection, but also coaching and managing the England team for the forthcoming home series against the West Indies and for the subsequent tour to South Africa. Ironically, it was the kind of responsibility and accountability Illingworth had first demanded in 1986, and which the board had then refused.

While this was going on, I was in limbo, unsure whether I too would suffer Fletcher's fate. Despite some justifiable criticism of my captaincy during the winter, the press felt that there was no other obvious candidate for the job. I always think that is a fatuous argument; that there is no one else to do a job is the worst reason for remaining in it. In any case, there is always somebody ready to step up to the mark – even the most unlikely candidates can prove to be surprisingly adaptable, given extra responsibility. But at this point, I genuinely felt I was the best man for the job and I had only really been off the boil, captaincy wise, in Melbourne. Fred Titmus was less sure. He was unimpressed with my remarks about the age of our selectors and had Brian Bolus still been on the panel I feel I would probably have been sacked. But David Graveney had replaced Bolus and he argued strongly for my retention.

I met Illingworth privately at the Pennine Hilton on 14 March. The meeting was not a good omen for the start of a new relationship. I got horribly lost, turned up an age late and we proceeded to have an ill-tempered meeting as we picked over the bones of the winter. I met the selectors again on 25 April and this time their main concern was my appearance. They wanted to see me clean-shaven more often and more smartly dressed. As I had always abided by the team's dress regulations it seemed an unimportant matter to me so I agreed to cooperate. I recalled Ted Dexter's comments about 'facial hair' in India – hadn't we been here before?

On 30 April, during Lancashire's one-day friendly against Yorkshire, Illingworth announced my reappointment for the first half of the summer. The announcement itself was a shambles and a PR disaster. It should have been a good opportunity for us to present a united front, but nobody had bothered to tell me of the press conference and, since I wasn't playing in the friendly, I had gone off to Allwoodley to play golf. The announcement presaged some of the problems to come. How would the captain and manager work together? Was it a partnership of equals? Illingworth's year in control of England's affairs raised the fundamental question that cricket has often failed to answer in recent years – who is in ultimate charge, the captain or the coach?

In rugby and football the answer is obvious – it is the manager or coach who has ultimate control, leaving the captain as nothing more than a glorified cheerleader on the field. Sven-Goran Eriksson appointed David Beckham and Michael Owen as England football captain because they were both, in his own words, young, good role models and widely popular – not because of any inherent leadership qualities. In cricket, the captain's role is so much more. He controls the decision-making and tactics on the field as well as trying to be the glue that holds the disparate elements of his team together.

It was obvious that the TCCB had failed to give sufficient thought to the problem. By vesting sole authority in Illingworth, they fundamentally altered the role of the captain without consultation. Between us, it was a question that was never satisfactorily answered. I recognised that Illingworth had a deep well of cricketing knowledge, and I was keen to draw on it. He saw in me, I think, an honest, straightforward and talented cricketer in a similar mould to himself. As a result, we developed a mutual grudging respect, and that sustained us through some difficult times. But, at the outset, we never really marked out our respective territories, so each knew who was responsible for what. We bumbled along and the resultant lack of clarity was no help to the team throughout the year. As a manager, this division of labour should have been his first role, but Illingworth was always a cricketer first and foremost.

I have no doubt that Illingworth would have wanted to be in charge when he was captain of England, but when he came back to manage Yorkshire in the early 1980s, it seemed he wanted to control things. It was Illingworth, apparently, who gave the captain, Chris Old, the twelve names on the morning of the match. Such was Illingworth's frustration at having to sit and watch that he came back and captained Yorkshire for part of 1982, aged fifty, and all of 1983. In the end, I believe that Illingworth felt he had to be in charge, whichever position he occupied, captain or manager.

Illingworth's style of decision-making was certainly autocratic and gave the impression, to the outside world at least, that he was in control. At Lord's, for the Second Test against the West Indies, the selectors had settled on Steven Rhodes as the specialist wicketkeeper after Alec Stewart had indicated to me that he didn't want to open and keep wicket. When Illingworth asked Alec the same question he told him it wasn't his preference but that he would do it if asked. Despite the apparent volte-face, which made us look foolish, and the uproar it caused in the press, Illingworth changed the team on the eve of the match without consultation.

You had to admire his determination to back his judgement against everything. In the event, we won the match and Alec took a brilliant catch to dismiss Lara in the second innings.

But other than occasionally stamping his feet over selection, and keeping time in the nets, I wasn't sure what else the 'supremo' was supposed to be doing. There was no doubt that during Illingworth's year in charge my workload increased enormously. There seemed to be a void where a coach should be, and I took up most of the slack. By the time the World Cup had finished, I was physically and mentally exhausted. Raymond did ask me if we needed a specialist fielding coach, but I didn't want an extra body in the dressing room, on top of the batting and bowling coaches. As a result, I organised all the fielding drills as well as analysed the opposition and gave the team-talks, although in Wayne Morton, the physiotherapist, and John Barclay, the tour manager, I had valuable help. As the team left for its first training session in Lahore, Illingworth could be seen spreading out his towel by the swimming pool, tanning lotion at the ready. All the irritating jobs that a captain ought not to be bothered with fell to me – organising video clips of the opposition, making sure we had enough baseball mitts and the right type of cricket balls. My view was that the captain was there to make the important cricketing decisions and the manager was there to reduce the hassle. Raymond obviously thought it was the other way around!

Who then should run a modern cricket team, the captain or the coach? I believe the final responsibility for decision-making should be left to the captain because he is the one who controls the play on the field, and who, if things go wrong, is held ultimately accountable. But clearly a captain's workload, with his own game and ten others to worry about, is immense and he needs help. The role of a coach is vital, especially in helping to prepare the team in the two or three days prior to the match. A partnership, then, not of equals but where each knows his role and egos don't clash.

At the outset Illingworth stressed that his first priority was to improve the spirit within the dressing room. The implication, of course, was that it had deteriorated in Australia, during his absence. Poor team spirit and a sour dressing-room atmosphere was a charge levied against the team at various times down the years. Aftab Habib complained that he was not made to feel welcome in Nasser Hussain's England team in 1999 and Devon Malcolm was clearly unhappy during the 1995–96 tour to South Africa.

I am never quite sure what is meant by the term 'team spirit'. I agree with Steve Archibald, the former Tottenham Hotspur striker, who famously said that team spirit is the illusion glimpsed in the aftermath of victory. Players don't have to send each other Christmas cards, or even like each other, although clearly it helps, but respect for each other's ability is essential. Lancashire's team of 1996 had the best team spirit I experienced – we won the double of NatWest Trophy and Benson & Hedges Cup with ten Lancashire-born players (the eleventh, Jason Gallian, was an adopted Lancastrian) and our shared upbringing and background was a strong binding force. Yet we won the double because we had the best players, not the best team spirit, and later when our ability began to wane, team spirit could not help us and, in fact, disintegrated as well. For that reason, I don't go along with the oft-made assertion that a champion team will always beat a team of champions. Team spirit can only carry you so far.

My experience was that team spirit was never a factor in our various defeats, more a limp excuse. Even in the team's worst run of form, it was never bad. Habib's complaints told me more about his vulnerability and weakness; Malcolm's comments failed to reflect the fact that the 1995–96 South African tour was, for 90 per cent of the time, among the happiest I have known.

It is the captain's job to look carefully at the mechanics of the dressing room and to act swiftly to deal with any problem areas. In doing so, he has to know the players, their quirks and foibles, their likes and dislikes. To an outsider, England's dressing room during the run of success in 2000–01 might have seemed too quiet and intense. In reality, it was a reflection of the individuals within the team. Gough was probably the only outgoing and loud character in there. Graham Thorpe, for example, offered little in the way of words and was criticised for that, unfairly in my opinion, by Mike Gatting when he was a selector. More often than not during the day, Thorpe would sit quietly in his corner fiddling with his bat handles and grips (batting can drive a man to lunacy). Yet when the time came for Thorpe to perform, his actions spoke louder than any words and you could guarantee he would never shy away from a challenge.

A good dressing room not only accepts people as they are, but is a place where honest opinions can be expressed, and criticism is taken in the way it is intended. In my early years at Old Trafford this was a definite strength of the team. There were some strong characters and mostly it was a mature dressing room. You knew that forthright opinions could be given and no grudges would be held. In a team meeting in Cheltenham in 1989, Jack Simmons told David Hughes to his face that he was wasting a place in the team, and yet they were seen eating together (fish and chips no doubt) later that evening. In my later years at Lancashire it became less so, largely because of the influx of some younger less mature players. Criticism was not as easily accepted and therefore less often made and the dressing room was less open and poorer for it.

Above all, the dressing room needs to be a place where players can feel absolutely at home and act naturally. Because of that, I rarely allowed outsiders in. Once, when I was at a football match at Manchester United, I was taken in to the dressing room just before the start of play. I felt dreadfully uncomfortable and couldn't wait to leave. It was not my place to be there, nor should it have been.

With television cameras increasingly intrusive, the dressing room is the only place a player can be guaranteed some privacy.

After a particularly bad defeat in the Benson & Hedges Cup at Derby, I smashed the brick surround to a bath. I once saw an England player dismantle showerheads with his bat, one by one, in a fit of temper. Both of us may have regretted our actions afterwards, but the dressing room was the best place to make fools of ourselves.

My own view, as a captain who had observed these things, was that team spirit had not been a problem in Australia. Injuries had, and the coming and going of the injured and their replacements had, more than anything, upset the rhythm of our tour. The dressing-room atmosphere, then, was not my most pressing concern at the start of the 1995 season.

Our one-day form was high on my list of priorities. In Australia we had failed to make the finals of the World Series, and with the World Cup less than a year away I was keen to get back on track. The three one-day internationals against the West Indies, prior to the six Tests, gave us that opportunity.

We triumphed 2–1 and, in the final match at Lord's, I played my best-ever one-day innings to silence those who doubted my one-day credentials. Ambrose was unplayable early on, and I remained rooted on nought for an age; thereafter I took the West Indies attack apart in an innings that must have surprised many. I walked off after scoring 127 to the type of ovation that for most of my career had been denied me at Lord's.

The Test series that followed was an up-and-down affair. Twice we came from behind, proving our resilience, and 'team spirit', to an approving and on-looking Illingworth. Dominic Cork's introduction to Test cricket was instrumental in our revival. I had played against Cork many times in domestic cricket and admired his spunky attitude. He looked like a winner to me, the type of cricketer you would much rather have with than against you. Before his debut I spoke briefly to him on the Lord's balcony; I told him I didn't want him to change and that he should continue to irritate the opposition as much as he irritated me during our frequent county battles.

Crucially, Cork looked like the bowler most likely to get Brian Lara out. As was so often the case with Lara, he was not quite at peak form early in the series. He usually moved back and across at the crease, but when he was out of form he jumped rather than moved, causing his head to bob around too much. A bowler who bowled close to the stumps and moved the ball back into Lara, like Cork did, could have success. It was clear to me that Lara held the key to the series, and I was quick to introduce Cork into the attack whenever Lara came to the crease. Setting up a personal duel against Lara, in any event, was never a bad ploy because such was his pride, or arrogance, he never liked to be dominated and could often take unnecessary risks against a bowler whom he perceived to be a threat.

Lara was an opponent a captain had to think carefully about, not just tactically, where to bowl to him, but also how to react to him. His character was far from constant and his batting often reflected the mood he was in. Later I came to the conclusion that the best approach was a neutral one – you certainly didn't want to fire him up with sledging. Michael Slater told me that it was an altercation before the start of play in Jamaica that sparked off Lara's form in the 1999 series against Australia. The visitors had hogged the nets at Sabina Park and refused to let Lara practise. It riled him and he went on to smash a thrilling double century. Later, in Bridgetown, Glenn McGrath again showed the futility of winding Lara up when he scored a brilliant, match-winning 100.

I fell into the trap during our home series in 2000. Lara had been in moderate form and had looked vulnerable to Gough in the early games. During the Third Test, just as Lara came to the crease, I made mention of the fact that he was becoming Gough's 'bunny'. As I passed Lara at the end of the over he said, 'Thanks Mike, that's just what I needed,' and he proceeded to take Gough and the rest of our attack apart.

In the First Test of the 1995 series at Headingley, we were soundly beaten. Then in the second innings at Lord's, after I had switched Cork to the Nursery End, he took seven wickets as we won a close match and levelled the series. It was the first time as captain I had to control a tight fourth-innings game. We set the West Indies 296 to win, but on the fourth evening they were 68–1 with Lara ominously 38 not out. We won by 72 runs although for much of the time it was touch and go, and I was pleased with the way I kept my head and marshalled the side.

Although the force was with us, and our confidence was high after Lord's, we suffered a catastrophic defeat at Edgbaston. The pitch was rock hard, multi-coloured and piebald. Ambrose's first ball to me ballooned over my head, and the wicket-keeper's, for four wides. He stood in the middle of the wicket for an age, his eyes bulging and grinning from ear to ear. 'I like it, Amby! I like it, Amby!' came Lara's shrill cry from the slips. He knew, and I knew, that on a fast, uneven wicket there was only one winner.

We were beaten in just over two days, with a full house denied much cricket on the Saturday. The crowd vented their frustration on the team, and as we ate lunch in the downstairs dining area, they banged on the windows, mouthing obscenities – 'Piss off back to Yorkshire!' Darren Gough, Peter Martin and Richard Illingworth were all Yorkshire born and looked a little concerned although I rather think the abuse was aimed at the other Yorkshireman, Raymond Illingworth.

As I stepped out to walk the 200 yards to the press conference, which was held in the old indoor school, I too bore the brunt of some of the crowd's anger, and I needed a police escort for safety. I remember one gentleman in particular, who walked beside us all the way, red-faced and frothing at the mouth, hurling all kinds of vitriolic abuse. A month later, he wrote to me apologetically; he had since had a heart attack and wanted a signed shirt for charity!

At Old Trafford, Cork's run of success and good fortune

continued. He scored his maiden Test 50, during which, as he set off for an all-run 4, he stood on his stumps and knocked off a bail. He brazenly picked it up and, like W.G. Grace in his prime, placed it back on the stumps and continued batting as if the whole crowd had indeed come to watch him play. Then, in an astonishing start to the fourth day, before the Lancastrian crowd had settled down, Cork took the first Test hat-trick by an England bowler for thirty-eight years. We needed 94 to win, and after I needlessly ran myself out, the tension was high. We lost three quick wickets, and my memory is of each ingoing batsman squeezing by Robin Smith who was being slowly carried down the stairs on a stretcher, his jaw badly broken by a Bishop bouncer.

Lara really found his form in the second innings at Old Trafford although it was too late to save his team. Thereafter he scored brilliant, successive 100s at Trent Bridge and The Oval, condemning us to bat out each game, and condemning the series to a 2–2 draw when, after our first innings in each game, we were contemplating victory. In those two games it was almost impossible to contain him. With most players, the captain and bowler have a get-out clause, so that even if you don't look like getting a player out you can always stop him scoring. Steve Waugh, for example, never hooks so a short ball is always a dot ball. There was no such relief with Lara. There was little margin for error and I asked the bowlers to bowl a tight middle and leg line to give him no width. After that, all you could do was set the field accordingly, hope for the best and admire his play. Carl Hooper joined in the fun in the high-scoring draw at The Oval. He was an easy batsman on the eye, and he hit Angus Fraser for a straight 6 with the minimum of effort. The ball landed on the committee-room balcony, in John Major's lap.

Given that we had twice come from behind and that Gallian, Illingworth, Stewart and Smith had all suffered broken bones, the 2–2 result against the West Indies represented fair progress. We moved on to South Africa for the 1995–96 winter tour, the first England tour there for thirty-one years, with confidence.

The tour began in low-key and relaxed fashion and within the first week we experienced the opposite ends of the social spectrum. It started amid the beautiful surroundings of Nicky Oppenheimer's golf course and Raymond Illingworth was announced on to the first tee to get the tour under way. Raymond had frequently talked up his golfing game so we gathered around expectantly. He swung back gracefully but just as the club ought to have begun its downswing, it took on a life of its own and did a double whirl at the top. He heeled the ball into a bush, twenty yards due west of the tee.

As it was England's first tour post apartheid, we knew that there would be political obligations in the early weeks. I, for one, was keen to get out and about to try to understand the years of apartheid and the system's brutal effects. I opened a cricket pavilion near the township of Alexandra in the first week. The far side of the ground overlooked the township – thousands of tiny corrugated huts surrounded by thick coils of barbed wire; a single square mile of massed humanity and seething discontent.

Our opening first-class match was the first ever to be played in a black township, and although the facilities were not really up to first-class standard, we were all keen to get a look at Soweto. Alec Stewart and I put on 163 for the first wicket and we were going well when the game was interrupted by a visit from the South African President. Usually, cricketers are unenthusiastic about visits from local dignitaries or even royalty, but we were all eager to meet Nelson Mandela. He chatted mostly to Devon Malcolm. I stood two away in the line and overheard him say, in that grainy and faltering voice, 'You . . . are . . . the . . . destroyer!' Devon beamed and nodded in agreement.

Raymond Illingworth's handling of Devon Malcolm on that tour was rather less satisfactory, and highlighted his main weakness, which was the man-management of the players under his control. He was as poor as Duncan Fletcher, later, was excellent. I had asked a number of players who had played under Illingworth about his style of captaincy. To a man, they said he had wonderful tactical knowledge and in a tight situation he was among the best, but that his man-management skills were less good. I don't think he actually gave any thought to the fact that he had a variety of different characters in his charge. He adopted the same honest, hard-nosed and abrasive style with them all, and with Graeme Hick and Devon Malcolm he had differing results.

Before the Fifth Test of the previous summer, Graeme Hick demanded to see Illingworth. He had been dropped for the previous match, but Robin Smith's broken jaw had got him a recall. Hick wanted to know where he stood with the manager and went to see Illingworth in the coach's small enclave that adjoins the main dressing room at Trent Bridge. Illingworth's bluntness made even me wince. 'I think you've got a soft centre,' he said, 'and it's because you've had a mollycoddled upbringing. Go out and prove me wrong.' Quite what Raymond knew of Hick's upbringing I am not sure, but Hick certainly proved him wrong with a wonderful 100.

This uncompromising approach didn't work with Malcolm. The two had 'previous', following Malcolm's early release before the Lord's Test against New Zealand in 1994 – a slight Malcolm had never forgotten. Nevertheless, Malcolm was back in the team for the final Test of the summer against the West Indies, and Illingworth assured him of his place on the winter tour to South Africa, provided that the fast bowler would work on his follow-through with the bowling coach, Peter Lever, in the build-up to it.

At the start of the tour, however, Malcolm seemed unwilling to work with Lever. He also seemed strangely preoccupied. There were doubts over his fitness (fluid on the knee), he failed to turn up at a match in Springs to support the team when asked, and his performances in the nets were uninspiring. Lever and Illingworth vented their frustration in a press conference scheduled on the last day of the match in Soweto. In saying that Malcolm had little to offer other than his ability to bowl quick, the press inferred that he was viewed as a nonentity and they went to town. Illingworth simply could not understand the effect public criticism had on a player, and Malcolm was naturally incensed.

Discontent simmered between the two throughout the tour and erupted into the open after the end of the deciding Test in Cape Town. Rain in Pretoria and Durban, and battling draws in Johannesburg and Port Elizabeth, had left the series tantalisingly poised at 0–0 before the final Test. We were bowled out for 153 in our first innings but had fought back superbly to restrict South Africa to 171–9. As Paul Adams, their number eleven, walked in, I threw the new ball to Malcolm. It proved to be a disastrous move. Forty minutes of mayhem followed, begun by Dominic Cork's wild overthrows and completed by Malcolm's four insipid overs which cost 26 runs. South Africa took a commanding first-innings lead; we lost the match in three days and the series 1–0.

At the end of the game the players congregated on the field for the presentations. The public-address system announced that England had agreed to play an extra one-day game to make up for the lost two days. It was another example of Illingworth's autocratic style – I knew nothing of it and made my objections known in the dressing room. Illingworth dismissed my objections, turned to Malcolm and said, red-faced and spluttering, 'As for you, you bowled crap and you've cost us the Test match!' I thought at that moment that either Raymond was about to suffer a seizure, or that Devon was going to throttle him. Either way, his prospects didn't look good; but the moment passed.

The bad blood between them continued after the tour. Inevitably, and depressingly, both had to have their say in various newspaper columns. Malcolm escaped censure and Illingworth was fined £2,000. The fine was later rescinded. I was glad, as I had no desire to see a man who had given much to English cricket leave with a black mark against his name.

The feud between Malcolm and Illingworth was a new kind

of problem for me. Malcolm was a key part of the squad and his heroics against South Africa at The Oval seventeen months previously were fresh in my mind (and no doubt in the South Africans'). But I was in an invidious position because I could see both sides of the argument and it was clear that both parties were to some extent at fault. Malcolm's attitude in practice was poor and he looked far from fully fit at any stage. Equally, Illingworth's propensity to wash our dirty linen in public was damaging not only to Malcolm but to the team as a whole.

I tried to steer a middle ground. I got them together early on in the tour and tried to sort the problems out. At the same time, I tried to reassure Malcolm of my faith in him. Clearly, it was a policy that did not work and later Malcolm criticised me for failing to give him unequivocal support. Maybe he was right, but I was under the impression that we were all on the same side and I was keen that we worked together rather than tore ourselves apart.

After the Fifth Test we played seven one-day internationals in thirteen days and took a pounding. We then flew home for a week, before setting out for the World Cup in India and Pakistan. I knew that the team's confidence had been badly affected by the last fortnight in South Africa and that we desperately needed a good start to the tournament. But despite the fact that we trained hard and well in Lahore, our World Cup campaign was a disaster from start to finish. It began with Graham Thorpe dropping two straightforward chances at slip in Ahmedabad on the way to defeat against New Zealand, and ended with Phillip DeFreitas being smashed all over Faisalabad as we were humiliated in the quarter-final by the eventual champions, Sri Lanka. In between, we won two matches only, against Holland and the United Arab Emirates, two of the minnows of the tournament.

Off the field things did not go much better. In an attempt to obtain decent practice facilities our amiable manager John Barclay found himself at the centre of a bribery incident. Days later my patience snapped with a local journalist. Once again I gave the press another excuse to jump on the critical bandwagon. Raymond Illingworth was feeling his age and the effects of a long winter, and our tired and ultimately dispirited squad dragged its feet from Peshawar in the north to Karachi in the south with little reward.

We had regular team meetings to try to sort out our problems, but often they succeeded in making people more confused. During our meeting before the Pakistan game, Illingworth was concerned about their spinners. 'Who can pick Mushie?' he asked. Out of the silence a lone hand, belonging to Dermot Reeve, offered itself. Reeve went on to espouse his theories about sweeping and reverse sweeping Mushtaq. The next day Mushtaq bowled Reeve a googly; Reeve advanced down the wicket, aimed a huge drive through extra-cover and was comprehensively bowled through the gate. I was all for team meetings and tactical theories, but sometimes they obscured the need to play good cricket and do the basics well.

Sri Lanka's bold and aggressive approach bundled us out of the tournament in the quarter-final and secured them victory in the final against Australia. It was a personal triumph for their captain, Arjuna Ranatunga. Ranatunga may not have been everyone's cup of tea, and wasn't mine, but I admired the way he changed his team's outlook. As so often happens with powerful captains, the team took on its leader's image. Previously they had been talented but timid. Ranatunga encouraged the talent and turned them into tigers, snarling and ultimately successful.

Criticism was quick to follow our exit from the tournament, and my critics pointed to the World Cup as evidence that neither my batting nor my captaincy was suited to the one-day game. I was criticised for being 'off the pace' tactically when it came to the use of pinch-hitters of the kind that Sri Lanka were using to dominate the tournament. It didn't help, of course, that so few of us were experienced in Asian conditions – I had never played a one-day international there before. But, in fact, looking back, I think we were too concerned with what Sri Lanka were doing, and it only confused us over our best opening combination even further.

I was horribly out of form during the tournament. Since the fourth Test of the winter in South Africa I had gone off the boil and other than a half-century against Pakistan, few runs flowed from my bat. We also made the mistake of chopping and changing too frequently. Both in South Africa and the World Cup, we couldn't work out what our best combination actually was, and during that time we used half a dozen or more different opening partnerships. The resultant lack of clarity in selection was disconcerting for the players.

Certainly we made mistakes, but I felt and still feel that I had plenty to offer in one-day cricket. Throughout the decade I was, along with Neil Fairbrother, the most influential batsman in the best one-day team in the country, and my ability to pick the gaps and work the ball around outweighed my lack of power. It was less than a year previously that I had played an outstanding one-day innings at Lord's against the West Indies. Throughout my captaincy, England were unbeaten in the Texaco Trophy series at home, beating New Zealand, South Africa, West Indies, India, Pakistan and Australia, losing only two out of sixteen matches in the process. Those are not bad one-day credentials.

Ultimately, I felt that England's administrators had not given our players the best chance of success and this was part of a growing problem throughout the nineties. It seemed ludicrous to me that we should prepare for a prestigious one-day tournament with a gruelling four-month Test match tour of South Africa, with only a week off in between. Moreover, the rules of our domestic one-day cricket failed to mirror the playing conditions we were to encounter in the World Cup, which put our players at a disadvantage. Every other country played their domestic one-day cricket to fifty overs, with white balls, coloured clothing and fielding restrictions in the first fifteen overs. In

England, we continued to play sixty, fifty-five and forty overs, in white clothing with red balls, and none of the fielding restrictions we encountered in the World Cup. England was the only country where an off-spinner could still bowl to six on the leg side.

In a way, the 1996 World Cup highlighted a problem that England's administrators were slow to come to terms with throughout the decade. Other countries were playing forty or fifty one-day internationals a year, while we were playing, if we were lucky, a dozen or so. While our players were tied up in meaningless domestic games, other countries were sharpening their talents in tournaments in Sharjah, Kenya and elsewhere. We stood haughtily by. In the quarter-final against Sri Lanka, six of their players had a hundred caps or more. Only Phillip DeFreitas had reached that landmark for us. Despite our previous good record in World Cups, in the 1990s other countries passed England by in one-day cricket.

Even in the 1999 World Cup, under Alec Stewart, when England had all the benefits of sound preparation and home advantage, we failed to reach the second stage of the tournament. We were just as disappointing as we had been three years previously. Under Duncan Fletcher and Nasser Hussain, England has suffered its worst run of one-day defeats ever, and Fletcher has gone on record as saying that unless our players get more exposure to one-day international cricket, we will have no chance in the next World Cup. Fletcher has deliberately committed our players to over thirty one-day international games in the year before the next World Cup (February and March 2003). Gradually we are committing our players more, at the expense of their domestic involvement, but it has taken the administrators a long time to listen.

Those arguments would have fallen on deaf ears as I returned from the World Cup to face the flak. I was wise enough not to offer excuses, and big enough to accept that I had made mistakes and that criticism was inevitable and justifiable given our recent run of results. One tabloid newspaper sent a reporter dressed as a giant, furry, white rabbit to intercept my arrival at Heathrow and embarrass me. It was a far cry from four months previously, after Johannesburg, when every newspaper, tabloid and broadsheet alike, had hailed me as a hero.

12

JOHANNESBURG

If he is lucky, a batsman may once play an innings that defines him; that, whether he likes it or not, he will be remembered for. The greats play them more than once, of course, but in any generation they number but a few. In my fifty-third Test, and twenty-sixth as captain, I played mine: a match-saving 185* against South Africa, an innings that lasted 492 balls and spanned nearly eleven hours.

At that particular time I was in good form, probably the best of my career. Since taking over the captaincy I had scored runs regularly and had gone from being a fringe player to a regular; someone who was regarded as a certain pick, who was important to his team's chances of doing well and who was occasionally targeted by the opposition. The captaincy had undoubtedly been a positive influence on my batting; I found that responsibility and pressure, at this early stage, were empowering. Eventually they would take their toll but that was still some way off. At this stage, the responsibility of captaincy was forcing me to look more at other players and therefore worry less about my own game. As a result, I played more instinctively and naturally. I was still determined to make a success of the captaincy, and the vision of a dynamic and successful team was a strong motivation for my batting at the time.

In the West Indies in 1993–94 I had scored 510 runs at 51.66; against New Zealand 273 at 68.25; against South Africa 207 at

34.50; in Australia 407 at 40.70 and against the West Indies in 1995, 488 at 40.66. It was an impressive and consistent run for an opener against the best new ball bowlers in the world. Moreover, I felt my game was developing and my repertoire expanding. In the previous twelve months I had also been more of a force in one-day cricket than before. My 127 against the West Indies at Lord's showed that when it came to inventiveness and stroke-play I could occasionally eat at the same table as the best.

Due to the constant diet of international cricket, there had been little chance to work on my technique since the Boycott sessions of 1991. But a couple of changes had crept into my game, one consciously, the other less so. Before the West Indies tour in 1993–94 I had felt strangely cramped and powerless at the crease and I decided to pick my bat up earlier and higher. The constant repetition, both in practice and matches, meant it was now an ingrained habit.

On that same tour I developed a tendency, almost unknowingly, to plant my front foot earlier against the quick bowlers. Mostly batsmen are advised to stand still, but I moved early enough to be still at the point of delivery and my balance was evenly distributed so that I was not committed on to the front foot. As a result, I felt I could rock back to pull and cut, and I had more time to play on the front foot to a ball of full length. It had served me well, and had again become an ingrained habit.

Other than those changes, my game was essentially the same one that stuttered into Test cricket for the first time against Australia in 1989. But since then I had played fifty-one Tests against the best bowlers in the world in a variety of conditions. I had played spin in India and reverse swing against Pakistan, suffered bombardments at the hands of the West Indies and been toughened up in Australia. In short, I was experienced.

This then was the background to my batting as we arrived in Johannesburg for the Second Test of the 1995–96 South African series. I was in good form (I had just scored 78 in the First Test), technically 'grooved', young, fit, motivated and experienced. It was a happy combination.

The preparation for my innings, as always, had taken place in the two days' practice before the match. We travelled to Centurion Park to net, which was an hour away from Johannesburg but had the better practice facilities. Throughout my career I never had a set routine for practice; mostly it depended on how I was feeling at the time. Before the First Test in New Zealand in 1997, for example, I batted for nearly four hours in practice, so out of form did I feel. Here, though, I felt good and I asked Raymond Illingworth for a ten-minute net only.

It was an important ten minutes. I always tried to net with a purpose and here I wanted to replicate my first ten minutes in the match. As I walked into the net, therefore, I transplanted myself into a match situation, imagined I was about to face the first ball of the game and I went through my ritual: I scraped the crease to make sure I had a good footing; stretched and visualised the umbrella field that was likely to be awaiting Allan Donald's first ball.

Practising with a purpose was vital, and it varied according to the conditions and the match. Before a one-day game I would imagine the field in my head and practise manoeuvring the ball and hitting the gaps. In Pakistan during the 2000–01 tour, Graham Thorpe deliberately scuffed the net surfaces up with his spikes on a length in order to replicate the likely spin-friendly conditions.

In Johannesburg, though, fast bowling would be the order of the day, so I asked to face Devon Malcolm with a new ball. I wanted both to check on his fitness, as we were thinking of playing him, and also to put my reflexes briefly to the test for I was sure the Wanderers' pitch would be quick and bouncy. My reactions and movements felt good and I left the net in confident mood.

After practice, in the changing room, I went through South Africa's bowlers in my mind.

(a) Allan Donald: wide of the crease; generally moves the ball in; length usually short or full; first spell quick; lots of bouncers; can go flat if you get on top of him; attack off back foot and defend off the front.

(b) Shaun Pollock: close to the stumps; bounce and away movement; bouncer difficult to take on; stay still and avoid going across the crease; first spell quick, not so after that.

(c) Meyrick Pringle: medium pace; genuine swing bowler; usually away swing with an obvious change of action for the inner; wait and play late; bit of a joker – avoid getting into a chat.

(d) Brian McMillan: straight, no swing; bouncer quicker; sledger – don't get involved!

(e) Clive Eksteen: orthodox left-armer; not much spin; very accurate; bowls over the wicket a lot; place under threat from Paul Adams.

My pre-match mental preparation had to be supplemented halfway through the game. On a greenish-looking wicket, I had put South Africa in to bat, and by the fourth day they were more than 400 on. Moreover, early in my first innings I had left a delivery from Allan Donald that had clipped my off stump and I had been dismissed cheaply.

Before play on that fourth day, I stood on the wicket oblivious to the camera crews and former players who were chatting convivially. I played a few air shots and envisaged the task ahead of me. I reminded myself I was still in good form despite the first innings blip, and that the second innings would require me to dig deep. As their coach Bob Woolmer had said on the third evening, they had some extremely quick bowlers and they were keen to unleash them around lunchtime. We would have to bat five sessions to save the game.

As a captain and opener I hated the period before the end of an innings. As a captain you felt your bowlers ought to be able to knock over tailenders without too much trouble, although it rarely happened like that. As a batsman you needed to get your mind switched on to bat. It was always a difficult time.

South Africa declared half an hour before lunch on the fourth day, and I ran off the field to prepare to bat. As with most things, I had a set routine in padding up, mostly out of superstition – box first, chest guard, inside thigh-pad, outside thigh-pad, left pad, right pad, arm guard and finally I would put my gloves and helmet on as I walked out to bat. I didn't always wear a chest and arm guard, but on this pitch against this attack I was happy to have the extra protection.

I never worried about noise as I was padding up. Some did – Nasser Hussain, for example, would often bark at the bowlers who were celebrating the end of their endeavours a little too fiercely. I was happy to hear music and general noise – rather that than nervy silence. Nice, too, to hear the good wishes of your team-mates as you walk out to bat – of course, a batsman's task is a solitary one but it is good to feel the dressing room is with you.

I walked out to bat with my regular opening partner at that time, Alec Stewart. The dressing rooms at the Wanderers are side on to the ground and the player's first view of the stadium is the old wooden stand that looms up on the far side, the solitary concession to the old days of the 'Mean Machine' and Rice, Pollock and Van Der Bijl.

To get to the playing area you have to walk across the grassy knoll, from where late in the afternoon the smells of the traditional braai waft on to the ground. Then it is down the players' tunnel, which is encased in wire fencing for protection. The locals lean on the fence and leer at you, usually mouthing obscenities. It was here that Merv Hughes and Shane Warne memorably lost their cool and part of their match fees in fines. Outside India, there is probably no more hostile stadium in the world than the Bull Ring.

Then it's on to the oval itself. Later on in my career, I came to have the ridiculous superstition that I had to get on to the field first. Why I developed that superstition I don't know – batting can play funny tricks on your mind. The first time I opened with Marcus Trescothick he was taken aback when I barged past him on the steps at Old Trafford. But I didn't have that superstition in 1995, and I probably sauntered on to the pitch in Alec Stewart's shadow. The noise was immense as we walked out to the middle, with the crowd banging on the metal hoardings incessantly.

At such times it was good to be accompanied by Alec Stewart – a proud fighter and someone you knew would never take a backward step. I had thirteen opening partners in my time as an England player and all the regulars (Gooch, Stewart, Butcher and Trescothick) were good to have by your side. Others were less so. As I opened with Mark Lathwell against Australia at Headingley in 1993, I said to him, 'Good luck, the crowd are rooting for you.' 'They won't be in a minute when I'm on my way back,' he replied. As Stewart approached the crease with his chest puffed out, walking bow-legged on the sides of his heels, his bat twirling, I was reassured to have him on, and by, my side.

Before the first ball, I went through my routine – scratched the crease, stretched and checked the field. I always took first ball when I batted with Stewart. With Gooch, I always took second. Later, as I became the senior partner, I always gave a debutant the choice, and it was a kind of test for them. Marcus Trescothick showed no preference whatsoever and I thought that indicative of his self-confidence. Others were not so sure. Darren Maddy was adamant in the two days prior to his debut that he wanted the first ball, and then as we were walking to the middle at The Oval against New Zealand he changed his mind and asked me to take it. His prevarication was indicative of his nerves and uncertainty.

By preference, I took the first ball although I hated the moments before it. My mouth was usually dry and my heart pounding. I never heard the noise of the crowd when I batted but invariably, before the first ball, I could feel the tension and the silence. Graham Gooch was the only cricketer I knew who said he never got nervous before batting. As someone who batted with him often, he never seemed nervous, but I knew that if I wasn't at all nervous it was a bad sign.

Sports psychologists would argue that to perform at a peak, a certain level of anxiety is necessary. A complete absence of anxiety can lead to poor performance, as can too much. A state of controlled nervousness is generally considered the best pre-performance state. I knew I needed to be a little nervous to play well. Gooch was clearly the exception to the rule.

My natural temperament is calm and laid back. The stimulus provided by a big match, with the crowd and media attention, lifted me into the perfect pre-performance state. A county game with fewer stimuli failed to make me nervous enough and so if I didn't find a way of artificially pumping myself up – sledging a bowler for example to provoke a confrontation – my performance was often flat. Conversely, for highly strung types such as Nasser Hussain and Mark Ramprakash, the big match often pushed them over the limit and they had to find ways to control their nerves and 'de-pump' with relaxation and breathing in order to be in the right frame of mind. As Ramprakash demonstrated in his two innings in Johannesburg when he scored a becalmed 4 in the first and a frenetic nought in the second, it took him quite some time to find the right balance.

We were batting ostensibly to save the match, although I had the same mental attitude as if it was the first innings of a Test. Geoff Boycott often spoke of the need to be positive in defence as well as attack – the kind of committed block that would break a bowler's heart. But also it was important to score runs and take advantage of South Africa's attacking field.

Back then, although I was nervous before the first ball, I was relaxed about not being off the mark. Later, as I became aware of the growing number of ducks I had scored in Test cricket, I was less composed and more eager to score that first run. In the corresponding Test match at this very ground four years later, I was to get a couple of unplayable deliveries on a brute of a wicket to register a pair. It took me to holding the joint record (with Derek Underwood) for the number of ducks scored by an England player in Test cricket. Of course, the more you play the more you are likely to hold records, both wanted and unwanted. This one was definitely unwanted and for the remainder of my Test career I was paranoid about getting off the mark. On the Sri Lanka tour of 2001, I was almost hitting and running in order to get off the mark. Of course, eventually I did get one more duck (against Australia at Trent Bridge) and so hold the unenviable record of having scored more ducks in Test cricket than any other England player.

This time I got off the mark readily and in fine style. Meyrick Pringle bowled an outswinger of full length. I leaned out to it and, with a high elbow, punched it through extra-cover for 4. It was a solid shot – good footwork and timing – and a good start.

At the start of the innings South Africa's bowlers bowled too short; Donald's bouncers were often ill directed, allowing me width, and I decided to take him on. I cut him hard over point and then pulled him over wide mid-on. To hit the pull so early and so far in front of square shows that while I might not exactly have been premeditating the short ball, I was certainly on the lookout for it. He stood mid-pitch nodding his approval and no doubt was happy to see me taking the risk. But I was happy with my positive outlook. I was moving early to Donald, forcing myself down the wicket, but quick to rock back and score off anything short.

Pollock's bouncers were invariably straighter, at the body, and I felt less comfortable having a go. There was nothing to be done other than to try to tough it out. Both were bowling quickly. At one point Alec Stewart was hit above the heart and even this tough cricketer flinched and was obviously hurt. The adrenalin was flowing and I was pumped up, but it was crucial to stay in control and not make a mistake. Deep breaths and a cool, analytical mind were the key. The first hour was the hardest part – it would get easier after that.

The Kookaburra ball, unlike its English counterpart, goes noticeably softer after around fifteen overs. It is the opener's task still to be there then. At that point he can say he is 'in' and he can settle down to play in a rhythm. Occasionally, a wicket at the other end broke the rhythm. McMillan bowled Stewart, driving loosely, and Ramprakash looked all at sea. Thorpe, his head too far over to the off side, was lbw as Pringle swung one back into his pads.

Although batting is a solitary, lonely business it takes place within a partnership and each new arrival to the crease demands something from you. I was a kind of chameleon, adapting and changing to my partner's character and needs. Stewart was experienced and tough and needed little; Ramprakash lasted two balls, but would have been the junior partner, needing to be coaxed through the difficult periods.

I looked closely at Thorpe because I reckoned I could judge his mental state from the way he was playing. I was always happy to see him playing aggressively, but within the limitations of his game. He was a good puller, hooker and cutter, but here he was trying to hit on the up through the covers from the start. He was too frenetic, similar to the way he had batted at the start of an innings in Melbourne in 1995; it indicated he wasn't quite focused and he needed reminding.

Robin Smith batted with me until the close of play and he rarely wanted to talk cricket between overs. He was always tense, constantly stretching and fidgeting, muttering to himself, 'Come on, Judgey, be strong!' He needed the opportunity to relax, maybe to talk of the evening's activities ahead, or about a mate in the crowd. We got through to the close: 167–4 and I was 82 not out.

I rarely overnighted well. Too often I did the right thing and went to bed early, but with the adrenalin still flowing I got little sleep. Twice I was not out overnight in Test cricket with 100 to my name and twice I got out the next morning in the first over – against New Zealand at Trent Bridge in 1994 and later against South Africa at Edgbaston in 1998. In the middle of this innings I made sure I went out and tried to forget about the game over some pasta and a few glasses of wine in the Sandton Sun, the hotel where we were staying. As a result, I had a long, dreamless sleep.

The next morning I wanted to preserve my energy as much as possible. After a stretch and a couple of throw downs, it was time to pad up and go through the routine again. Superstition demanded that I wore the same clothes; I must have smelt like a polecat but superstition was stronger than the smell or the discomfort.

I was conscious, as I walked out, that I was near my 100 and in the past I had tensed up near that landmark – I was one of only three players to have been dismissed twice in Test cricket for 99. The run-out at Lord's was hardly my fault, but at Headingley against South Africa I had snatched at the ball and hit it too early. I told myself to relax, and that I wasn't interested in the 100, I was in for the long haul.

On 99, Donald bowled a short delivery and I was up on my toes to turn it away. I played it well, but the ball hit high on my bat and I saw it spoon to Gary Kirsten at short-leg and hit him in the chest. He snatched at the rebound and I was still alive. I instinctively knew that Donald would try another short ball. Predetermination in batting is never a good thing but I was ready for it and quickly into position. The ball crashed into the boundary fence at square-leg and brought up my first 100 against South Africa. It was a rare moment to relax, to soak up the crowd's applause and release some emotion, which I did by hugging a startled Robin Smith. He recoiled, no doubt at the smell. Time to settle; I retook my guard and focused again.

During the morning Robin Smith departed, caught unluckily at third man. Jack Russell came to the crease; I knew Russell demanded nothing from me – he was the one who was constantly niggling, snarling through his moustache and snapping at my heels. 'Don't give it away now,' he said, 'it's not finished yet, remember Barbados,' (when Curtly Ambrose demolished the end of the England innings in 1990). It was wise to let him carry on, and when he had finished ranting, he had to superstitiously touch my pads with his bat before the start of the next over.

Despite Jack's idiosyncrasies he gave his all that game, as he always did. He was at the peak of his career having also taken eleven catches in the match – a new world record. He was a great fighter and a worthy companion.

By mid morning I was 'in' again. I had seen off the second new ball, and there was little spin for Clive Eksteen – only a lapse in concentration could end my stay, and concentration was always the strongest part of my game. The key to concentration, and therefore to playing long innings, is the ability to focus intensely for short periods of time and then switch off completely.

My trigger to switch on was when the bowler was halfway through his run. I would then focus intensely on the ball until it was dead – a period of seven seconds, say. In between deliveries or at the end of each over, I would switch off completely, and by doing so I saved energy. This was my biggest strength as a batsman. Gary Kirsten was a batsman who matched me in this respect – compare his body language in between deliveries to that of, say, Robin Smith. Kirsten, calm and neutral; Smith, pumped up, talking to himself, forever jigging about and wasting energy.

It was also important not to look too far ahead. At the start of my innings, batting for five sessions seemed a long way off. I tried to break it down into small periods – a two-hour session until lunch, tea or the close of play; an hour up to the drinks break; a bowler's spell, which might be forty minutes; each over; then to the smallest unit, each delivery. It boils down to the old cliché, one ball at a time.

By the afternoon, and for the only time in my career, I was in the zone. It is a state of being much talked about by sports psychologists and while I can describe my feeling that afternoon, I couldn't begin to explain how to replicate it. I don't think I ever completely experienced it again. The zone for me was a feeling of absolute control. It is a rare feeling for a batsman, who is usually at the mercy of forces outside his control – the bowler, the pitch and the umpire, for example.

I was in an almost trance-like state. Everything happened dreamily, in slow motion, although I was still alert and picking up the cues around me. Picking up cues can be an instinctive thing – against the West Indies at Lord's in 1995 I *knew* the last ball of Curtly Ambrose's spell was going to be a yorker. Quite how I don't know, except that he had not bowled me one all spell, and he usually bowled at least one. The insight didn't help me – the ball was perfectly pitched and knocked my middle stump flat.

With some bowlers, predicting the next ball came down to experience; by playing against them often, you got used to certain signals. I could always see, for example, when Winston Benjamin was going to bowl a bouncer. There was something different in his run-up and approach to the crease. Devon Malcolm had a reverse cock of his wrists, i.e. his wrist would point downwards not upwards, which could alert a batsman to his bouncer.

In Johannesburg I was alert to the cues. Eksteen went over the wicket and I instinctively opened my stance and changed my game plan. McMillan's slower ball was bowled from wide of the crease. The peripheral awareness was there, too – I knew when the wicket-keeper and slips would be walking up, and that the outfielders would be moving straighter as a result of a slower-ball call. Pringle bowled an over of inswingers; the change of action (open-chested, with a floppy wrist) was easy to spot. The zone was a state of both inertia and intense concentration, and I *knew* that I was in total control and they couldn't get me out.

By late afternoon, the crowd became quieter and began to

drift away. South Africa took the third new ball, but tired limbs betrayed their unflinching desire. I was dimly aware that we were approaching our goal and got slightly more nervous, at both the anticipation of success and the fear of failing so close to the finish line. But I was also enjoying batting, the feeling of total control and seeing South Africa's bowlers tired and defeated. Suddenly Hansie Cronje came up and offered his hand. It was all over.

Instinctively, I turned to Jack, who had stayed with me until the end. We embraced each other and there was little that needed saying. We rushed off the field, just as the England supporters ran on and I remember being chased by a huge Union Jack that seemed to have a life of its own. Back in the changing room there was a good reception. A cool beer with your mates and the knowledge of a job well done – there is no better feeling in sport than that.

For those two days I played a great innings. I was in the middle of my best period as a batsman. For a short time in the mid nineties, I was the best player in the England team and the wicket most prized by the opposition. I was solid and consistent and undoubtedly one of the best openers around. More than that, it was as if my efforts were a complete reflection of my character. All the self-sufficiency of my youth, the stubbornness and single-mindedness of my cricket, had come together in an innings that would stand as a testimony to my character as much as my batting.

I was by no means a great player, however – I had too many bad games and bad series to be considered that. My final Test record shows that I was nothing more than a good Test batsman. Johannesburg was the pinnacle for me, and afterwards the curve of the graph was mainly downwards, although its gradient was shallow. I still had good series and played many match-winning innings for England, but I don't think I ever played with the same strength, solidity or certainty again. Maybe, in its immediate aftermath, the innings took more out of me than I realised, or maybe even I got carried away with my own publicity for a while. I remember saying to Nasser Hussain that the hardest innings to play is the one after your great one. His decline in form started after his monumental innings in Durban. It is so difficult to climb Everest twice.

But as I sat in the dressing room at the Wanderers that day, sipping cold beer and soaking up the congratulations, I wasn't worried about the future. Just as an opening batsman knows he has to make it count when he is in because the unplayable delivery with the new ball might be just around the corner, so I was determined to appreciate that good moment. It was just as well. Before I retired I was to play three more innings at the Wanderers; I lasted four balls and got three ducks.

13

BUMBLING ALONG

I had known of David Lloyd for many years. He had been an integral part of the successful Lancashire team of the 1970s, whose names roll as easily off my tongue now as they did as a youngster. Lloyd (D), Wood, Pilling, Hayes, Lloyd (C), Engineer ... I had known 'Bumble' personally ever since I had run out his son Graham in a Lancashire Schools Under 13 match against Yorkshire at Old Trafford. Neither of us could have conceivably guessed that fifteen years after he quietly admonished me for my running between the wickets, in defence of his son's honour, we would be working together as captain and coach of England.

Since that unpromising start, we had got on well. I enjoyed his company. He had an infectious enthusiasm for the game and the players within it. Some people radiate warmth and are good to be around and Lloyd was one of them. Not only did we have a passion for Lancashire and cricket we also shared an enthusiasm for fishing and racing. My interest in racing is a relatively recent one. It began in the mid 1990s when I began to buy the *Racing Post* because it was the only newspaper without in-depth cricket coverage, and therefore criticism. From these unlikely beginnings, a passion was formed and now I am an avid follower and punter.

Our first foray into racehorse ownership was completely unsuccessful. We purchased a quarter-share in a horse called Mephitis (Latin for 'evil smell' – not a good start) trained by

Venetia Williams in Herefordshire. One glorious autumn morning we went down to see our equine investment. We looked
around the fantastic stables on the banks of the River Wye,
watched the horses on the gallops and saw a couple of stable
stars. No sign of Mephitis. Suddenly, out of the corner of his
eye, Bumble saw a grey being brought towards us. 'Look at this
hairy-arsed runt,' he whispered to me. Mephitis was made to do
a couple of turns in front of us; he bucked constantly and looked
anything other than a trained racehorse. 'How's he doing?' we
asked Venetia. 'Well, at the moment he's got sore shins, a hanging head and won't go up the gallops. Apart from that he's doing
well.' He was sold shortly afterwards.

After that our luck didn't improve. We bought a quarter-share
in an ex-German flat horse called Golden Goal. We followed it
over hurdles for a couple of years, and it proved hard to win
with. During the winter of 2001, we decided that instead of
shelling out for training fees, we would sell our share. Within
three months it had won two Grade One chases and over
£50,000 in prize money. It ran at the Cheltenham Festival and
was touted as one of the top novice chasers in the country.

Lloyd had been appointed Lancashire's coach in 1992. He
cared passionately about the players under his control, as his
appearance in 1994 in the Lake District on my behalf had shown.
He obviously realised that the winter of 1995–96 had been a
tough one for me and he agreed to pick me up from Manchester
airport after the World Cup. I warned him to keep his ear to the
ground because a job vacancy might be coming up within the
England set-up and he should have no hesitation in applying.
'We need you,' I told him. Nobody from the board spoke to me
about Lloyd, but I would have had no hesitation in rec-
ommending him had they done so.

As a naturally humorous after-dinner speaker and popular
commentator on 'Test Match Special', Lloyd had a reputation as
a bit of a joker. When it came to business, however, he was
passionate and serious about the game, as I had seen at Old

Trafford. During the winter, I had talked with John Barclay at length about the attributes the new England coach would need. We agreed on the four 'e's: experience, expertise, enthusiasm and energy. Lloyd fitted the bill. I was sure we would be good for each other, his fire contrasting well with my phlegm.

But my first task on returning from the World Cup was to write my captain's report (see appendix), which I duly sent to the board. I was never quite sure who looked at these reports, or if they were read at all, although I didn't see any point in being anything other than honest. Reading through it now, it is obvious that I felt some frustration at the lack of progression and direction within the England set-up, but that I still had a clear vision of what needed to be done to improve it. The report not only looked back at the South African tour and the World Cup, but also looked forward to the need for change.

I feel it is always instructive to look at how other countries run things and in this instance I offered something of a comparison with South Africa. The holier-than-thou, image-conscious attitude of some of their players irritated me intensely (although I got on famously with the likes of Donald and Kirsten) and was later shown to be a shattering illusion. Nevertheless, the structure within which their team operated was a good one; I felt they made the best use of their resources while we did not.

I made certain recommendations – the need for more rest, shorter tours, more preparation time, better press management, central contracts and the appointment of a full-time coach were the main ones. Over time most will have been seen to be sensible proposals; some were even swiftly acted upon. But the most important – central contracts – took another four years to arrive, and was even rejected by the Acfield Committee the very year I recommended it. They moved quickly, however, to appoint a coach.

I knew that Raymond Illingworth wanted to finish his day-to-day involvement with the team. He rang me on 20 March and he sounded tired and depressed. It had been a long winter, the

Devon Malcolm affair was rumbling on and Warwickshire and Surrey had moved to put forward David Graveney as an alternative chairman of selectors. 'All right lad, I'm thinking of chucking it in. I'm tired of the backstabbing and I want to know where you stand.' I told him honestly that I was happy for him to remain as chairman of selectors but that the team needed a younger, full-time coach.

In the end, Illingworth stood down as manager but remained as chairman of selectors when David Graveney, who felt his role as general secretary of the Professional Cricketers' Association (PCA) was a conflict of interest, withdrew from the contest. Graveney was coopted on to the selection panel, along with Graham Gooch, and Raymond's power base was very much eroded. A very different, and less autocratic, Illingworth was in evidence during the next twelve months. He had been genuinely hurt by the criticism, and now that he was no longer head honcho, he was happy to see out his time quietly.

The board appointed Lloyd as coach while we were both in Jamaica with Lancashire on our pre-season tour. I heard the news during a Sunday match in Montego Bay. Opposite the ground was a Baptist church and as I wandered over to hear the wonderful singing at first-hand, I was ready to offer up a prayer of thanks that I was about to work with someone whom I knew had similar views to my own on how the England team should be run.

Like me, Lloyd did not believe in over-coaching, especially once the players had reached international level. Further down the scale, Lloyd was much more interventionist. Richard Green arrived at Lancashire as a promising young batsman but after two years under Lloyd he was making people sit up and take notice of his lively outswingers. At international level, Lloyd felt it was important to manage the players, and create an atmosphere in which they could enjoy their cricket without fear of public criticism.

We quickly marked out our respective territories. Lloyd would be in charge of the preparation of the team before a Test and he would run the practice sessions. He would also look closely at the strengths and weaknesses of the opposition. Once the game started, I was in charge. It was an arrangement that suited us both well and was virtually the same understanding that Hussain and Fletcher came to have years later.

If the players wanted technical help, there would be specialist coaches and video analysis on hand for them. Lloyd was keen to give the players whatever they needed to succeed. He set up Team England, a backroom staff consisting of a nutritionist, sports psychologist, press liaison officer and fitness trainer, as well as various specialist coaches but, in the end, it was down to the players to use whatever they felt necessary.

In setting up his backroom staff, Lloyd dragged England forward so that in our preparation we did not suffer in comparison with any other country. Within a year, much of what I had recommended in my captain's report had come to pass. It was not his fault that he was continually hamstrung by not having full-time control over the players. It was Duncan Fletcher, the next England coach, who was to benefit from central contracts, and from the system that Lloyd worked so hard to set up.

Like anybody, Lloyd had his faults, and as is so often the case, his strength was also his weakness. Occasionally, his passion and intensity translated into a lack of calmness in a tight situation. During one close cup-tie at Old Trafford, his constant pacing and muttering did little to ease already frayed nerves and the players dragged Lloyd into the room next door and bound, gagged and trussed him up in a straitjacket (where did we get that from?) until the match was over and had been won.

Sometimes he found it difficult to watch dispassionately, as I discovered while sitting out a one-day international in Barbados on our 1997–98 tour. Dean Headley had been bowling too many no-balls and Lloyd had worked with him for a couple of hours the day before the game. They had found a solution whereby if Headley's left foot landed in a box that they marked out, he would land on rather than beyond the line, curing the no-ball problem.

Lloyd marked out the box with sawdust on the morning of the match and settled down to watch the game. When Headley came on to bowl, Lloyd tensed up, grabbed his binoculars and sat glued to proceedings. 'Hit your mark, Headless, hit your mark,' he kept muttering. As Headley ran in, Bumble's face got redder and the veins on his neck began to stand out. 'He's going to miss it, the fucker's going to miss it!' Headley missed it and a no-ball was called. Bumble slumped back, head in hands, in despair. 'Headless, Headless, what are you doing to me?' he whimpered, as if his favourite son had just been caught smoking for the umpteenth time.

I knew there was a chance that Lloyd's passion would occasionally boil over and that he might land himself in hot water, especially with the press. He was ticking when he made his 'flippin' murdered 'em' comment in Zimbabwe in 1996 and when he questioned Muralitharan's bowling action at The Oval in 1998, both of which landed him in hot water with Tim Lamb, the new chief executive of the board. It strained relations between them for good, and brought a premature end to Lloyd's tenure shortly after the World Cup in 1999.

Lloyd's first summer in charge went well. We won three out of the four series (two one-day and two Test) on offer, losing to Pakistan in the Tests in the second half of the summer. In Wasim, Waqar and Mushtaq, Pakistan had three world-class bowlers, and we extended our hospitality too far by preparing pitches at Lord's and The Oval that were drier and more grassless than Lahore or Faisalabad. That summer we also offered the opposition the choice of which balls they wanted to use. Wasim wanted Readers because they reversed and I wanted Dukes because they swung conventionally. I lost every toss for choice of balls. Generally, however, I was pleased with the new set-up and with my relationship with David Lloyd, and I looked forward to us making progress.

The warning signs that I had not long left in the job were all too evident. In statistical terms I had a good summer, scoring

425 Test runs and averaging over 40, but I knew that, technically, I wasn't playing well. The Second Test against India at Lord's was Dickie Bird's farewell match. On the first morning, I organised both teams to line up and applaud him on to the playing surface, and afterwards Alec Stewart and I followed the Indian team out. Bird was in tears. He hugged Mohammad Azharuddin, waved his hankie to all four corners of the ground and thanked me profusely. 'Eh lad, what an honour. I'm so grateful, Mike.' Srinath bowled the first over of the match to me from Bird's end. He jagged the fifth ball down the Lord's slope and I shuffled across my crease and was trapped in front. Dickie's eyes were still red and he had scarcely wiped the tears from his cheeks, but he rightly waved his forefinger high above his head and shouted, practically bellowed, 'That's aht!' Another failure at Lord's.

Bird was a popular but notoriously nervous umpire. Rain and bad weather seemed to follow him as inevitably as night follows day. During a Test match at Old Trafford in 1995, he astonished the natives by bringing off the players because the light was too bright. (It was reflecting off a greenhouse on the practice ground.) Earlier in that match he interrupted play when he dropped the marbles that he used to count the number of deliveries that had been bowled. Play was halted momentarily while Bird scrambled around on his hands and knees looking for his counters. 'I've lost me marbles! I've lost me marbles!' he cried. Most of us thought he had lost his marbles a long time ago.

The next match against India was at Trent Bridge and I scored 160. I didn't feel in any sort of form until I had passed three figures and had batted for three hours or more. I suppose it said something for my mental strength and stickability but it was damned ugly to watch. 'That's the worst hundred I've ever seen,' said Anil Kumble, congratulating me. 'Yeah, but at least it keeps coming off the middle of the bat when you're bowling,' I retorted. We were both right. It was a terrible 100 but Kumble only ever spun the ball on a dustbowl and he did provide some light relief from India's opening bowlers, Javagal Srinath and Venkatesh Prasad.

India went home beaten, Pakistan arrived and the week before the start of that series, Lancashire played Derbyshire at Old Trafford. As I was wandering around the back of the pavilion, a biker, clad in leathers, handed me a brown envelope. I opened it and was surprised to find a wad of notes, and even more surprised to find a subpoena from Imran Khan to testify in his highly publicised libel action against Ian Botham. I wondered briefly if the money was a bribe and accepted it warily only when the courier assured me it was for travelling expenses to the High Court.

The court case was a hassle. It did get me out of the end of a dull county fixture, but it also threatened my participation in the Lord's Test, which was three days later. I sat in court for two days and was not called. Thankfully, I was allowed to testify on the third day. I was understandably nervous, but George Carman QC put me at ease by enquiring after the Manchester Grammar School (his son went there). I fared better than some; Robin Smith was confounded by the advocate's use of long words. 'Jeez, your honour,' he pleaded. 'I'm only a simple cricketer.' The case was complex and it seemed to me that the jurors were totally confused by the intricacies of reverse swing and ball tampering, and they sat uninterested and doodling. As I stood in the witness box, with Jemima Khan's big doey eyes looking balefully, first at the jurors and then at me, I feared for Botham and the outcome of the case. He duly lost.

The fourth day of the final Test at The Oval was a Sunday and it was the kind of day that made me wonder for the first time whether the captaincy of England was worth all the bother. We were 1–0 down and needed a win to level the series, but most of my energies seemed to be needed elsewhere. The selectors had picked the squad for the one-day internationals the evening before and I had to tell three players who were playing in the Test (Hussain, Crawley and Cork) that they were surplus to requirements.

Sunday dawned overcast and soggy and I went down to

breakfast at the Conrad, Chelsea Harbour, where we were staying. Hussain, as was his custom, was already there (he was usually too highly strung to sleep) and I broke the news to him. He took it badly, told me it was bad man-management to select a one-day party in the middle of a Test match and stormed off. I thought so too, but five years later during the Australia Test at The Oval, Nasser, as captain, had similar problems with Stewart and Gough over their winter plans. Sometimes it was just unavoidable. Crawley was more philosophical. Cork had already left for the ground.

When I got to The Oval, Cork was practising in the middle. I went up to him and told him that he had been left out of the one-day squad and, without warning, he broke down in floods of tears. He was having marital problems and was also struggling to come to terms with the fame and attention that had been his constant bedfellow since his introduction into international cricket. Simply, he was a young man struggling to cope with various things in his life and he needed help. Shortly afterwards, Cork recognised his problems and pulled out of the first leg of the winter tour to Zimbabwe.

Eventually he calmed down and we went over to join the rest of the team at 9.30 a.m. for our warm-up. There was no Chris Lewis. It was not the first time that summer that Lewis had been late; he had been forty minutes late for a practice day before the first Test of the summer. This, however, was a matchday. He was due to open the bowling that morning and by 10.20 a.m. he was still not there. He sauntered in at 10.30, explaining that he had a flat tyre, but there was no apology. It was a feeble excuse. I thought it was unacceptable and told him so in the captain's room next to the dressing room. After consulting with David Lloyd and Ray Illingworth we dropped him from the one-day squad.

Play began on time and Pakistan were pushing hard for a substantial first-innings lead. Lewis ran out Asif Mujtaba early on with a fine, fast throw from the boundary, but seemed not to share the rest of the team's joy. The bowling needed constant attention. Mullally was bowling steadily but too wide; Salisbury continued to bowl nervously, sending down one or two bad balls an over; Croft was a debutant and I needed to stand at mid-off, although thankfully he needed little nursing; Lewis bowled at medium pace. At one point, Cork, Crawley and Hussain were all in the covers continuously making sarcastic comments about their omission from the one-day team. I felt a headache coming on.

By mid afternoon, Salim Malik was nudging his way towards 100, and at the other end Wasim Akram was slogging, violently. A right-hander nudging, and a left-hander slogging meant about six field changes every other ball. I felt under siege from all directions, from my own team and the opposition. Eventually, Wasim declared. I now had to go out and face Wasim and Waqar for twenty-three torrid overs on a typically fast Oval pitch. Alec and I withstood the barrage and we walked off 74–0.

That day the crowd saw an insipid performance in the field from England, but what did they know of the background? The problems, the frictions, the dynamics of human relationships – they all made for a particularly fraught day and left me with a thumping headache. On top of that, we were losing the game. I suppose it was one of my great strengths that I could still go out at the end of such a day, put it all to one side, and keep my own game intact.

Afterwards, Alec and I sat in the dressing room and shared a drink with our two county colleagues, Wasim and Waqar. Everyone left and I sat there on my own until David Lloyd returned from the press conference. He must have sensed my mood. 'You're thinking of jacking it in, aren't you?' he said. I looked at him and said nothing; it was a momentary feeling and it would pass. But I realised that I was fatigued, and I could see myself lasting for only another year in the job. It had been a tough summer on the back of a heavy winter. This was before central contracts and before international players were routinely pulled out of county games, and so I had little rest. Moreover Lancashire won both one-day finals that year and so there was a big cup-tie the day after each Test. This was my intended schedule mid summer:

30 May–3 June: Gloucestershire at Old Trafford
4/5 June: practice before First Test
6–10 June: First Test v. India
11 June: Benson & Hedges semi-final
12 June: travel to Durham
13–17 June: championship v. Durham away
18/19 June: practice before Second Test
20–24 June: Second test v. India
25 June: NatWest third round v. Oxfordshire
26 June: DAY OFF
27 June–1 July: championship v. Somerset at Old Trafford
2/3 July: practice before Third Test
4–9 July: Third Test v. India (Sunday rest day)
10 July: NatWest fourth round v. Northants

Bob Bennett (the Lancashire Chairman) also knew that I was exhausted by the end of the summer, and he arranged for me to miss the last three championship games. I forgot about cricket for a while and rested, and then looked forward to my first winter tour with David Lloyd.

In Zimbabwe, we played two Tests and three one-day internationals. In New Zealand, five one-day internationals followed three Tests. The tour as a whole was a microcosm of the England team under my captaincy. Our cricket veered from awful (during the one-day games in Zimbabwe) to excellent (during the Tests in New Zealand) with not much in between. I went from batting in binary in Zimbabwe – 0, 1, 0, 1, if you get my drift – to averaging 100 in the three-match series in New Zealand. I lurched from villain to hero, and it was certainly never dull.

The feelings of uncertainty about my game from the summer continued throughout Zimbabwe and up until the First Test against New Zealand. But whereas in the summer I was in the habit of scoring runs, despite my poor form, gradually that habit left me and it resulted, for the first time during my captaincy, in a horror trot. Other than a half-century in the second innings against Matabeleland, few runs flowed from my bat. By the time the First Test against New Zealand came around, I had scored 126 runs in eleven first-class innings on tour, and I began seriously to doubt my ability to regain my touch. I was also having increasing problems with my back.

Two matches before the First Test in New Zealand, we netted in New Plymouth. I was desperate to practise away from the limelight – away from cameras, television crews and well-intentioned supporters who winced and groaned every time I got out – but it was impossible. I had a terrible net and became hugely frustrated at my inability and at all the other things I had no control over, such as the standard of practice facilities and the presence of the press.

It was unusual for me to worry about such incidentals and is indicative of the kind of pressure I felt under. In a way, that practice session was a complete contrast to the 'perfect practice scenario' I described before the Johannesburg game. In Johannesburg, I was in full control; in Auckland, events seemed to be controlling me. When I emerged from my horror net I overheard Ralph Middlebrook, a Yorkshire Academy coach, say to David Lloyd, 'He is in a mess, isn't he?' He was right.

There were some glaring technical deficiencies in my batting. I was moving around too much before the ball was bowled. I was planting my front foot as before, but now it was going across the crease instead of down the wicket. I tried to compensate for being closed off by opening up my stance and withdrawing my left leg but that put my hips and body and shoulders out of alignment. As so often happens, correct one fault and another one appears.

When bowlers bowled outside off stump I was fine. The problems came when the ball was straight because my left leg was invariably in the line of the ball and prevented my bat from coming down straight. As a result my bat had to come down across the ball – 'doing a scissors' as Nasser Hussain used to say, chuckling, as he did an impression that looked like a cross between me, out of form, and Devon Malcolm, in form, the bat coming down at right-angles to the delivery, stumps everywhere.

That was the fundamental technical problem. Instead of keeping things simple, watching the ball, standing still and trusting my talent, I constantly tinkered with my game and made things worse. Along with those problems came the mental anguish and loss of confidence that are the inevitable result of a run of low scores. In form, a batsman thinks of little and plays his favourite shots naturally. Out of form, too many things crowd the six inches between the ears and he goes searching for his shots too eagerly. By the time the First Test in New Zealand came around, I was definitely in the second category.

I think that fatigue and the constant diet of international and domestic cricket were, in my case, to blame. I had been on the international treadmill non-stop since 1993. The winter in South Africa had taken a heavy toll and the following summer was equally tough with Lancashire and England commitments. There was no time to take stock, to reflect on the problems and work them out away from the pressure of international cricket; gradually and unknowingly, faults had crept into my game.

Looking back, it is clear that the captaincy was a factor. Now, it is easy for me to analyse the problems but I couldn't back then because I was totally preoccupied. In Zimbabwe there were myriad issues to consider – Graham Thorpe's moodiness; the clique of Irani, Tufnell, Thorpe and Hussain that was beginning to develop; whether Alec should keep wicket or not; everything other than my own game.

At the start of my captaincy, not being able to spend time on my own game was a benefit because it prevented me from being too insular. Initially, also, the added responsibility and pressure were empowering and resulted in better personal performances. Eventually, however, as pressure increased over time, my ability to cope clearly decreased. Now, I needed extra time to put my game in order and the captaincy was a hindrance. I was not the only captain whose game suffered; most other captains in my era found that the extra responsibilities sat heavily on them and it affected their game in varying degrees – Richie Richardson, Mark Taylor and even Sachin Tendulkar, to name but three.

On top of my poor form, the team struggled in Zimbabwe. We were beaten by Mashonaland and whitewashed in the one-day internationals. We were pilloried in the press in Zimbabwe and England ('send them home' roared Tory MP Terry Dicks). The impression was given that we were beaten by a bunch of farmers. Eddo Brandes, our destroyer in the third one-day international, was a chicken farmer, but when he wasn't feeding his chooks, he was a fine outswing bowler.

All this obscured the fact that the fundamentals of our Test form were sound. Bulawayo was the scene of the First Test. We played some good cricket and chased the 205 in thirty-seven overs we needed to win the match. Mostly, people doubted that we would accept the challenge but there was no doubt in my mind that we should go for it. We would have won handsomely but for some cynical, but understandable, tactics by Zimbabwe's bowlers who bowled as wide as possible in the last few overs so that we could not hit the ball. For the only time in Test history, scores were level and the match was drawn. Only three wides were called. I was incensed and I raised the matter with one of the umpires. The reply I received astonished me. 'In a Test match,' I was told, 'the ball has to land beyond the return crease for me to call a wide.'

Hanumant Singh, the match referee, was nowhere to be seen. Before the match, his presence had been an irritation. He had walked into the dressing room with a huge dollop of bird-shit on his shoulder. 'You're all fine,' he said. 'Yes thank you, Mr

Referee, we're all fine,' we replied. 'No, no, no!' he said. 'You're all *fined*!' He insisted the advertising logos on our bats were too big and threatened to fine the whole team although later he withdrew his complaint. It was typical of the kind of irrelevancies that ICC match referees worried about.

The Zimbabwe tour was characterised by mistakes and misconceptions and at the end of it I found myself the subject of severe criticism. A captain who is short of runs needs his team to win; a dearth of runs and victories is a situation no captain can survive for too long. On our flight to New Zealand I reflected upon this.

The journey from Zimbabwe to New Zealand took thirty-six hours. When we landed in Auckland we were not sure, with the time difference, whether it was early morning or late evening, or whether we had landed a day later, or a day earlier, or even, for that matter, on the same day. There was an all-night bar just around the corner and it seemed the only solution.

The release from the tension of Zimbabwe was palpable and it was quite a session. Walking to work that morning, Aucklanders were greeted by nearly the whole squad, in full uniform, drunkenly spilling out on to the sidewalk watching Phil Tufnell learning to surf on Wayne Morton's backside as he, Morton, lay face down on the pavement. The more adventurous shelved their plans for a sober morning in the office and joined in the fun.

I staggered back to the hotel in a pleasant haze and was greeted by John Barclay, the tour manager, who announced that there would be a lunchtime press conference. I slept, showered and two hours later breezed into the press conference, blithely accepted a glass of Buck's fizz, and steadied myself for the usual inanities and soundbites. My mouth was dry and the first dull poundings of a hangover were beginning to appear.

A man whom I vaguely recognised but could not quite place stood up. 'Michael Nicholson, ITN,' he announced rather pompously. Oh my God! A *news* reporter! 'Are you going to resign?' 'Well . . . no actually . . .' 'Don't you think you should?' 'Well . . .' 'If you were the chief executive of a public company you would have been kicked out by now.' No argument there. Michael Nicholson, ITN, was known in the trade as a 'heavy' and wasn't to be placated by soundbites and inanities. I got through as best I could with nobody any the wiser as to my condition. At the end of it all, Jonathan Agnew, possibly feeling sorry for me, said it was the best press conference I had given. I had given some shockers, mind you.

Michael Nicholson, ITN, hung around for another week or so. He was on standby to fly to Russia if Boris Yeltsin's health deteriorated any further. I fervently wished Boris would take a turn for the worse. If Michael Nicholson, ITN, had been there much longer, *my* health would have deteriorated. When we started winning, he left as suddenly as he had arrived. A winning team is no story.

Before the First Test, we played in Hamilton and it was there that I rediscovered my touch – not out in the middle but in an old indoor school at the back of the ground where I was able, at last, to practise away from the limelight. I took Wayne Morton, the physiotherapist, to feed the bowling machine and I practised one afternoon for four hours. Away from the media, supporters and even my own team, I was able to clear my head and practise with purpose. It helped that I had someone with me who knew nothing about batting – I was left to sort out the problems on my own.

What did I do? Nothing more than simple repetition and certainly nothing fancy. I was so out of rhythm that all I wanted to do was show the full face of the bat to the ball and hit it straight. I did that monotonously for four hours and gradually my natural movements and timing returned. I emerged feeling much better within myself and I confidently looked forward to the First Test in Auckland.

I put New Zealand in on a damp-looking pitch tinged with green. None of the bowlers could find their rhythm and we had a disastrous morning. At lunch David Lloyd sat alone and refused to talk to us, and I was left to try to repair the damage. Later I was asked if the pitch had played how I imagined it would; I could only reply, 'We'll never know.'

Dominic Cork was proving troublesome. After pulling out of Zimbabwe, and refusing to attend pre-tour fitness tests, Cork arrived in New Zealand, but his failing marriage was still at the front of his mind and he was in no state to play. On that first morning I suggested a field change and he told me frankly to 'fuck off'. I thought an extra slip was quite a good idea. Lord MacLaurin suggested we send Cork home but I was against it. I thought Cork was fundamentally a decent bloke and the type of cricketer we simply couldn't afford to lose. I argued that we needed to be more understanding and give him time to come around. A month later, Cork scored the winning runs in Christchurch to seal our victory.

I scored 83 in the First Test and was out in unfortunate circumstances when I slog-swept Dipak Patel only to see the ball cannon off short midwicket's shoulder straight back to the bowler. The cycle of low scores had been broken.

Nathan Astle and Danny Morrison held out for three hours to prevent our victory and increase the criticism of my captaincy. I was unconcerned now; my form had returned, we had erred in not selecting a second spinner and I knew we had played good cricket after a wayward first morning. My faith was rewarded with a comprehensive victory in the Second Test in Wellington.

The series hung in the balance by the fourth evening of the Third Test in Christchurch. We needed 305 to win batting last, and at the end of the fourth day we were 118–2. I had spent every second on the field, having carried my bat for 94 in the first innings, and being 65* in the second. I was feeling good about myself. Not only was I playing well but I had enjoyed captaining Tufnell and Croft who bowled so well together, and I felt my positive attitude in the field had helped get us back into the game having conceded a first-innings lead of 118.

I knew the target was a stiff one; England had only ever once chased more than 300 to win and there was plenty of rough outside the right-hander's leg stump for New Zealand's young spinner, Daniel Vettori, to exploit. I ate alone, nervously, that evening; then I wandered around Christchurch for a while, bumped into Hussain and Thorpe in the casino and later slept fitfully. I knew that a 1–1 draw would be poor reward for our efforts and 2–0 would be a much fairer reflection of the cricket we had played. Everything hinged on the next day.

As I walked out the next morning with Andrew Caddick, the nightwatchman, the tension was high. Vettori was the main threat and I had thought carefully about how to combat him. He was bowling mostly over the wicket into the rough. I decided to open my stance, stand taller rather than crouched and bat outside leg stump to try to open up the off side. Above all, I didn't want to hit against the spin.

Caddick lasted a valuable fifty minutes. Hussain's arrival and New Zealand's decision to take the new ball brought a brief flurry of runs and I reached my eleventh Test 100 before lunch with an on-drive off Simon Doull. An on-drive, with a straight bat and good balance, was always a sign that I was playing well. We lunched at 203–3, 102 more needed.

After lunch, I nibbled at Astle, Hussain got a snorter from Vettori and Thorpe, all aggression, went quickly, caught and bowled. We were 231–6, 74 more needed with Cork and Crawley in and not much to come.

I watched from the balcony next to John Emburey. I was reading *Fly Fishing in the West Country* in a vain attempt to give off relaxed vibes. David Lloyd was sitting two away from me and was far from relaxed – he was chewing gum furiously, the veins in his forehead throbbing, and he looked on edge. Occasionally, I went down into the dressing room to check on things. Tufnell, Thorpe and Hussain were huddled together on an old worn sofa, smoking nervously and unable to watch. A dense fug hung over them.

Crawley and Cork were cool under pressure and slowly but

surely with few alarms they took us to victory. Cork hit the winning runs and the relief on the balcony was palpable. The terrified three from downstairs emerged to join in the celebrations and as John Crawley ran off, he gave me a match stump as a souvenir.

As always, the winning dressing room was a good place to be. Before the fun began, Crawley called the dressing room to a hush. 'Goughy, you've got to shut your cricket case.' Gough looked puzzled and annoyed that his celebrations had been interrupted. 'What do you mean? What are you on about?' 'Well, I know you've never won much at Yorkshire, but our experience at Lancashire is that when you win a trophy you spray champagne around and it invariably ruins your kit. So shut your case.' Not for the first time, Gough and Yorkshire were the butt of the team's humour.

The next day David Lloyd, John Barclay and I fished the Hope River, two hours north of Christchurch, in an attempt to lure New Zealand's elusive trout. Lloyd could reflect on a turbulent year in charge. Firstly, he had been hailed as a breath of fresh air; then, after his 'flippin' murdered 'em' comment in Bulawayo, he had been vilified. He had fallen out with his employers, and occasionally with the team, but he had also shown himself to be compassionate and caring when Phil Tufnell was falsely accused of smoking dope in Christchurch. He had endured much, as had I.

Lloyd could also reflect on a team that had progressed more, in my estimation, than at any time since the Illingworth era had begun. The fielding was sharp and the standard of catching better on that tour than with any England team I played in. The batting (Atherton, Knight, Stewart, Hussain, Thorpe and Crawley) looked solid while the bowling (Gough, Caddick, Cork, Tufnell and Croft) was varied and incisive. Lloyd had transformed England's backroom staff and made sure that in our preparation we suffered in comparison to no one. He could reflect on all that and more, and he could look forward to the fact that the Australians were coming.

14

THE ASHES, AGAIN

Australia. The Ashes. While I was growing up I thought little about either. Clive Lloyd was Lancashire's overseas player, and one of my heroes, and it was his West Indies team that was the dominant force in world cricket. Their fast bowlers terrorised all before them and their batsmen, eschewing helmets and defence, played with an uninhibited joy that reflected their cricket in general. Australia, weakened by defections to Packer, seemed pale and dull in comparison. It was the maroon caps rather than the 'baggy greens' that I looked forward to seeing as a boy.

As a player that perspective quickly changed, and the Ashes became the Holy Grail – and just as elusive. At the start of my career, the long history and tradition of the Ashes infected me like a virus and by 1997 it had become a full-blown disease. By that time, Australia had also become the standard bearers of cricketing excellence. I knew that I would never be truly recognised as a top-flight England player unless I played in a victorious Ashes team, and as captain, I always had half an eye on our next Ashes challenge.

At the start of the summer I was concerned about the fact that Lancashire had awarded me a benefit year. While I obviously needed to try to take advantage of that, I didn't want it to deflect my energy from the business in hand. I asked Bob Wilson, an old friend from Lancashire, to run the benefit and I remain extremely grateful for the fact that he took on the entire burden. We had a successful year, and I was left to concentrate on the cricket.

As we returned from New Zealand it felt, for the first time in my experience, as though we had a team ready to challenge for cricket's ultimate prize. I had captained well in New Zealand and my batting was back to its best. The management of the team was strong and the side had developed. The only queries were over Nick Knight as my opening partner, and Dominic Cork whose injuries and off-the-field problems threatened his place as the back-up seamer to Gough and Caddick. Other than that, everything was in place.

Moreover, the appointment of Ian MacLaurin as chairman of the ECB six months earlier signalled a change in attitude from the game's administrators. Someone once said to me, 'Never trust a man with shiny shoes and a perma-tan.' MacLaurin had both and he could, at times, be a little smooth and political. But he did recognise that the national team was the shop window of our summer game, and that it was vital to put its needs above everything else. Prior to his appointment, the interests of county cricket dominated. MacLaurin set out to chart a different course, one that culminated in central contracts three years later – the beginning, in my opinion, of England's resurgence as a cricketing nation.

Finally, the England team, or 'Team England' as fashioned by David Lloyd, began to be viewed as exactly that – a team rather than a disparate group of individuals whose primary loyalty was to their counties. For the first time, I felt confident that the team that finished the winter tour would be the same one that convened for the first Test of the following summer – continuity at last.

Lloyd organised an early season get-together at the NatWest Training Centre at Heythrop in Oxfordshire. It was a team-building exercise run by Will Carling's company, Insights. There were lectures by Frank Dick, the former national athletics coach, and Steve Bull, the team's psychologist. Such seminars could not make bad players into good ones overnight but it was one brick in the edifice that David Lloyd was trying to build, and I was entirely in favour.

I didn't agree with everything the ECB was trying to do, however. Simon Pack, who had been appointed as the International Team's Director, was concerned about the team's poor public image during the Zimbabwe tour, and reports of our unsociability. Instead of speaking to those players who were actually there, he appeared to accept the press reports as gospel and set about ways of improving our social skills.

His solution was a staged 'cocktail party' at the Heythrop gathering. In order to get the players used to small talk in social situations, each player was given a list of questions that he had to find the answers to by going around and talking to the props who had been invited to attend. I viewed this little game with distaste, more suited to eight year olds and the diplomatic corps than professional sportsmen, and I was quick to let Tim Lamb know.

Six months later, prior to the West Indies tour, Pack organised a meeting in Manchester to avoid a repeat of the problems in Zimbabwe. He was keen that, before each tour, the team be given a lecture on the mores of the host country. I suppose the idea was fine but it soon became clear that the gentleman who gave the lecture (I will spare his blushes) knew less than most of us about the Caribbean and spoke mostly of racial stereotypes. Mark Butcher, Dean Headley and Mark Ramprakash, all of Caribbean extraction, were in the squad and as the atmosphere degenerated I had to bring the meeting to a premature, abrupt and embarrassing end.

These blips notwithstanding, I felt the ECB was at last making progress in the right direction. For the first time, Tim Lamb and Ian MacLaurin spoke to the players about what needed to be done to make us more successful. I was left in no doubt that privately they wanted to see fundamental reform of our domestic game although publicly they could never say so.

So the stage was set and Australia arrived. At the start of the summer we played the best cricket that we played under my captaincy. We won the Texaco Trophy 3–0 and the First Test by nine wickets. We continued in the same vein as in New Zealand, and our general confidence was reflected on the first morning of the series when, at Edgbaston, we reduced Australia to 54–8. Mark Taylor had, as usual, opted to bat first. The humid conditions and the new stand, which created a more enclosed atmosphere than before, combined to provide perfect conditions for swing bowling, and Darren Gough and Andrew Caddick took full advantage. During one over, Gough dismissed Greg Blewett with successive deliveries, the first a no-ball. After the second, Gough jumped a mile high, both arms raised aloft, a huge smile on his face, and at that moment he reflected the character of the team, which was confident and happy.

Alec Stewart and I finished off the match, our third Test match victory in a row, with a flurry of boundaries and as I ran off the field on that fourth evening, Ian Healy grabbed my arm and said, 'Jeez, Athers, what the hell have you been on?' Whatever it was, it didn't last.

Since retirement, I have not looked back with regret at all. But if I could play one game in my career again, it would be the Third Test of that series at Old Trafford. If I could magically walk through the revolving glass doors of the Old Trafford pavilion and emerge, in brilliant sunlight, five years younger, on the morning of 3 July 1997, I would. For, although Australia fought back in the Second Test at Lord's, rain resulted in the match being drawn, and a win at Old Trafford would have left us two up with three to play, and strong favourites for the series. Old Trafford was the pivotal match; it was our chance to stake a claim for the Ashes and we fluffed it.

Australia won the match by 268 runs, comfortably in the end although for the first two days it was touch and go. They won because four of their fine players – Mark Taylor, Ian Healy, Shane Warne and Steve Waugh – produced the goods when required, as they so often did. All were thorns in our side for a decade. Healy, Warne and Waugh were great players and throughout they had the guiding hand of Mark Taylor, the best captain I have played against.

Taylor had come into the series under enormous pressure, due to an horrendous run of form that had resulted in him failing to score a 50 in twenty Test innings or more. Australia have always picked their captain from the best eleven and Taylor must have been close to exhausting the selectors' patience. I also felt he was under more pressure from his own team than was publicly acknowledged. During the second one-day international, I was sitting on the balcony with two young Australian players while we were batting. Adam Hollioake pushed a ball towards Taylor at midwicket. Taylor was an atypical Australian cricketer in that he was very unathletic, and as he flopped over the ball, landed like a beached whale, and missed it, the two young players next to me giggled and gave each other the kind of look that suggested Taylor was fast losing some respect in his own dressing room. He dropped himself for the next one-day international at Lord's and Steve Waugh took over.

But throughout his batting problems, Taylor kept his cool and his dignity. I watched him carefully and his batting technique never altered – an indication that he wasn't tinkering with his game and wasn't panicking, even if the rest of his team were. The *Daily Mirror* tried to play a stupid prank on him by presenting him with an oversized bat. Taylor said he didn't have to prove either his cricketing ability or that his sense of humour was intact and he brushed the slight away.

Good players and good people usually come through in the end, and Taylor ended his drought with 100 in the second innings of the First Test at Edgbaston. At the end of play, I went into the Australian dressing room to congratulate Taylor (for I knew what he had gone through) and the relief on his face was obvious.

Taylor was a good player, not one of Australia's best, but a good player nonetheless. He was also a fine slip fieldsman and a fine captain. As captain, he was orthodox rather than flashy, undemonstrative rather than showy. His game plan was simple – he knew he had the best bowler in the world at his disposal in Shane Warne, and he always tried to bat first and have Warne bowling last. Steve Waugh reversed this policy when he became captain, largely because he recognised that, with Warne's ability on the wane, the strength of his team was based more around pace than spin. Waugh's team bullied opponents more effectively than Taylor's, but in a tight situation Taylor was, in my opinion, the better captain.

Taylor always seemed to have something up his sleeve. In Brisbane on the 1994–95 tour, for example, Graham Thorpe and Graeme Hick built a big second-innings partnership that threatened to make a mockery of his decision not to enforce the follow-on. In the middle of a Warne over, Taylor deliberately took time out to walk ponderously from first slip to the bowler and chat to him, animatedly, for a lengthy time. Then he slowly walked back to his position. Warne bowled Thorpe next ball. I have no idea what Taylor said, and he probably said nothing of interest, but it distracted Thorpe and, by doing so, turned the match for Australia.

At Old Trafford, Taylor scored 2 and 1 and did not contribute with the bat, but he did have an awkward decision at the toss. It severely tested his usually sound judgement and was critical to the outcome of the game. The Old Trafford pitch was mottled and damp, with a tinge of green, and was sure to help the seam bowlers on the first day. Later, Taylor admitted to me that he looked at the pitch three times before the start of play. Twice he thought he should bowl, but after the pitch had been rolled for the final time, it lost some of its green tinge, and the third time he looked at it he decided, with great trepidation, to bat. It was a brave decision and ultimately the right one; the dampness in the pitch created deep follow-through marks, which Shane Warne exploited as the match wore on.

In batting first, Taylor hoped to get enough runs in the first innings to stay competitive. He did, thanks to a brilliant century from Steve Waugh, who added another to his tally in the second innings. These twin 100s, both scored with painful bat-jar of his right hand, were perhaps the most telling of Waugh's many Ashes contributions.

I saw Waugh for the first time on our 1990–91 tour, and like many others I thought he flinched and looked unsure against short, quick bowling. Indeed, so unsure did he look that he was dropped at Adelaide in favour of his twin brother Mark. Six months before our next tour there, I unwisely mentioned this flaw in a newspaper interview. He hadn't forgotten the comment, and when I was batting against Shane Warne in the First Test of the '95 series, Waugh asked Mark Taylor if he could field at silly point for me. 'I've waited a long time for this,' he snarled, as he took up residence under my nose, and he continued to growl and snarl throughout my stay.

That was unusual for Waugh. His sledging, or 'mental deterioration' as he called it, was usually indirect. He would often pass comment to a team-mate, designed of course for the opposition player and within his earshot. 'Hey, Warnie,' he might say, as he passed Nasser mid-pitch, 'Hussain plays with a really open face, doesn't he?' He avoided full-on confrontation, and by picking his comments and his targets carefully he was much more effective.

That was as much communication as we had in the thirteen years we played against each other until after my last match at The Oval when we chatted and shared a beer. It was not that either of us was unwilling to talk, or that we didn't get on, but that we were both essentially shy people and not naturally gregarious or garrulous.

By the time the 1997 series came around, I had realised that while Waugh may have looked uncomfortable against the short ball, and didn't score off it, it rarely got him out. I told all our seamers that they had to attack Waugh full and straight when he first came in. He often moved a long way back and across as if he was expecting a bouncer, leaving him vulnerable to the full ball. At Old Trafford, Caddick did exactly that and he trapped Waugh bang in front with a full-toss first ball. George Sharp thought it was just sliding down the leg side and gave Waugh the benefit of the doubt. It was a decisive moment.

We also decided at Old Trafford not to sledge Waugh or engage him in any way. We felt he revelled in a hostile atmosphere and sledging merely fuelled his adrenalin. He arrived at the crease and soon realised this: 'Okay, you're not talking to me are you? Well, I'll talk to myself then.' And he did, for 240 minutes in the first innings, and 382 minutes in the second.

Waugh gave a great performance at Old Trafford. His first-innings century kept his side in the match; his second took the game away from us. He has the quickest hands in the modern game and allows bowlers no margin for error. Any width is flayed through the covers, while his iron wrists and low back-lift pick off the leg-side ball with clinical efficiency. He isn't the prettiest player of my generation, but he is the most effective.

Waugh's 108 in the first innings helped Australia score 235, a competitive but hardly daunting total on a pitch that was flattening out. Our first innings was our big chance to put pressure on Australia, and we began well. Mark Butcher and Alec Stewart put on 66 for the second wicket and looked set. Taylor had bowled McGrath and Warne, his bankers, for over an hour. They had strangled the scoring but Butcher and Stewart had held firm, and Taylor had to try something different. Not for the first or last time, he had a trick up his sleeve.

He turned to Michael Bevan, a part-time bowler, who usually reeled off a combination of chinamen, googlies, full tosses and long-hops. Bevan bowled Butcher a leg-side full toss. Butcher tried to flick it to leg, missed and overbalanced. The ball reached Ian Healy on the half-volley, the most difficult take for a wicket-keeper. Healy gathered the ball and in one motion whipped off the bails while Butcher was still unbalanced and out of his ground. It was a brilliant stumping.

Healy's contribution that game went unnoticed, as wicket-keepers often are. Keen observers of the game would have seen Healy at his very best, and appreciated a wicket-keeper who was, in my estimation, the best in the world. His catches to dismiss Crawley in the first innings, and Thorpe in the second, as both deliveries spat out of the rough, were two of the best that I saw. In Australia's second innings, as they tottered at 132–5, Healy counter-attacked, as he so often did, with a brisk 47 and took the game away from us.

Healy kept wicket wearing a gum shield that game because of the deep rough that Warne was bowling into. The resultant silence was a shame – it meant he wasn't able to sledge, and Healy's sledges were always humorous and worth listening to. Once, when captaining Queensland, he told the bowler he wanted a fielder 'right under Nasser's nose' and he proceeded to place him about six yards away. They always liked winding up the highly strung Hussain. In Melbourne in 1998–99, Mark Butcher had moved down to number three from his usual opening berth, but each innings he was in by the second over. As he took guard in the second innings, Healy gleefully piped up, 'Not much different at number three, is it Butch!' I enjoyed playing against Ian Healy. I admired his play and his combativeness, and the fact that he never took himself or the game too seriously.

Taylor, Waugh and Healy all made significant contributions in this critical match, as did Shane Warne. Warne wrapped up the game when he had Andrew Caddick caught by Jason Gillespie, giving him match figures of 9 for 111 off sixty overs. Old Trafford, with its hard, abrasive surface, suited Warne more than any other ground in England, and he always bowled well there. Indeed it was at Old Trafford in 1993 that Warne announced himself on the Ashes stage. With his first ball in Ashes cricket, he spun and swerved one past Mike Gatting's forward prod. Gatting could scarcely believe it and lingered momentarily as if he was about to be awakened from a nightmare, and then he trudged off disconsolately like a bear that had just had his porridge swiped from under his nose.

But it was not just at Old Trafford that Warne tormented us. He was the biggest single difference between England and Australia in every Ashes series that I played in. That is not to say that we would have automatically won without him, but things would have been a damn sight closer.

Warne revitalised the art of leg-spin when it was in danger of dying, and then he mastered it. Often you would see him go through his repertoire in a single over, gradually varying the amount of side and over-spin on the ball, and throwing in a flipper and a googly for good measure. Warne had the full armoury; it always amazed me, in contrast, that after a career as a professional leg-spinner, Ian Salisbury never added a flipper to his repertoire. It was like being a fast bowler without a bouncer. Apart from Muralitharan, Warne was also the biggest spinner of the ball, and the most accurate; it was a deadly combination.

On top of his ability he was by far the smartest bowler that I played against. His close catchers – Healy, Taylor and Mark Waugh – were his extra eyes and ears, but he could usually work out a batsman's weakness without much help. In the second innings at Lord's, for example, in 2001, I took guard on middle stump. Warne quickly worked out that I had exposed my leg stump and he attacked me behind my legs, eventually bowling me. In the next match, at Trent Bridge, I took a leg-stump guard to protect against that line of attack, and Warne quickly switched to bowling outside off stump, making me reach for the ball. He soon spun one past my outside edge and I was adjudged caught behind.

He knew instinctively which batsmen to goad. I never saw him say much to Sachin Tendulkar, the only batsman who made him look ordinary, but he was always ready with some choice words to batsmen whom he suspected he could rattle. In the second innings at Trent Bridge in 2001, Warne constantly baited Mark Ramprakash who looked eager to attack him. 'Come on Ramps, you know you want to.' 'That's the way Ramps, keep coming down the wicket!' Ramprakash fretted, caught between the desire to attack and waiting to see out the day. Eventually, just before the close, he ran down the wicket, had a mighty heave and Warne had his man.

Warne's variations were easier to pick than, say, Mushtaq's, but he was more difficult to play. I liked to use my feet against the spinners, but I found Warne the hardest to come down the wicket to because of the amount of drift he used to get in the air. As a result, when I came down the wicket to him, I felt unbalanced, as though my head was too far to the off side of the ball. Of course, being marooned in your crease was a short cut to disaster as well. Leg-spinners had occasionally attacked around the wicket (Richie Benaud memorably against England in 1957) but nobody had bowled a leg-stump line so often before, or used the rough outside the right-hander's leg stump as successfully as Warne did.

It was hard enough for good players, so imagine the tangle tailenders got into. Phil Tufnell was constantly in a flap. For a start, Warne spun the ball twice as far as Tufnell, who often looked innocuous in comparison. 'That bloke's making me look crap! He's ruining my career!' Tufnell constantly complained. To add insult to injury, Warne would have some fun when Tufnell came in to bat. At Melbourne in 1995, Warne continually bowled around the wicket at him, creating such confusion that Tufnell decided the only answer was to sit on the ball as it pitched, which he did, and then he lost his balance and crumpled backwards in a heap. Even the inscrutable Boon at short-leg cracked a smile.

Having witnessed Warne's control, craftiness and competitiveness over a decade or more, having seen him embarrass us on numerous occasions, and having watched him raise his game when the stakes were highest, there is no doubt in my mind that he must be one of the greatest bowlers to have played the game. His golden period was 1993–97, before his shoulder gave way. Like Tufnell, I bemoaned the fact that it coincided exactly with the period of my captaincy.

I suppose if I had been able to walk through those revolving doors at Old Trafford to have another crack at that vital match, the result might still have been the same. For, in truth, Australia were a better side than we were throughout the decade that I played. Each Ashes series seemed to follow a particular pattern – we would lose the first three Tests, regain some confidence in the middle and win a Test match at the end when the series was done. In 1997, there was a slight change. We won the first, folded in the middle, and won the last Test when, again, the Ashes were gone and the series was done.

Although Australia's victory at Old Trafford meant that the series was tied at 1–1, secretly I knew that the fortunes of the respective sides were going in opposite directions, and after that we would have our work cut out. Thereafter the selectors huffed and puffed and altered our side a little. The Hollioakes were brought in for Trent Bridge in the hope they could rekindle some of the spark we had at the beginning of the summer. It made little difference. Ben Hollioake found that Test cricket was a tough game and when he edged the ball early in his first Test innings, Mark Waugh jubilantly caught the ball and Ian Healy sent him on his way. 'Back to the nets, idiot!' he crowed. Australia retained the Ashes at Trent Bridge and we were left to dream again.

I suppose I was unfortunate to have played in a decade that will be remembered as one of Australia's best. They had some wonderful players. Apart from Healy, Warne and Steve Waugh who would be considered great in any era, Mark Waugh was close to that category and Glenn McGrath would be in it next time we met, eighteen months later. In the likes of Alec Stewart, Graham Thorpe and me, England had some good, solid Test cricketers but none of us would be considered great.

The reasons for Australia's hegemony went deeper than that. Their grade and state cricket produced tougher, hungrier cricketers than our system. You only had to see the difference in a young English professional after a winter down under. They might return with an irritating Australian twang, saying 'you beauty' every other phrase, but they were more confident, aggressive and ready to take on the world.

Consider a promising eighteen-year-old English cricketer. After looking good in schoolboy representative games, he is offered a contract by a county club. That means a full-time job, decent salary, sponsored car, name on his locker, sponsored kit, sunglasses, mobile phone and all the lingo – all the trappings, in fact, of the professional game. Of course, at the moment he isn't very good, but he's happy and contented, of limited ambition, and he kicks around the second-eleven circuit for a few years until he realises that his chance has passed him by and the grim reality of life and a proper job await him.

His Australian counterpart has been brought up playing against men in grade cricket. Good grade cricket in Sydney and Perth is of a better standard than county second-eleven cricket in England, but not as good as first-class cricket. He practises with his club side on three nights a week – hard practice on good-quality net wickets (grass in the cities, concrete in the suburbs). Club games are spread over two weekends and in some months he may bat once or twice only, and so when the opportunity arises he is hungry to take it. He also has a job and knows at first-hand about life beyond cricket. When the chance comes to play state cricket, he knows it is the opportunity of a lifetime and that he is but a good innings or two away from representing his country.

The Australian doesn't really respect his English counterpart. During the last Ashes series that I played, I arrived at Edgbaston at the same time as one of our debutants and the Australian team bus. The rookie arrived in his convertible Saab, with his sunglasses perched on his head, and as he swaggered into the dressing room I saw one or two of the older Australian players nod at each other with the kind of meaningful look that said they were looking forward to exposing another impostor, as they termed them. And, of course, they did.

So Australia have good players and a good system. But more than that, sport, and cricket in particular, seems to occupy a far more central and important place in Australian society. Rod Kafer, the Wallabies' reserve stand-off, made this telling remark before the World Cup final, which Australia went on to win: 'Sport is in the Australian character. We're an outdoor race and we pride ourselves on being physically robust.' Australia uses sporting success as a way of getting the rest of the world to sit up and take notice. Between 1998 and 2001, Australia were world champions in at least half a dozen disciplines, and that from a population a third of the size of Great Britain's. As the author Thomas Keneally famously said, 'It was our way out of cultural ignominy. No Australian ever wrote "Paradise Lost" but Don Bradman did make a hundred before lunch at Lord's.'

In the same way as New Zealand always raise their game against Australia, so Australia, in turn, are most motivated against the Poms. Psychologically I suppose, the Australians are always keen to put one over the 'mother country' to show just how far they have travelled. When Allan Border asked Ian Chappell for some advice on taking the Australian captaincy, Chappell growled, 'You can do anything but don't lose to the Poms.' In the decade that I played against them, they rarely looked like doing so.

15

THE END OF THE AFFAIR

I made some bad decisions as England captain – when you make several hundred decisions a day, it's hard not to – but not resigning immediately after the last Test of the 1997 Ashes series was by far the worst. 'Take your time. Don't rush things. Don't be rash,' was the general advice I received, and like a fool I listened. My reputation as a stubborn man is fair enough but I have always listened to advice, sometimes too readily. In this instance, I should have followed my instincts and jacked it in the moment we ran off The Oval in triumph.

I had already tried to resign after the Trent Bridge Test when the Ashes had been lost. I felt the time was right. I had done the four-year cycle that took in every Test playing nation, and The Oval Test would have been a good opportunity for the next captain to dip his toe in the water before the West Indies tour. I told David Lloyd and he reluctantly agreed. Ian MacLaurin was less easy to persuade. 'I don't want you to resign. In fact, I won't let you resign,' he said. 'At the start of the summer you agreed to see the series through. I expect you to do that, and if you still feel the same way after the end of The Oval Test, then fair enough.' He made me feel as though I would be letting people down and running away, which clearly I didn't want to do. Reluctantly, I agreed to stay until after The Oval.

The truth was that I had had enough and that the criticism was getting to me. Previously I have said how the media were totally unimportant to me as a player. That was true, and, in part, it was my defence mechanism, my way of coping with the criticism. But by the middle of the summer, the vilification was almost universal and hard to ignore.

'Captain Grumpy' was a tag that had been given to me by the South African team and media on the South African tour of 1995–96. I played up to the reputation as much as I could because, in a perverse kind of way, it gave me some pleasure. The result was that in public I was perceived as, not to put too fine a point on it, a miserable sod; someone who smiled at himself in the mirror first thing in the morning in order to get it over and done with for the day. I have quite lugubrious features anyway; I am the person on the tube that old ladies come up to and say, 'Don't worry, it might never happen!' But I certainly didn't try very hard to disabuse people of the notion.

Privately, among my close-knit circle of friends, it was never a problem. I was never Jimmy Tarbuck but I was always quick to smile and ready to laugh. I never took myself, or the game, too seriously and never for one moment worried about my reputation or my place in the history of the game. The ability to switch off and relax is critical to success in the pressurised atmosphere of international sport, and for most of the time I could switch on and off easily.

By the end of the summer of 1997, however, I was becoming Captain Grumpy in private; I couldn't switch off and the people closest to me started to worry. One evening during The Oval Test I went to 192, a restaurant in West London, with Isabelle and Nick Broughton, a close friend from university. Later Nick told me that I just sat through the meal glumly and didn't utter a word. I didn't realise that at the time because my mind was obsessed with cricket and the captaincy. I was becoming completely self-absorbed, to the detriment of those around me. The same thing happened the next evening as I sat staring out on to Chelsea Harbour for hours on end. I needed sleeping tablets at night; it was time to get my life back.

I don't think that I was in any fit mental state to be captaining England at that point. Yet, remarkably, when Australia chased 124 for victory in the last Test at The Oval, I gave a flawless performance in the field. Tactically, it was near perfect. I found exactly the right blend of attack and defence and made all the right moves.

Good cricket captains have retentive memories for the obvious things – that Mark Waugh is a good player off his legs, or that Carl Hooper plays spin (especially left-arm spin) better than he plays pace – and for the more specific things – that Jimmy Adams drives through the off side with a stiff front leg and as a result hits the ball in the air, to short extra-cover's right hand, for about ten yards; or that the man at point for me should always be five yards behind square. After 1990, the Australians always had him there but it amazed me that I could play on the county circuit for fifteen years and not one county captain would have a man in the right position. I reckoned I had a good retentive memory and it was crucial in the second innings at The Oval because, defending 124, every run would be vital.

As we waited for the umpires to make their way on to the field, I reminded the team of the obvious – that Australia were vulnerable chasing small fourth-innings totals. It was their well-known Achilles heel and one they had demonstrated often down the years, most memorably at Headingley in 1981, and more recently against South Africa in Sydney in 1993–94, when they fell short chasing 117. Having been bowled out ourselves for 163, this knowledge, and the fact that we knew that they knew, gave us an important psychological boost. It gave us hope.

The pitch was typical of The Oval in the second half of the 1990s – the soil was dark brown rather than white as it had been in the first half of the decade, and it was excessively dry and crumbly, a spinner's paradise. Phil Tufnell had taken seven wickets in Australia's first innings and I knew he would be my match-winner in the second. He was tetchy and nervous before we went out. He knew the pressure was on him to perform, so I said nothing to him and quietly encouraged the others to leave him alone and let him get on with it.

I was concerned about Caddick and Malcolm opening the bowling together. At times they could both be profligate with the new ball, and above all we needed a disciplined start so that we could stay in the game as long as possible and give Tufnell maximum time to work his magic. I decided to let Peter Martin share the new ball with Devon Malcolm, hoping his accuracy would counter-balance Malcolm's occasional waywardness.

When defending a small total, an early psychological lift is crucial, and Malcolm trapped Matthew Elliott early on to give us just that. It also got rid of one of the left-handers, which was important because they would have a better chance than the right-handers of counter-attacking Tufnell, by hitting with the spin.

After an otherwise uneventful seven overs, I brought on both Caddick and Tufnell. Mark Taylor and Greg Blewett had put on 31 for the second wicket – hardly a huge partnership, but in the context of the game it was a worrying one and we needed a breakthrough. Caddick dismissed Taylor immediately. Good bowling changes are never random, and often produce the required result. A captain has to know instinctively when a batsman has entered the comfort zone and should be asked a different question, hence the advantage of a varied attack. He also needs to know if a certain batsman is less comfortable against a particular bowler. In 2001 at Trent Bridge, it was my job to know that Darren Gough had dismissed Ricky Ponting in his previous five Test innings against England. As soon as Ponting came in, Gough came on.

Now that both the openers had gone we were into the meat of the Australian batting line-up, the middle order of Blewett, Mark Waugh, Steve Waugh and Ricky Ponting.

Blewett was a better player of pace than spin. He loved to drive through extra-cover, and anything short he liked to pull, just in front of square. For Caddick, then, the key was length – not too

Above: Checking out the form at Aintree.

Right: Playing golf in Australia 1995.

Below: When in Rome – trying my hand at Aussie Rules on the beach in Newcastle, New South Wales 1995.

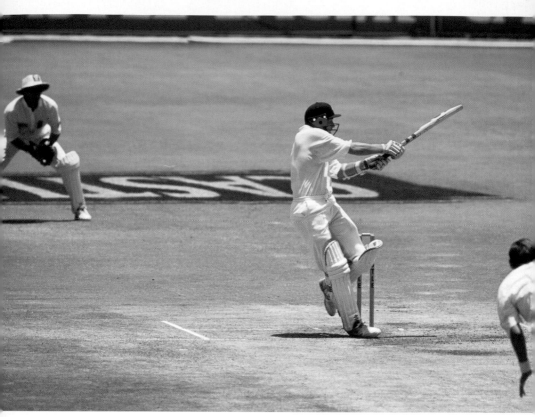

Bringing up my hundred at Johannesburg, off Allan Donald.

'We're not there yet!' Jack Russell keeps me going during our long partnership.

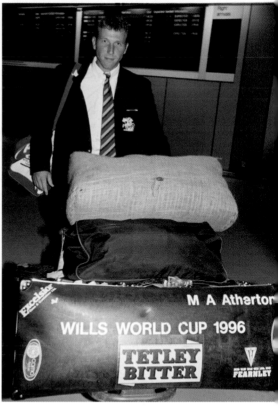

ready for the celebrations in Johannesburg.

Returning from the World Cup to face the flak. At least I had a few carpets (in the hessian sack) for my troubles.

Meeting Nelson Mandela in South Africa. He was eager to talk to the 'destroyer', Devon Malcolm.

'What's gone wrong?' Attempting to put things right with coach David Lloyd and vice-captain Nasser Hussain, Zimbabwe 1996.

Trying to get through a press conference with a hangover, and placate Michael Nicholson, ITN, hours after our arrival in New Zealand, 1997.

Celebrating our series victory over New Zealand with a united and happy team.

Fishing the Hope River the day after our series win.

Darren Gough reflects the mood of the team at Edgbaston in 1997, after dismissing Greg Blewett.

Sharing a joke with a fine Australian captain, Mark Taylor.

Handing first Test caps to Adam (*left*) and Ben Hollioake at Trent Bridge in 1997. Ben will be sadly missed.

Andrew Caddick (*right*) and Phil Tufnell, architects of our victory over Australia at The Oval 1997. Both bowled beautifully.

Above: Quick hands and an unflinching attitude –
Australia's Steve Waugh.

Left: My nemesis Glenn McGrath tastes more success
against me.

Below: The great Shane Warne bowls to Graham
Thorpe. Ian Healy waits expectantly.

full or too short, and I needed my two most agile outfielders at extra-cover and square-leg. For Tufnell, Blewett's get-out-of-jail shots would be the sweep and the drive over mid-off (he rarely went over mid-on). So I gave Tufnell two sweepers to cut off those big shots, two catchers (slip, silly point), and the rest saving one, hoping we could frustrate him. We did and eventually he tried to pull a ball off Caddick that was not short enough and gloved a catch down the leg side to Alec Stewart.

Mark Waugh was a danger because he was a good player of spin, and his natural instinct was to attack. Tufnell bowled less well to attacking players, and could be intimidated by someone who came down the wicket aggressively waving a big stick at him. Caddick needed to bowl a good line, six inches outside off stump, and keep away from leg stump. Even so, Waugh often fetched deliveries from outside off stump through midwicket and I sometimes liked to put two catchers at short midwicket to try to encourage him to play through his less favoured off side. Fortunately, Tufnell produced a beauty to Waugh early on, as he had done in the first innings. In both innings, Waugh played with low hands at Tufnell early on, giving a catch to silly point in the first, and to slip in the second. I quietly fancied us now.

But it was obviously going to be a tight game and, as the team that holds its nerve invariably wins, Steve Waugh's was a big wicket. He wasn't as aggressive as Mark, and therefore not as dangerous, but he was Australia's mentally toughest player. Caddick knew to bowl full and straight early on, and the fielders knew not to engage him in any chitchat. As we gathered around at the fall of the previous wicket, I reminded the fielders to be sharp – Waugh had played tip and run with us early in his innings for most of the summer. I felt that Waugh would not take any risks against Tufnell, and would aim to grind the situation out. Apart from the catchers around the bat, therefore, I had everybody in on the single, even the sweeper at deep backward square. The invitation was there for Waugh to play a big shot early. He declined and could not break the shackles imposed by Tufnell, Caddick and the field setting. Frustrated, he slashed at a good length ball from Caddick, and Thorpe, at first slip, accepted the offering.

At 54–5 we were now the favourites, and this in turn brought specific problems. At the start of the innings we were not expected to win and could play with the freedom that underdogs often have. Now I could sense a growing expectation within the team, and with it, nervousness. I wasn't sure what to say, or whether to say anything at all, but at the fall of Waugh's wicket I reminded everybody to stay in the present, to concentrate on each delivery and not the scoreboard or the end result. That would take care of itself.

Ponting, like Blewett, was a better player of pace than spin. He was a typical Australian batsman. He played early with hard hands and loved to cut, pull and hook the quicker bowlers. I was sure that the unpredictable nature of The Oval pitch would not suit his style of play, and equally sure that Tufnell would cause him problems. Against a good spinner, and with men around the bat, Ponting was tortured. He looked anxious and fidgety rather than composed. He played big shots in order to rid himself of the close fielders, like a man swatting at troublesome flies in his native outback. I was sure Tufnell would get him, which he did, eventually, for 20.

Healy and Warne were both dangerous. Healy could bat, and neither were the type to go quietly or die wondering. Against Caddick, Healy would look for the cut, and try to swing anything straight over wide fine-leg. He had fewer shots against Tufnell. Warne was the opposite. Often he didn't like facing the quicker bowlers and stepped away to carve them over point or third man. But he played spin quite well and loved to slog-sweep against the turn to deep midwicket. Healy and Warne decided to risk some quick singles to upset our rhythm and break the stranglehold. Adam Hollioake shied at the stumps and missed, and the resultant overthrows were costly. Despite that, I needed to applaud and encourage Hollioake's attitude without worrying about the overthrows, hoping his aggression would continue to rub off on the team.

Caddick needed to concentrate against Healy, sticking to the basics of line and length, which he did. Healy attempted to drive at Caddick who juggled the return catch three times before throwing it up in triumph.

The field for Tufnell to Warne was important. We needed good, agile fielders with safe hands at deep square-leg and deep midwicket. We decided to drop mid-off out as well – not because Warne would hit there, but because we wanted to make it obvious that mid-on was up, and hitting with a straight bat against the spin was a tough and risky option. Warne took it on and hit the ball up in the air. Peter Martin caught it well, running backwards from mid-on towards the pavilion – 95–8.

Up until that point we had danced between attack and defence and had never committed to either. Tufnell never liked to over-attack at the start of his spell. 'Let me settle, let me settle,' was his constant refrain. But now with Australia's tailenders to come, we had to move in for the kill. We needed 'in-out' fields – that is plenty of close catchers and the odd sweeper with not much in between. Tailenders were usually all or nothing, block or slog, and rarely had the ability to work singles into the gaps. An 'in-out' field then.

I had never see Shaun Young play, nor had anybody else in the team, and so I had to set the field 'blind'. Nasser Hussain had played with Michael Kasprowicz at Essex and was a useful source of information. At first we had a leg-gully for him, but I quickly realised that there was not enough pace in the pitch to warrant such a position. I moved Adam Hollioake to short extra-cover, and Kasprowicz obliged the very next ball. When that type of thing happens, you just know it is your day – it made up for all the times I had removed third slip, only for the next ball to fly through there at catchable height – 99–9.

The sight of Glenn McGrath striding to the crease with Australia still 25 short of their target is a thing England captains can only dream of, and it was time to get the champagne on ice. He tried to work Tufnell through the leg side, against the spin. At that moment, at the completion of his shot, he froze, realising his error. Everyone else froze too, a frame of a moment in time, as the ball ballooned up off a leading edge towards Thorpe at mid-off. I can see it now in slow motion, gently arcing as eleven sets of eyes followed its path. There was a long silence as Thorpe moved in to take the catch, and when he did, pandemonium ensued. I raised both arms, fists clenched, issued a guttural cry and set off in pursuit, as did everyone else. We caught Thorpe halfway to the pavilion, the adrenalin surge giving speed to our limbs. Alec Stewart caught up with me and screamed in my ear, 'You've got to stay on now, Ath!'

In the dressing room afterwards, I enjoyed the moment like everyone else. Well, almost everyone – Phil Tufnell had a towel over his head and was shaking. The pressure on him had been immense, almost too much. Both he and Caddick had bowled beautifully, and had made my captaincy look impressive, as good bowlers always do. It was the perfect time to walk away – a victory and a memory to remind me, if no one else, that the captaincy hadn't been all warm beer, but some champagne as well. I was still determined to resign.

Quite how I came to be leading England in the Caribbean the following January is a mystery to me, even now. I left The Oval promising not to rush my decision, but knowing that resigning was the right thing to do. I met David Graveney a week later in the Regent's Park Hilton, and agreed to carry on. Why?

It is something I cannot explain. David Graveney was not that persuasive. He told me he would like me to carry on, but then watched me squirm and wriggle with indecision. It was entirely my fault. I prevaricated when I ought to have been strong. Money was not a factor. Unlike those who succeeded me, I naively never asked the board to raise the captain's fee. I didn't need the kudos; the status and added attention the England captain receives was one of the less welcome aspects of the job. Perhaps my week's fishing at the end of the season had restored me and renewed my hope. Maybe the challenge still excited me and energised me. Possibly I felt we had a great chance of success. Whatever the reason, it was a bad decision and one I knew I was going to regret.

Any notion that the 1997–98 West Indies tour would be uneventful was quashed in Jamaica – the First Test became the only Test match ever to be abandoned because of dangerous conditions. Nasser Hussain and I had gone to look at the pitch three days before the match. It was a strange sight – dark red in colour with cracks and fissures the length of it, and more undulations than Epsom Downs on Derby day. We looked at each other wide-eyed, and left saying nothing although I knew we were both thinking the same thing.

Cosmetics had improved its appearance on the morning of the match although the unevenness remained. Earlier I witnessed the groundsman laying a piece of string along the strip; the string touched the ground in parts but there was a three-inch gap elsewhere. It merely confirmed the undulations, which were obvious to the naked eye.

I won the toss and decided to bat on the basis that things could only get worse. I turned the first ball of the match off my toes for one and there normality ended. In the same over I got two deliveries from Courtney Walsh that pitched six inches apart – one flew past my shoulder and one passed my ankle. Hussain, Butcher and I were dismissed quickly and we sat down to watch the carnage with interest. Wayne Morton, the physiotherapist, completed his day's training within the half hour, and was called on to the ground six times in all. John Crawley was next in and looked agitated. He had already got through a packet of Benson & Hedges and could contain himself no longer. 'Jesus, someone's going to get killed out there.' No doubt he was concerned that that someone was going to be him.

Barry Jarman, the match referee, was equally concerned and was in constant touch with the umpires. Alec Stewart was hit again and he motioned me on to the pitch. I was in uncharted territory here, but I had little hesitation in answering Stewart's call. I walked over to Brian Lara, the West Indies captain.

'What do you think, Brian?'

'It's not fit.'

'I know. Shall we talk to the umpires?'

'Shit. You'll have to do it. It's my first game as captain, and they already hate me here.' Lara had just replaced the Jamaican favourite, Courtney Walsh.

'Okay. Come with me though.'

We went over to the umpires. Venkat looked worried and hopped from one foot to the other, like a nervous sparrow. Steve Bucknor took control. He looked up, sniffed the air and announced, in his sonorous way, that we would leave the field.

Within an hour the match had been abandoned and an extra Test had been scheduled for Trinidad. Bob Bennett, the tour manager, was flapping. He had been in contact with the ECB and they were concerned to present the abandonment in the best possible light. It was the only spin the spectators would see that day. He told the players to be careful about their public pronouncements and to avoid criticising the pitch. Adam Hollioake grunted his disapproval.

'The Test has just been abandoned because of a dangerous pitch. What do you want us to do, sing its praises?' He had a point.

It was a disaster, both for West Indies cricket and the Jamaican tourist industry. Prime Minister P.J. Patterson hastily arranged a cocktail party at Government House for disgruntled spectators, which the players also attended. As we were leaving, an elderly, courteous English gentleman came up to me and told me that he had been saving up for twenty years to watch England play abroad, and this was the game he had chosen. I felt terrible, but I knew the right decision had been made. The next day I went to Sabina Park on my own to look at the pitch again. It had dried a little and now the fissures had risen and opened and, like burnt paper, they had folded at the ends. I touched them and they crumbled to nothing. It was definitely the right decision.

Before the tour, I felt the West Indies were definitely there for the taking. They had just been beaten 3–0 in Pakistan, and there was clearly some disquiet within their camp. It was rumoured that Brian Lara was after the captaincy. Courtney Walsh had had a tough time as West Indies captain, leading a team that was clearly in decline. Nevertheless, I felt he lost nothing in comparison with one of his illustrious predecessors, Clive Lloyd, who recognised that unity was the key to West Indian success. Lancashire's players were always adamant that Lloyd was a relatively poor tactician. Yet he was a great West Indies captain, forging unity and a sense of purpose where none had existed before.

Like Lloyd, Walsh was a big man in stature and character. Before the First Test Lara did indeed replace the Jamaican, much to the disgruntlement of the Sabina Park crowd, and out of solidarity with their hero, they threatened to boycott the match. On the first morning Walsh walked out arm in arm with Lara to give the new captain his support and to show that you don't have to be captain to be a leader of men.

A new England captain may well have achieved a different result from the 3–1 defeat that we ultimately suffered. A different captain may well have had a fresh outlook, and have been able to drag a little extra out of the players, as that was all that was needed. He may have had that vital spark, or energy, that I felt on my fifth tour as captain was lacking. Nasser Hussain commented on it at the end of the tour when he said to me, 'You've got to get that fire back in your belly, Ath.'

I had a poor tactical match in the first of the Trinidad encounters. We had set the West Indies 282 to win on a capricious pitch on which balls alternatively shot along the floor or reared past your chin. Like everyone else in the team, I assumed that we would win, but assumptions are always dangerous for captains. In a way, the fact that it was such a poor pitch was a disadvantage. Instead of being proactive, and setting batsmen different challenges, I waited for wickets to happen. And of course when you wait passively for things to happen, they rarely do.

The back-to-back Test matches in Trinidad, in searing temperatures, were the most energy-sapping and nerve-racking that I played in. Each evening the players would drag their weary bodies through the foyer of the Trinidad Hilton, past the bar and groups of journalists and spectators blithely discussing the day's see-sawing events. Most evenings I stopped off for a drink before retiring to my room for a usually sleepless and anxious night.

We won a thrilling encounter in the second Trinidad match, and the series was finely poised at 1–1. Thereafter, three hammer-blows of misfortune ensured that, after the last match in Antigua, my resignation was a formality. The Test matches in Guyana and Antigua were the most crucial tosses in my time as an England player – and of course I lost them both. Guyana had not seen rain for months due to the El Niño phenomenon, and the acute water shortage meant the pitch was unusually dry. After the second day it crumbled to dust, with the West Indies already in a strong first-innings position. In Antigua, by contrast, the groundsman miscalculated his watering and on the first day, when we batted, you could stick half a thumb in the surface. No team would have coped with such misfortune.

In between, in even conditions in Barbados we played good cricket and had the better of the game. Mark Ramprakash finally scored his first Test 100 after six years of trying, and on the fourth evening I was able to declare, setting the West Indies 375 to win in ninety minutes and a day. With the pitch turning I was confident of victory, but unseasonal rains arrived to ruin the final day, and our chances of squaring the series.

These three hammer-blows, and the absence of Darren Gough through injury, meant that we were staring defeat in the face on the final morning in Antigua. I was staring squarely at resignation and on the fifth morning I sat on the lush outfield and rang David Graveney in Barbados, where he was supervising the one-day squad. I had already indicated to Graveney that defeat was unpalatable and this time he didn't try to dissuade me.

Once the post-match ceremonies were complete, I motioned the players into the dressing room and gave the shortest but most difficult speech in five years as captain. My voice cracking with emotion, I announced my resignation and thanked all the players for their support and efforts over the years. Some – Fraser, Stewart, Thorpe and Hussain – had endured much on the long journey with me and because of that the bonds forged are strong and long-lasting. For a while, some tears flowed – not just because of my situation but because the series result barely reflected the cricket we had played. Then I composed myself and faced the press, emotionless and inscrutable. I was damned if I was going to let them take a peek at my soul.

I stayed on to fight for my place in the one-day team. My changed circumstances were quickly brought home to me, and despite England's poor run of form in the one-day internationals, I could not get a game. Most of the time I carried drinks as twelfth man. In Barbados, the captain was always provided with the use of a car. As I waited in vain for a taxi at the Rockley Resort, I saw Adam Hollioake drive by in a flashy green Ford. The King is dead. Long live the King!

My reign as England's captain lasted a record fifty-two games and almost five years and rarely suffered from a neutral reaction. This, for example, was the team manager's report after the 1996–97 winter tour:

> His was a performance of genuine depth and character. Poor personal form, poor team performances and poor press initially combined to test even the most durable of characters.

217

That he did ultimately withstand and see off the storm was as tough a task as he will ever have to face. He is a good listener, absorbs information well and reaches a decision. He cares for his players and never shirks the issue.

On the other side was criticism from a variety of characters, the most damning of which was probably from Fred Titmus who, on the day I passed Peter May's record for captaining England the most times, said I was a nonentity as a captain. What to make of it?

Before my first tour abroad I expressed a desire that I might develop a team – a group of young, talented and athletic players who would stick together through the inevitable tough times and come through the other side. In that England were never consistently successful under my captaincy, I obviously failed to achieve that vision. Given that Illingworth, Bolus and Titmus were responsible for selection within six months and none of them shared my vision, I am not sure that it was attainable. It was certainly never given a proper chance. In the absence of central contracts, I don't know whether it was ever a realistic vision.

In statistical terms, my win ratio of 25 per cent fits neatly into the period. It was neither much better nor much worse than my immediate predecessors, or those who followed. Gower's win ratio was 15 per cent, Gatting's 8 per cent, Gooch's 29 per cent and Stewart's 30 per cent. Botham never won a match as England captain and Brearley has by far the best, winning 58 per cent of matches he captained. Of the twenty-one series (both Test and one-day) that I captained, we won nine, lost eight and four were drawn.

Statistics, in any case, tell you only so much. So, as objectively as I can, here is my own verdict. I had some obvious strengths. My fitness record was good (I was ever present in Tests) and, by and large, my form held up and my place in the team was not in question. Tactically, I felt I was good – at least as good as anybody I played under, before or since. Of course I had a couple of poor matches (Melbourne '95 and Trinidad '98 stand out) but generally I was happy with my efforts. I had a good retentive memory and was able to assess the opposition and conditions quickly and easily.

I would like to think that I had the respect of the dressing room, as a player, leader and human being. I was honest and fair, loyal and supportive. I was always aware of other members of the team when they were going through difficult times. Hours after probably my finest moment in Johannesburg, I was in Mark Ramprakash's room trying to lift him in the knowledge that he would be feeling low after his performance that day. In so much as I captained over a lengthy period, unless I am very much mistaken, the players played for me.

The most damning thing, looking back, was the failure to win games we ought to have won. I remember Richie Benaud once saying that England had yet again found a way not to win a match we ought to have won. In Trinidad in 1994–95 and 1997–98, Auckland in 1996–97 and at Headingley in 1994 against South Africa, we should have turned two defeats and two draws into four victories. Why this was so, I don't know – maybe we were just not used to victory, and we shied away from crossing the finishing line first. As captain, I have to take my share of the blame for that.

I think one or two players felt that I never rated them and that, of course, is a black mark for any captain. After Andrew Caddick had destroyed the West Indies at Lord's in 2000, I overheard him say, 'I think that Athers finally rates me now.' The irony is that I always rated Caddick, and when he was fit he was a near automatic selection. Nevertheless, it is the *impression* that is crucial, and if he felt I didn't rate him, it would hardly have helped his confidence.

In that regard, it took me a long time to learn that the face we see every morning in the mirror and think we show to the world is not necessarily the face that the rest of the world sees. The difference between perception and reality can be cavernous. Caddick for that reason misread me. More recently, Angus Fraser wrote that I was 'cold and distant' and he is a good friend of mine! I never thought of myself like that but clearly some people did. If that was so, they probably felt I was unapproachable, which again is never a good thing for a captain.

Obviously I went on too long, and people tend to remember the failure and criticism at the end rather than the hope and praise at the beginning. Most of our heroes who don't die young or don't fade away at the peak of their powers are afflicted by this, and if I had ducked out a year earlier, when I ought to have done, maybe I would have a slightly better reputation than I suspect I have. And, of course, through a complete lack of effort or desire, I was useless with the media.

Overall it was a mixed bag – good and bad, success and failure, celebration and heartbreak in near equal measure. But I think that in time 1993–98 will go down as a peculiarly difficult period, one before England's administrators realised that fundamental reform was necessary for both survival and sustained success. Four years later, I look upon my contemporary Nasser Hussain with some envy. He has good people around him, in a structure solely designed for the success of the England team, and all his best players are centrally contracted to the board. He and Duncan Fletcher are able to develop players, and teams, quicker. I had to rely on natural evolution.

My workload at times was enormous. Occasionally there was no coach, until 1997 there was no press-liaison officer, and when I did sit on the selection committee, it was left to me to tell those who had been dropped. All these responsibilities are now taken care of by others. In the circumstances of the time I think I did a pretty good job. Whether anybody else would have done better I don't know. The captaincy, possibly, came too soon, but none of us is master of our own destiny or the timing of such things. Speculation is a wonderful thing, but I shall stick to the only truth I know: I was appointed at twenty-five with little or no team in place, in a system not conducive to success. I gave it my all for nearly five years and there I will leave it.

16
WINNING THE MIND GAMES

Opening the batting in Test cricket is a tough and lonely business. As a result, there exists a kind of unofficial special relationship between openers. It cuts across national enmities and is reserved for those who know about the hardships of facing the new ball – not for us the chance to stroll to the crease at 200–2, a couple of ineffective spinners lobbing the ball high and the fielders looking at their watches, ready for tea; not for us the chance to get to 20 before a serious question is asked. For the opener, it's always a new ball, fresh limbs, fast bowlers and a pitch of unknown quantity. Are you feeling sorry for us yet?

It is also, as Graham Gooch never tired of telling me, the best place to bat, giving you a chance to set the tone for your team and get a really big score. You need a semblance of technique and a little courage for sure, but you also need, above all else, a strong mind.

An opener has to be able to shrug off the occasional but inevitable unplayable delivery– the dreaded 'jaffa'. In South Africa in 1999, I played beautifully in the matches prior to the First Test and I felt in prime touch. The First Test was at Johannesburg, the scene of a former triumph, and so all my vibes were good. The pitch, however, was poor and the light was worse, and Allan Donald bowled me a vicious inswinger second ball that knocked my off stump flat. I was on the dreaded pair, and I had two days in the field to think about it. In the second innings, Shaun

Pollock bowled me a brutish, lifting leg-cutter first ball, which brushed my glove on the way to the wicket-keeper. I was in the form of my life and, through little fault of my own, I had got a pair, and now I had a fortnight to think about things before the next Test.

It is then that your mind begins to play its tricks – the little voice in your head is constantly nattering away and you try not to listen to it: *'I've lost it; my eyes have gone; how am I ever going to get another run; I'll do anything to get off the mark.'* Somehow you need to put that voice to the furthest reaches of your mind and bombard it into submission with positive thoughts and good visualisations. Thirteen days later I walked out to bat at Port Elizabeth, to face Donald and Pollock again, aware that 10,000 people wanted to see another duck, aware of their sarcastic applause when I finally got off the mark for the series, and then aware that I had subdued them as I turned the ball to fine-leg to bring up my thirteenth Test century.

It is why opening batsmen as a rule make good slip fielders. We are prepared to concentrate all day for the one chance, and should we muff it, we'll still want the batsman to edge the next ball to us. I knew I was mentally tough; it was one of my biggest strengths. I would not have survived twelve years as an opener in Test cricket without it.

It was clear to other people that my temperament was one of my strengths. Two months after retirement I met Dr Steve Bull at Lord's. Bull is the sports psychologist responsible for the development of mental skills for all the England teams, juniors upwards. Under my captaincy, we had often asked him to talk to the squad about temperament and toughness in international sport. Now he was doing a study, for the new Academy, of the mental attributes of a number of England cricketers whom regional and national coaches had commended for their 'mental toughness'. I had been chosen by every coach, and was therefore top of his list to interview.

Afterwards I got to wondering why this was so. Perhaps it was because I had often played with injury; perhaps it was because I was so obviously less talented than, say, a Gower or a Gooch and therefore there must be some other explanation for how I became eleventh (at the time of writing) on the list of all-time run scorers in Test cricket. I thought that, most probably, the majority of those asked had in mind my famous duel with Allan Donald at Trent Bridge, during the 1998 South African series.

That duel was what sports psychologists would call a 'clutch' situation. Donald and I instinctively realised that it was the crucial phase of the day, the match and therefore possibly the series. We both stepped up a gear to give a performance at the peak of our respective abilities; something that was immediately obvious to those who were watching. The result was a passage of play, just forty minutes in length, which was so absorbing that when people talk to me about my career, it is that confrontation they remember the most.

But before all that I had to retain, or regain, my place in the England team. A month after my resignation, the white smoke had gone up over Lord's and Alec Stewart had been appointed England's new Test match captain. I was sure that Stewart would be well disposed to my presence at the top of the order for the forthcoming series against South Africa, but in the early part of the season I didn't make things easy for him, the coach or the selectors. The round-robin stage of the Benson & Hedges Cup was a nightmare for me. It culminated at Old Trafford against Northants when I succumbed to the second ball of the day and walked off to an eerie silence, apart from the odd boo, from the members. David Lloyd had arrived at 11.05, ostensibly to watch me play, but when he walked into the changing room I was already in my corner, unfurling the pages of the *Racing Post*. There was a pained look on his face. 'Shit, Ath, you've got to get through the turnstiles early to see you play these days,' were his none-too-comforting words.

Thankfully, I was able to give Stewart, Lloyd and the selectors (Graveney, Gooch and Gatting) something to cheer at Canterbury in the championship and in the quarter-final of the Benson & Hedges at The Oval, with 152 and 93 respectively. My place at the head of affairs for the First Test at Edgbaston seemed assured.

David Lloyd had asked Alec Stewart whether he wanted to change dramatically the way things were run within the England set-up. Stewart indicated not, which meant I had, at least in his eyes, not been doing everything wrong. He approached the task in a different manner from me; he was more calculating in his public pronouncements and keener to give team-talks although at times he spoke in clichéd tones, like a form master addressing a class of attentive schoolchildren. He was, however, experienced, aggressive and determined to win, and the players played for him.

Halfway through the series, the change of captaincy had apparently failed to lift the team and an air of gloom pervaded the whole country. My form was good. I had completed my rehabilitation with my twelfth Test century at Edgbaston. At Lord's, however, I failed as usual and we went 1–0 down in the series. England's record at the home of cricket for much of the decade was a poor one, much like my own. There were the usual theories about Lord's inspiring the opposition more than us because we played there more often and were, as a result, blasé about the place. Possibly this is true. It is a wonderful ground, and the recent architectural additions a credit to those in charge, but it does have a touch of self-importance and pomposity that irritated me whenever I played there.

In the next match, at Old Trafford, we faced defeat again. At the end of the first day, South Africa had scored 237–1 and were in complete control on a faultless, if slow, pitch. We followed on and I helped Alec Stewart to put on 226 for the third wicket, a courageous and aggressive partnership against some fierce fast bowling. The match was played to a half-empty stadium under leaden grey skies. As defeat loomed, not for the first time the press presaged the death of English cricket and tales abounded of empty stadiums and declining interest.

We avoided defeat thanks to our third-wicket effort and to Angus Fraser and Robert Croft who repelled Allan Donald for the final, tense hour of the match. South Africa, though, had only themselves to blame for failing to win. Instead of pressing on after the first day, they added only 250 the next day for the loss of three more wickets. Most of the batsmen appeared to be playing for personal gain. In general, South Africa were the least interesting team in international cricket to play against. They rarely did anything off the hoof, or unexpected, always playing predictably, as if constantly following a pre-determined plan. Of course, they had some fine players, and as a side they were tough and efficient and hard to beat, but, in my opinion, their caution prevented them fulfilling their potential.

Australia, for example, would have pressed on, declaring on the second evening instead of an hour before lunch on the third day, giving themselves extra time to bowl us out, win the match and with it the series. It was not the first time that South Africa had removed their foot from our throat before they had expunged our final breath. In Johannesburg in 1995 they came off for bad light on the third evening when we were at their mercy. On our next tour, 1999–2000, at Port Elizabeth, Jacques Kallis and Jonty Rhodes dawdled at less than 2 an over when they should have been pushing for victory; the result was that South Africa declared on the final morning instead of the previous evening, and again we escaped their grasp. Their unwillingness to take risks in search of victory hindered their play throughout the 1990s. Until they change that approach it will continue to inhibit them and they will constantly finish bridesmaids in their battles against Australia. It is no surprise that an unpredictable team such as Pakistan, one that is prepared to counter-attack, has had most success against the Australians.

As Angus Fraser survived Donald's despairing final over at Old Trafford, Alec Stewart jumped to his feet on the balcony, punched the air with clenched fists and rushed down on to the field to embrace Croft and Fraser. It was a touch melodramatic, but he knew, as did I, that South Africa had fluffed their chance, and sport is invariably cruel to those who do. We went to Trent Bridge, confidence restored, with renewed hope.

The Trent Bridge Test would eventually be remembered for that elevated passage of play between Allan Donald and me on the fourth evening. Before that it was a moderate affair. On a flat wicket, batsmen got themselves in and got themselves out. Fraser's ten wickets owed as much to their batsmen's profligacy as his own perseverance or wicket-taking ability. South Africa had the better of the early exchanges and led by 38 on first innings. We bowled them out for 208 in their second, so needing 247 in a day and a half to win the match and level the series.

Mark Butcher departed in the eighteenth over after an uneventful start to our second innings, and Nasser Hussain joined me at the crease. Midway through the final session on Sunday evening, Hansie Cronje walked over to Allan Donald. They stood for a while and talked in animated fashion, and then Donald peeled off his sweater and marked out his long run. Not for the first time, or the last, the South African captain had called upon his great fast bowler at the crucial phase of the game.

I tell myself: *this is now the critical period; the game will be won or lost here; the responsibility is mine, and mine alone, to win this little battle and to get through tonight unscathed.* The first over is a loosener, and no indication of the barrage to come: not slow but certainly not quick by Donald's standards (about 85–88 mph on the speedometer). He offers up a juicy long-hop, short and wide, which I cut for four past Gary Kirsten in the gully and Jonty Rhodes at point. *I'm feeling good – standing tall, bat coming down straight and I'm seeing it well.*

After one ball of the next over, umpire Dunne indicates that Donald is going to come around the wicket – a sign that he is fully loose and ready to step up a gear. *Open up my stance – I don't want a blind spot from around the wicket; careful of the change of angle, the ball going across, rather than into, my stumps; try and leave anything outside of my eye-line and make him bowl at me, and then pick him off through the leg side.* He bowls one short and at me, hip height, and I turn it around the corner and get up the other end. *That's good – remember Boycott's advice to rotate the strike against fast bowlers ('the best way to play fast bowling is from t'other end, lad'). He's right – let Nasser take the heat for a while. The trouble is, in Shaun Pollock, they've got a fast bowler at the other end too.*

The barrage begins in Donald's next over. It's short and at me, from around the wicket, and I'm in a tangle and can't get out of the way. Instinctively I try to protect myself with my bat and the ball cannons into my right hand and balloons up to Mark Boucher behind the stumps. Huge appeal – I stand my ground and Donald runs straight past me, right arm raised aloft in triumph. I dare not look up, but when I do umpire Dunne remains unmoved – *surely he's going to raise his finger any second now.* But he remains unmoved, as do I. I can't believe my good fortune. Donald can't believe his misfortune and he stands in the middle of the pitch glowering at me, and screaming, 'You fucking cheat!' *Don't take a backward step here – body language is important. Keep staring at him – he's got to turn away first.* The moment passes although there's plenty of abuse flying from behind the stumps. *Stay calm now; got to stay composed; there will be plenty of short stuff coming and plenty of abuse too. Don't react. Stay in your own bubble. This is why they call it Test cricket.*

The next ball is fast and on target and I get a thick inside edge past my leg stump and fine-leg for four. *Luck is with me today. I think it's going to be my day.* The next ball is the quickest yet – mid 90s on the speedometer – the ball a blur. Initially, I look to play but realise it has got too big, too quickly, and do a kind of jump/duck to get out of the way. *Shit, that was close! Reactions must be good, though, to get out of the way of that one. Stick in now.* Another short one; again I get in a tangle, but this time I drop my hands and take it on the chest. *Got to take some blows here.* Plenty of abuse from Daryll Cullinan as he walks to the other end. *Ignore him.*

At the start of the next over, Hansie Cronje changes the field. He brings in a short-leg and a leg-gully. *Plenty of short stuff on the way. Stay strong. Remember Walsh in Jamaica. If there's no man out on the hook, I'll take it on – better than being a punchbag.* It's short and I hook, but it's a little too far outside the off stump and I mishit it in the air although it is safe. Cronje changes the field, chasing the ball, and puts a man on the hook, just where I've hit the ball. That horse has bolted. *That's good – moral victory to me. He's had to move away a catcher. Now that there's a man back there's no point hooking. Try to ride the short ball and turn it around the corner and get up the other end.* The next is a short ball, which I turn to square-leg for an easy single. *Relax for a while.*

Donald bowls a full ball, from around the wicket, to Hussain who, forward, nicks it to Boucher. Boucher snatches and spills the simplest of chances. The slip fielders have started to celebrate prematurely and miss the chance of the rebound. Donald stands mid-pitch screaming 'No!' at the top of his voice, the veins on his neck bulging and about to burst. Up until now, Boucher has been his usual vociferous self, niggling and irritating, but he is much quieter now. His team-mates try to pick him up, and during the next over Donald runs all the way from fine-leg to give him some words of encouragement. *Impressive – they are a tough and united team and not beaten yet, not by a long chalk.*

I chat with Nasser mid-pitch before the start of Donald's next over. 'Keep going, Nass. Forget what's happened. This will be his last over.' Donald steams in again, but the Boucher drop has knocked something out of him, and he starts to look tired. *Stick in now. This will be his last over. Don't take any risks – no hooking, just duck and weave and survive. Paul Adams is warming up.* The spell is broken and Dunne calls out the change of bowling. *Don't relax now, keep concentrating* . . .

That short duel with Allan Donald was by far the most intense period of cricket I experienced in my career. Both of us gave our all, laying ourselves bare, with nothing in reserve. In that forty minutes we showed some mental attributes that successful athletes in all sports strive hard to achieve. Competing and winning is as much a mental as a physical state.

We both recognised the critical phase of competition and were able to raise our game for it. Later, Donald wrote, 'I felt we were entering a decisive phase of the Test . . . I felt in my bones that the game would be decided by the next few overs . . . I needed to get my adrenalin flowing straightaway.' Both of us took on the responsibility of winning the battle for our team, and both of us were equally determined. There is a lot of talk of cricket being a team game, but in essence it is a battle of individuals, of batsmen against bowlers. At that precise moment, each batsman and bowler *is* his team – the hopes and aspirations of the others rest on one man, and are out of their control.

Amid the intense emotion, the sledging and the noise of the crowd, both of us remained calm and focused. I decided not to get involved in a war of words, to stay in my own bubble. He would stop and gather himself at the end of his run and take a few deep breaths before setting off again. He had to control his aggression and anger and make sure the next ball was in the right place, which it invariably was.

Both of us clearly loved the battle and the intensity of it, neither willing to give way. I used my experience of Jamaica and Courtney Walsh four years before to help me through. I was able to think quickly, on my feet, about technical changes I should make and the options I should take. In such a physical contest, body language is important – I didn't want to take a backward step, and by countering Donald's staring with my own,

I knew it was a battle I was bound to win because he had to turn away first.

On that day, we were equally mentally tough. It was only a huge slice of luck that saw me through. On another day, with a different umpire, Donald would have been accepting the plaudits. We had some great battles over the years, and he was a respected opponent, on and off the field. I like to think we brought out the best in each other.

At this stage of my career I was definitely a tough player. I wanted to face the best bowlers and revelled in the tense situation. Physically I was fit and I have no doubt that there is a connection between physical and mental fitness. Mental toughness, however, was never a constant for me. Towards the end of my career I was definitely less strong. Like a boxer who has taken too many blows, by the end, mentally, I had had enough. But that was much later.

In 1998, I knew my game and my strengths: I didn't smash huge sixes like Ian Botham did; I didn't have an insatiable appetite for runs like Graham Gooch had; I didn't destroy county attacks like Graeme Hick did; I didn't time the ball as well as Alec Stewart, or make it look as easy or elegant as David Gower, but I knew I could raise my performance for a big game and, for the most part, I was good under big-match pressure. That season, for example, I averaged 54 for England and 29 for Lancashire.

I didn't have Mark Ramprakash's obvious class or ability, but for most of the decade I had more of an impact on the England team. I had known Mark for a long time, since the England Young Cricketers tour of Sri Lanka in 1987, and I admired him as a player. But for most of the decade he struggled to establish himself in the team and to translate his dominance in the county championship for Middlesex on to the international stage. Batting in the three lions sweater he often looked strangely hesitant, and rarely dominant. In that same year, in contrast to me, he averaged nearly 50 for Middlesex and only 34 for England. I was sure it was his mental approach that was holding him back.

In the Johannesburg chapter I tried to explain why it was harder for a highly strung player such as Ramprakash to get in the right frame of mind for a big game. The extra nerves induced by the occasion took him beyond what would be considered the ideal pre-performance zone. He was also apt to approach challenges too cautiously. In 1993–94 in the Caribbean, I asked him to bat at number three. It didn't go well and before the final Test in Antigua, I talked to him and emphasised the enormous opportunities in that position. He screwed up his face and told me that he thought a senior player should be batting there and he would feel much happier at number six. Considering the lack of opportunity to get big scores at number six, I always considered it the worst position in the order. Later when he did bat at number six, Mark worried about the limited opportunities on offer, and then when Nasser Hussain asked him to open against the West Indies in 2000, he privately thought it was too tough a task. To me, he seemed to look for the negative aspects of each challenge rather than the positive, as though he didn't have the amount of faith in himself that his obvious ability demanded.

In Johannesburg in 1995, he approached two innings in the same match so differently it was a sure indication of his confused mental state, and that he hadn't quite worked out his game-plan for Test cricket. In the first innings he blocked for just under an hour, playing one scoring stroke off 35 balls, before he was bowled by Allan Donald for 4. Then, in the second, he aimed a huge expansive drive off the second ball he received, from McMillan, and got bowled for nought. It seemed it was all or nothing with not much in between.

He also seemed unbearably tense. Outwardly, at least, he seemed not to enjoy Test cricket. He would rarely laugh at himself, or other people, and he seemed weighed down by a burden of expectation, or something. Even after his breakthrough century in Bridgetown in 1998, I wasn't convinced he had cracked it, and his nadir was at Lord's in 2000 after a poor match against the West Indies. He sat in the shower area, glumly, for an age. 'I've had enough,' he said. 'I just can't take it any more.'

But within a year he was back in the England team against Australia, and immediately I sensed a totally different person, and consequently, player. I hope he has now unlocked the secret to a successful mental approach. He suddenly looked much more relaxed and much happier. He laughed more easily and at last was prepared to play his natural aggressive game. What brought on the change I am not sure. Maybe it was his move across the Thames to a different environment, maybe the realisation that he was in the 'last chance saloon'. Possibly he realised that, all told, it doesn't really matter that much. His ability and talent have never been in question, and if he continues to have a better mental approach he can go from strength to strength. His best years in international cricket can be ahead of him.

On the fifth day at Trent Bridge, neither Allan Donald nor I could repeat the heroics of the previous evening. Overnight we had come down too far to get back up again. Besides, he had had a cortisone injection in his ankle the previous evening and was feeling its effects the next day. He didn't have much more to give. I saw us home, cussedly, to the end, although I was never fluent. Nasser Hussain departed just after lunch and Alec Stewart came to the crease and put my struggles into perspective. Imperiously, he smashed 45 off thirty-four balls. He did relent for a moment and I hit the winning runs down the ground. It left me stranded on 98*. A century would have been nice, but the Rubicon had been crossed the previous evening.

After the match and the presentations, and enough cooling down time, I went down to the South African changing room to hunt out Allan Donald. It was clear that he was hurt not only by the defeat but also by my umpiring let-off the previous evening. Somewhat reluctantly, he agreed to my offer of a beer. 'What would you have done?' I asked, mischievously, knowing full well he too would have stood his ground if it meant his team winning. Later, he asked me for that particular glove and I readily gave it to him, my autograph neatly covering the offending red mark.

The series was poised at 1–1. Headingley was the decider. It was the nastiest, most ill-tempered match that I have ever played in and throughout it was clear that neither side had much regard for the other. Even the normally sane and placid types such as Jonty Rhodes were sucked into the fray. From our point of view, much of the hostility emanated from the amount of sledging directed at Mark Butcher as he and I walked to the crease the second time around. We were both quick to mention it to the rest of our dressing room – further motivation, if any were needed, to win the match.

As usual on Headingley's bowler-friendly surface, the match was compelling, and the margins were fine. We lost seven wickets in the last session of the first day and were restricted to 230 all out. Most of us sat despondently in the dressing room at the day's end, ruefully reflecting on missed opportunities. Darren Gough bounced in. 'Fuck me, it's like a morgue in here,' he announced. 'I'll lay anybody any money we get a first-innings lead tomorrow.'

Well, he would have been out of pocket, but he wasn't far wrong. South Africa were restricted to a lead of 22. In our second innings I got my inevitable come-uppance from Trent Bridge when I got a huge inside-edge on to my pads, only to be given out leg before by umpire Javed Akhtar. It does usually even itself out in the end.

A wonderful innings of 94 from Nasser Hussain enabled us to set South Africa 219 to win, and at the end of the fourth day they were, tantalisingly, 185–8, 34 short of victory. At that moment, South Africa had the chance to finish us off yet again by claiming the extra half hour as they were entitled to do. Alec Stewart was desperate to come off. He knew his pace bowlers were tired and he would have to turn to Ian Salisbury, and Shaun Pollock looked well set. Hansie Cronje sent out a message too late, Shaun Pollock made the decision to come off and, as usual, South Africa put off the decisive moment. Not for the first time, they gave us a second chance.

Despite the fact that there would be just an hour or so of play, the ground was full and expectant the next morning. Our bowlers returned refreshed and when Darren Gough trapped Makhaya Ntini leg before the series was ours. As I have mentioned elsewhere, I was at the hospital having a check-up and returned to the changing room with the champagne corks already popped and the celebrations in full swing.

Most of the after-match comment concerned the poor standard of umpiring during the final two games. There is no doubt that, at the end, South Africa did not get the rub of the green, although in the early matches we, too, had our share of misfortune. They could complain about the decisions against Rhodes at Trent Bridge, and Kirsten, Cronje, Liebenburg and Donald at Headingley. There can be no suggestion of bias, however. All umpires have bad matches from time to time, and, in any case, a few of the England team were also hard done by.

The two teams briefly mingled at the end of the series. There was not much warmth between the players but out of tradition we congregated together. It was clear that South Africa felt aggrieved. Their comments on the field left us in little doubt that the umpiring was a huge distraction for them. A few of their players were openly complaining and their chairman of selectors, Peter Pollock, sat thunderously, in conversation with Hansie Cronje. After they returned home, Dr Ali Bacher, amazingly, paid them their win bonus as if they had actually won the series.

But the good doctor had very much missed the point – South Africa ought to have won the series, but they lost it and deservedly too. They ought to have buried us at Old Trafford, but didn't through their own caution. Sloppy batting at Trent Bridge let us back into the match twice. Then, in the deciding match at Headingley, they put off the decisive moment and let the umpiring issue distract them. Any sports psychologist will tell you one of the first lessons in sport is to 'control the controllables' and ignore the rest. Old Trafford and Trent Bridge were within their control and they blew it. At Headingley, umpiring decisions were out of their control and should have been ignored. I had won the forty minutes of mind games with Allan Donald at Trent Bridge; at Headingley, South Africa lost them, and with them the series.

17

BLOOMING, WILTING ROSE

Throughout my career, Lancashire's fortunes travelled in opposite directions to England's. While the national side's results fluctuated wildly and success was intermittent, Lancashire was the most feared and successful one-day team in the land. Later on, as England finally turned the corner, Lancashire, both the team and the club, began a rapid descent into the doldrums. It was as if the notoriously capricious cricketing gods were willing to allow me some success – but never too much.

The Holy Grail, for Lancashire members at least, is the county championship. The club has not won it outright since 1934, when King George sat on the throne and Lancashire's team included such luminaries as Eddie Paynter and George Duckworth. I was never sure, however, it was ever that important to the players of my era. Of course, we tried to win it, and we finished runners-up four times during my spell at the club, but we never really committed ourselves to it. We never sat down at the beginning of any season and said, 'This can be our year, and we will do whatever it takes to make it so.' Before any endeavour, the goal must be set and a commitment made.

We really ought to have won the championship title in 1999. That year we won the National League for the second year in succession although, as our fielding had lost some of its sharpness, we were slightly past our best in one-day cricket. But I felt our time had come in the championship, if for no other reason than it was Muttiah Muralitharan's first year in county cricket and his impact was enormous. With his bobbing run and rubber wrist, he took an astonishing sixty-six wickets in seven games. Some of the efforts to counteract him were laughable. Most memorable was the stumping of Ben Spendlove, Derbyshire's young batsman, who hurtled down the wicket shouting 'Oh no!' before Murali had even released the ball. Somehow that year we lost at Southport to Warwickshire despite the fact that Muralitharan took 14–117 in sixty-nine overs of wizardry. A week later, we lost a critical game at The Oval, with Mark Butcher an unlikely second-innings wicket taker. Those defeats cost us the championship that our committee and membership so coveted. We never had a better chance.

It was a shame because halfway through that year Dav Whatmore left for his second stint as Sri Lanka's coach, and the players were left to run things themselves for the second half of the season. I thought the first eleven was better organised in those six months than at any other time in my career. It proved what I had long felt – that coaching is often overrated, and that with an experienced and good team such as Lancashire's there is rarely a need for one. It forced the captain, John Crawley, to engage the players more in decision-making and it forced the senior players to become more actively involved. The result was that everyone felt they had an input; decisions were more easily accepted and, therefore, more eagerly pursued.

But mostly we were regarded, by others and ourselves, as a one-day team. The championship is a long-haul affair, won over five months of hard cricket; not hard in the sense that the cricket is tough, but hard in the sense that there are so many days to feel unmotivated – the cold days, rainy days, hangover days and days when the players outnumber the spectators. Championship-winning teams have to be prepared to hang around in Derby in freezing April until the last hour to pick up that crucial extra point. In truth, we never were.

We were a 'playboy' team. We much preferred the fact that

the NatWest Trophy or Benson & Hedges Cup could be won after only five or six games, without having to put in too much effort. Of course, many of those games could be unbearably tense with nerve-jangling final overs in front of massive partisan crowds, but we enjoyed that pressure and we invariably came out on top. Until 2000, I had never lost a semi-final and the club was unbeaten in cup-ties at Old Trafford for over ten years. We were showmen, preferring the adulation and adoration of the crowds to the kind of clinical, professional performance required to beat Northants at an empty Wantage Road in May.

Throughout this period we regarded Lord's as our second home, and we appeared in eight one-day finals, emerging victorious six times. Our build-up became second nature and we never acknowledged the fact that we were about to play a big game. Other teams got to London two or three days in advance, to practise, prepare and grab the home changing room, and were thoroughly overcooked by the time the game finally got under way. We would blithely travel down the afternoon before, rarely practise and accept the away changing room, which we came to regard as lucky anyway. On the morning of the final, we would dress in the new suits that Phillip DeFreitas had procured, assuring us always of a 'good deal'; we would stick a blooming red rose in our lapels, and strut down St John's Wood Road in the way that winners do, taking in the good wishes of the hordes of Lancastrian supporters who had taken the well-worn path down from the north. We were supremely relaxed and always confident of victory.

We became the first team to win the NatWest and Benson & Hedges double, and for good measure we did it twice, in 1990 and 1996. Those were two distinct teams – Fowler, Allott, Mendis and Hughes were replaced by Gallian, Crawley, Martin and Chapple – although a hard core of Fairbrother, Austin, Watkinson, Hegg, Wasim and me, linked the two. We did lose two finals – to Worcester in 1991, and to Derbyshire in 1993. The 1991 final was rain-affected and carried over to a second day. The anti-climax in front of a half-full Lord's was never quite our scene.

Despite the changing personnel, we never changed our one-day style or tactics. We planned to bat around one of the first three in the order, keep wickets intact and use the tremendous depth in our batting to score heavily in the last ten to fifteen overs. Our opening bowlers aimed, above all else, to bowl tightly and get the opposition behind the rate as quickly as possible. We gave away few extras and applied the basics of pressure cricket. If ever we needed a wicket, we could always turn to Wasim Akram, and at the core of everything was aggressive and athletic fielding.

That was it – no flashy game plans or novel theories, no team meetings about the opposition or tactics to be employed. We were often not well coached, sometimes not coached at all, nor did we have wonderful captains. But we did have good players who knew their jobs and, more often than not, performed them. In the one-day game at least, we could call ourselves 'professional' and there was not a game in the mid 1990s that we were not supremely confident of winning.

Neil Fairbrother was a constant and vital presence (when he wasn't injured) in every Lancashire one-day team throughout the decade. For, 'like Hornby and Barlow of long ago', he was 'constantly flickering to and fro', always trying to score at a run a ball, pushing singles, picking the gaps, nudging here and there and rarely becalmed. It was fascinating to watch him in a run chase; his mind was like a computer, constantly analysing run-rates, where he needed to be at a certain stage and when he needed to play the big shot to relieve a moment's pressure. Early on in my career I often batted alongside him in a run chase, me at number three and him at number four, and I learnt that tight one-day games are won by those who keep their heads under pressure. He was a brilliant one-day player, England's equivalent of Australia's Dean Jones.

But if Fairbrother was cool and calm under pressure in the middle of a tight run chase, he was exactly the opposite in the changing room before his turn to bat. Whether it was 1989 or 1999, Fairbrother was incurably nervous. When he was next in, he was apt to seek refuge in the toilet, frequently. It was a nightmare for the man batting behind Fairbrother, and for most of the decade that man was Graham Lloyd. In the beginning, Fairbrother's loose bowels severely irritated Lloyd. 'Bumble!' came the cry when the urge came upon him. 'Shit, not again Harv,' and Lloyd would stub out his fag, put away the *Racing Post* and put on the rest of his gear. This would happen at regular ten-minute intervals and it was a mystery to me how Fairbrother was so rarely indisposed at the fall of a wicket. Superstitiously, I came to regard Fairbrother's motions as a good omen, a wicket-free zone, and a chance to relax. By the end of the decade, Lloyd was fully resigned to his fate and sat with full armour on at the fall of the first rather than the second wicket, oblivious to the demands of the bowels of Lancashire's number four.

We were lucky, by and large, to have excellent overseas players who integrated fully into the ways of Old Trafford life. The best was Wasim Akram, and he quickly became accepted as part of the furniture and very much a Lancastrian, as Clive Lloyd had been before him. But at first it wasn't easy for him or us. Most of us were ignorant in the ways of Islam, and Wasim's English was faltering and his knowledge of the West limited. During one of his first games for the club, the chef cooked pasta with pork at lunchtime, unaware that Wasim could not eat it. Not realising what was in it, Wasim started his lunch, and spat out the offending mouthful with a loud 'Aargh!' We all stopped, suddenly aware of what had happened, held our breath and waited for the inevitable explosion. Wasim sprinted out and forced himself to throw up. We were red faced and still holding our breath when he returned, cold-eyed, to survey his hosts. Then his face softened. 'Tasted bloody good, though!' he grinned, and we let out a collective sigh of relief. Once we had seen his unbelievable ability we were prepared to give him all the time in the world to integrate and we tried to meet him halfway. It helped that he was so popular, and there were no more problems after that.

For most of the decade the dressing-room atmosphere was wonderful. It helped that other than our overseas players the team was almost exclusively home-grown. Many of us had come through Lancashire's schoolboy teams together – Lloyd, Hegg, Martin, Speak, Austin, Titchard, Yates and I were all signed within two years from our Federation (under 19) side. It was a constant delight for me to be able to return to my mates, no matter how gruesome things got with England.

During that time, playing for Lancashire never seemed like a job, more an extension of our pre-professional days; just a bunch of mates having fun. It extended beyond cricket, to golf, soccer, cards and beer. Didsbury became the social hangout for most of the players in the days before marriage and children and other mature manifestations of life. The night of our Benson & Hedges semi-final victory over Worcester in 1995 summed up the spirit in the team. We had looked for all the world as if we were going to lose; those of us already out had quietly packed our bags and showered and prepared to watch the last rites. Not for the first time, our vaunted lower order, led by Wasim Akram, produced a miracle to keep our unbeaten semi-final record intact. At the moment of victory, pandemonium ensued, no doubt to the irritation of the dressing room next door, and we celebrated long and hard until the lights of Worcester's cathedral shone brightly in the night sky. Suddenly everyone realised they had had too much to drink to drive home, and so we booked ourselves into a nearby hotel and continued to celebrate our triumph. It was a wonderful evening, spontaneous and full of genuine friendship, and it summed up our team in a decade that will go down as one of the county's most successful.

Of course, in sport, good things never last forever. The warning signs for us were there in 1998 during our Benson & Hedges quarter-final defeat at The Oval; we came a distant second and looked way off the pace in the field. The following year we lost our twelve-year unbeaten home record in cup-ties to Yorkshire in the quarter-final of the NatWest. A year after that we lost not one, but two, semi-finals, both at Bristol against Gloucestershire. They squeezed us in the field in the way we had throttled countless other sides down the years, and we ruefully acknowledged that we had to pass on our title of one-day kings to a team we would have dispatched with ease in our pomp. We were relegated into the second division of the National League in the same year and a year later we flirted disastrously with relegation into division two of the championship – an unthinkable prospect for such a big club.

It ought to have been clear to the committee for a while that the majority of the players would come to the end of their shelf life around the same time. By the turn of the century we had already lost Watkinson and Wasim, and Gallian had left for Nottinghamshire. Ian Austin and I retired shortly afterwards and Fairbrother, Hegg and Martin are likely to follow soon enough. Some young players were brought in; Chris Schofield and Andrew Flintoff were good enough in a short space of time to attract the attention of the England selectors. But other than that, there seemed to be a complete absence of planning. The club signed, in the same year, Ryan Driver from Worcester and John Wood from Durham, neither of whom would be regarded as big-name players, or able to fill an ever-growing void.

As well as the passage of time, the oldest reason of them all, money, played a part in our decline. Throughout the 1990s the club operated a rigid pay structure. Every player knew what he had to achieve to be on a certain level. A newly capped player would be on level one; a capped player of three years on level two; of five years on level three; an international on level four, and so on, up to the captain, who was always the highest paid player at the club. It was adhered to strictly and resulted in a jealousy-free dressing room – always important when you rely on your team-mates as much as yourself to bring in the silverware.

It helped that the very senior players, Neil Fairbrother and me for example, accepted the system; it resulted in the dressing room as a whole being well paid although our top players were badly off in comparison with other counties. I don't remember ever negotiating a contract; it was sent through the post at the end of every year and returned the next day, duly signed.

This blissful state of affairs, for the club at least, could never last. With the new brigade of promising cricketers such as Andrew Flintoff, came agents, negotiations and contractual squabbles. His demands coincided with an end to the pay structure, and thus harmony within the dressing room. It was not the player's fault or the agent's, whose job it is to procure the best deal for his client. But the majority of players did not have agents and it meant the club weakly capitulated to the demands of someone who shouted the loudest rather than those whose performances merited such a pay rise. The club seemed unprepared for, and incapable of dealing with, this brave new world; their appeasement of Flintoff kept a promising young player at the club, but at the same time it alienated any number of senior players, who consequently felt undervalued.

An ageing team, with friction among the senior players over pay and their general lack of involvement in decision-making, resulted in a dressing room that was no longer a joy to walk into every morning. The enthusiasm, spark and commitment waned, and in sport as soon as you slip, there is always another team waiting to take your place. For some players it was obviously no longer fun but more of a job, and sometimes a complete chore. There was almost a loss of innocence, as cynicism and bitterness replaced enthusiasm and joy. I was glad to get out when I did, when most of my memories were sweet rather than sour.

The decline of the team and the dressing-room atmosphere seemed to be mirrored in a more general decline within the club. Some bad business decisions were taken resulting in a double-tiered stand that was empty 364 days of the year, and an indoor school that leaked money. The stadium itself began to look increasingly shabby and international matches were played to half-full stands. The club pleaded constant poverty – it was left to the players to do some fund-raising in order to go on the annual pre-season tour before the 2002 season. All in all, the year I left, the self-styled 'Manchester United of cricket' was looking in a sorry state and struggling to attract new young players to bolster its ageing team. The signing of David Byas prior to the start of the 2002 season was the clearest indication of the mess the club had got itself into.

The John Crawley saga summed up the whole problem. John is one of Lancashire's own, brought up through the system, a player of considerable gifts and a decent, straightforward person. By the end of 2001, he was so disaffected with what he had seen and experienced during his three-year stint as captain that he vowed never to play for the club again. Both sides became locked in a damaging legal dispute, the player trying to get a release from his contract and the club trying to hold him to it. It was easy to understand the club's desire to fight John's wish to leave and insist upon the sanctity of contract. But it was a sorry situation and, regardless of the rights or wrongs of the matter, it smacked of poor management that a player should find himself so alienated.

The afternoon before the last championship game of 2001, I walked into the Lancashire dressing room for the last time. The mess indicated that the players had practised in the morning, but they had left and now the place was empty and it had a cold, end-of-season feel. My locker was in the far corner and, as usual, only Andrew Flintoff's was messier. I had inherited my locker from Jack Simmons in 1989, and so it had served only two inhabitants in thirty-odd years of cricket. There was still a message pinned to the back for Simmons ('We knew you'd be back, Flat Jack' it said) but mostly it was filled with the debris of my fifteen-year career with the club. There were bats, pads and gloves, long-forgotten irate letters from England supporters, winner's medals and man of the match awards lazily unattended, and an old players' handbook with its bellicose seasonal message:

'the size of the fight in the man is bigger than the size of the man in the fight!' I emptied the locker in a wave of nostalgia. I threw most of my stuff away, keeping only the medals and a few mementos. Then I took one long look around a place that I associated with some of the happiest days of my career, and I walked out into the Manchester mizzle, a Lancashire player no longer.

On my return from South Africa in January 2000, I made some remarks about county cricket which threw me reluctantly into the spotlight and led to me being demonised by those who hold our domestic cricket dear. I said that county cricket *'in its present form* fulfils no useful purpose whatsoever'. Those who took offence at my remarks usually missed out the caveat. The chairman of the board's disciplinary committee threatened action for bringing the game into disrepute but nothing followed. The ECB's corporate affairs department rumbled into action, taking a 'dim view' of the whole situation. Ian MacLaurin and Tim Lamb came out in defence of our ailing county game, even though privately I knew they shared some of my views.

I must admit that the scale of the outcry surprised me. I was merely peddling an old line, one that I had trotted out on various occasions down the years. It is a view that I know the majority of current England players share, and judging by the responses to the annual questionnaire posed by the Professional Cricketers' Association, it is obviously a view shared by many within the county game itself. It seems to me to be startlingly obvious. The structure of our domestic game is an anachronism, bound by history and tradition, offering little, other than refuge to a tiny minority who turn up to watch and security to a number of cricketers who are professional in name only.

I am a passionate believer in English cricket and in our domestic cricket, but not in its present form. A great triviality such as county cricket must have its justification somewhere. It is entirely proper to ask the question 'what is it for?' Its justification could be in the entertainment it provides for a large number of people, either on television or through the turnstiles, or in the fact that it is financially self-sufficient through those monies and through sponsorship, or that it fulfils a role as a strong breeding ground for the national team, the 'shop window' of our game to use Ian MacLaurin's words.

It is clear that county championship cricket fits none of the above criteria. The number of people who turn up to watch is tiny. Even during the short time that I played for Lancashire, it was obvious that interest was dwindling. In 1988 nearly 46,000 people turned up to watch Lancashire's championship games. By 2001 that number had fallen to just under 27,000. The only time the car park is ever full is from the overspill when Manchester United are playing at home. The championship is not spectator-friendly. Most games are played midweek, when only those too young or too old to work, or those out of work, can find the opportunity to watch, and there are many weekends without scheduled cricket. There is no more depressing feeling for a professional sportsman than to play in a stadium that is virtually empty.

County cricket then is not a spectator sport; nor is it self-sufficient, depending as it does for survival on a financial hand-out each year from monies generated by international cricket. In itself, that is not a problem. No other country has a financially booming domestic game. The difference is that other countries have realised this and accept that the only *raison d'être* for their domestic game is to provide the strongest possible inter-national team. Even county cricket's staunchest supporters would not claim that it does that. The arguments are oft-repeated – poor pitches, poor practice facilities, too many matches with the best players too thinly spread to provide meaningful competition.

Looking back, I can remember with clarity virtually every Test match I played. Few, if any, championship matches spring to mind. The quality was often poor; the nature of it, whereby livelihoods depended on performance, encouraged a lack of enterprise and a risk-free attitude. The mind-numbing repetitiveness dulled the spark of even the most enthusiastic. The arrival of central contracts and the setting up of an Academy, so taking players out of the system, are tacit admissions from the administrators who run the game that the gap between Test and county cricket is ever-widening and that they need to look elsewhere to prepare their players for Test cricket.

In the near future, the county game will be pushed further into obscurity. International players are already under central contracts, and I am sure they will soon be exclusively contracted to the board. England's players will play more and more international cricket and less and less domestic cricket. With seven Tests every summer and a triangular one-day tournament, it is clear where the media focus will lie. Given that few people watch our county game, that it is a poor grounding for Test cricket, that sponsorship and television are not interested in it, surely it is valid to question the current structure of it. That is not attacking, but encouraging debate to ensure its future.

On becoming chairman of the ECB, Ian MacLaurin immediately announced that county cricket must do everything in its power to assist in the national team's success. He said that the bad old days of the counties' interests superseding England's must come to an end. I agree wholeheartedly with him – economic viability dictates that it should be so. To that end, in an attempt to raise standards, divisional cricket was introduced in the National League in 1999 and in the championship in 2000. Immediately, there were some beneficial results. Games that previously had been dead, end-of-season affairs now had much more riding on them, and became much more competitive. I believe that the administrators who run our game hope that, in time, divisional cricket will bring about a crystallisation of the best players in a smaller number of clubs. Although the administrators can never say it publicly, I think they hope that divisional cricket will, surreptitiously, force some smaller clubs to the wall, reducing our championship to a more manageable and efficient number.

They should not worry about that because there *are* too many county clubs. It is madness to continue to throw money at clubs who do not produce home-grown talent, and survive by filling their team with players on dubious EU passports and ageing players from elsewhere. There *are* too many professional players and there *is* too much first-class cricket. A reduction would bring some immediate rewards. The best players would find themselves playing against each other more than they do now, and they would have more time for quality practice and preparation. Meanwhile, those not striving quite so hard, or those having striven, those whom C.L.R. James would call the 'welfare staters', would be able to move to a semi-professional status, and develop interests outside the game, preparing for a life beyond cricket. They would help bridge the gap between the professional and the amateur game.

It is a change that would certainly bring about an end to the 'another-day-at-the-office' mindset. It would help prevent the kind of disillusionment and bitterness I saw so clearly in my last two years at Lancashire – players hanging on to their careers, waiting for a benefit and afraid to move on because a life in cricket meant no life afterwards. In a truly professional, competitive system, Lancashire should have moved on the moment our decline became clear. A lack of competition for places, and a system clogged up by those afraid to leave but no longer committed to being the best they could be, led to a stale team that was clearly past its best. It was a dressing room inhabited by some discontented, disillusioned and unfulfilled players, in a system that failed to engage them. Playing sport for a living should never come to that.

18

HUSSAIN'S ENGLAND

In time, Nasser Hussain would prove to be an excellent England captain. With the help of Duncan Fletcher, and an improved system as a result of the introduction of central contracts before the start of the 2000 season, he would lead England to four successive series victories, the kind of consistent success of which many of us had dreamed but secretly despaired. But at the end of May 1999, as Alec Stewart paid the price for a dismal World Cup showing, Hussain was not to know all that. No doubt he felt the same nerves and anticipation his predecessors had felt as he faced the press for the first time, even though a mouth-watering prospect of four Tests against New Zealand, tradition-ally lambs to England's slaughter, lay ahead.

I missed both the World Cup and the start of the New Zealand series with my increasingly troublesome back and took the first tentative steps towards preparing for life beyond playing. I signed to cover the World Cup for BBC radio and television, as well as continuing to write for the *Sunday Telegraph*, but I knew I was not ready to retire because I keenly missed the cricket. Only Saturdays, with six stints each on radio and television, as well as two editions for the paper, provided the adrenalin rush I was used to and still craved. Besides, I had no desire to finish my England career on the pair I had completed in Melbourne five months earlier.

In the absence of any help from the ECB, I enrolled on a Pilates course in South Kensington. The fact that it was full of female ballet dancers, and heavenly bodies, was not the only reason for my enthusiastic conversion. Fit again, I returned briefly for Lancashire's second eleven at Middlesbrough, scoring a century, and then for the first team at The Oval, where a half-century confirmed my progress. But I was back in the press box, and back in spasm again, when the First Test against New Zealand came around. For the first time I worried whether I would return to Test cricket at all, and during that game John Etheridge, cricket correspondent of the *Sun*, gave me a one in ten chance of doing so. Within weeks, a cortisone injection into a troublesome disc gave me prolonged relief, and 268* against Glamorgan shortly afterwards ensured me an enthusiastic welcome for the Third Test at Old Trafford.

Nasser Hussain's appointment had been greeted less than enthusiastically. Like many others, I felt Alec Stewart had been harshly treated; unlike many others, I was entirely in favour of Hussain as his replacement. I had been friendly with Hussain for many years, since our schoolboy days together, and I knew him to be a complex, occasionally difficult, but always interesting character. He had been out of favour during most of the Illingworth years. Illingworth felt that Hussain's technique was an impediment to him scoring consistently at Test level. As usual, he majored on what a player could not do rather than what he could do.

Hussain did have technical flaws, but I was always of the opinion that enough determination and spirit can overcome anything, and I knew he was lacking in neither. He quickly gained the respect of the team on his return for the India series in 1996; twin 100s enabled him to claim the number three position as his own, a rehabilitation he confirmed with a double century the following summer against Australia. He wasn't quite showing the level of brilliance I had seen from him as a teenager, but he was now established and respected and worth his place in the team.

I also knew Hussain to be a shrewd judge of a cricketer and someone with good tactical awareness to whom I often turned for advice when I was captain. It was at my suggestion that we appointed him vice-captain for the Zimbabwe and New Zealand tour of 1996–97 and the West Indies tour the following winter. I was sure that he was clever enough to know that he would have to change his previously self-absorbed approach should he be given the additional responsibility of the captain's armband.

Others were not so sure, and there is no doubt that Hussain had to work hard at first to gain the respect of the team as a leader of men. For, before the captaincy, he was completely self-absorbed, not usually to the detriment of those around him, but he was certainly unaware of the needs and problems of others. Some described him as selfish and it led to Angus Fraser announcing at the end of the 1998 Ashes tour, 'If he ever becomes captain, he'll need to look elsewhere for a new opening bowler.' Part of the problem I think was that Hussain was always ambitious; with his elevation to the highest honour in the game, he became less self-absorbed and an all-round nicer and better person.

Hussain was shrewd enough to know that he had to change his approach. Whereas before he had made life awkward for Andrew Caddick with his occasional barbed comments, now he put a long-needed arm around Caddick's shoulder. That, along with a slight technical change and Caddick's growing maturity as a cricketer, enabled Hussain to get the best out of the talented but mercurial Somerset fast bowler. As someone who had been tagged 'difficult', Hussain knew labels to be misleading as well as damaging, and he was fully prepared to incorporate so-called 'awkward' characters in the team.

He is a good motivator. During most team-talks I tended to switch off, keeping only half an ear open for the very occasional nugget that came our way. With Hussain, I was apt to listen more carefully, as he usually had something interesting and original to say. In the field, he liked to position himself at mid-off; to the bowlers he was like 'a horsefly on a plough horse' – always niggling them and 'keeping them up to their work'.

Tactically he was essentially defensive in outlook, possibly because of his upbringing at Essex under Keith Fletcher. That is not to say he was always orthodox. His tactics in India showed his willingness to eschew orthodoxy to get the most out of the occasionally limited resources at his disposal. It also laid bare his essential philosophy: whereas Australia would try to dominate and win the game from the first ball, Hussain believed in trying to stay in the game, hoping pressure would tell in the end. It was the difference, in footballing terms, between an attacking team and a team that liked to sit back and hit the opposition on the break. Those tactics worked especially well for him on the sub-continent; Pakistan, for example, would later succumb to our counter-attack and last-minute strike in the gathering gloom of Karachi.

Since Hussain often openly scoffed about captains such as New Zealand's Lee Germon, whose public relations skills far outweighed his cricketing ones, I was surprised how jealously he came to guard his own PR. I knew he was bright and articulate and that he would be excellent in press conferences, but he was more pro-active and sensitive to criticism than I thought he would be. In Pakistan and Sri Lanka he lounged in his room for most of the time, watching DVDs and complaining about touring life and saying how much he was missing home; the next day, without prompting, he would be praising the country, the people and its facilities. A year later when he toured India, Hussain genuinely felt it was the greatest experience of his cricketing career. Generally, he was far more media savvy than me, and he realised that it helped to get the media on your side, and how easily they could be sucked in. I actually enjoyed touring, but too often the teams I captained gave the impression that they didn't.

All in all, he was pretty much the ideal prototype of an England captain – he was the perfect age, thirty-one, experienced but also young enough to have the energy to do the job; he was worth his place in the team on merit; he was respected by the players, tactically sound, and articulate and aware of his media responsibilities. In May 1999, all he needed was a good start and a series victory over New Zealand.

By the time I returned for the Third Test of the summer at Old Trafford, the series was level at 1–1. The first flames of optimism that had risen in the aftermath of victory in Hussain's first Test as captain were swiftly doused, as usual, by a wet performance at Lord's. When I walked into the dressing room at Old Trafford, back in the international spotlight after more than six months in the wilderness, it was like starting over again. I was unduly nervous, and slightly concerned that I was still a fitness risk after being rushed back so quickly.

I was immediately aware that not all was well within the camp. Hussain had broken a finger at Lord's and, while he was off the field having treatment, he had passed responsibility to Graham Thorpe. A fortnight later at Old Trafford, the selectors overlooked Thorpe as captain and chose the relatively inexperienced Mark Butcher, who was by no means certain of his place in the team. Thorpe arrived in Manchester in a grim mood, his naturally iconoclastic nature fuelled by the snub, and he spent most of the match muttering darkly about his *bête noire*, Mike Gatting, and the other selectors.

Butcher was irritable too. The team he had been given looked unbalanced with only two seamers and two spinners. He wanted Alec Stewart to keep wicket to increase his options, but the selectors insisted on keeping faith with Nottinghamshire's young wicket-keeper Chris Read. The persistently damp and gloomy weather failed to break up the pitch as expected and Butcher found himself a seamer short for most of the game. The selectors themselves were under severe pressure. There had been the usual cries for new blood after the Lord's débâcle and they had responded by picking three over-thirty year olds – Graeme Hick, Peter Such and me. Hick's recall for the umpteenth time was a step too far for many scribes. Gatting and Gooch bore the brunt of the unfair criticism and resigned before the end of the summer.

The Manchester weather saved us from possible embarrassment. Then, on the last day of the next and final Test at The Oval, a fierce attack from Chris Cairns changed the course of that match and clinched the series for his team. Cairns smashed 80 off ninety-four balls, including a violent assault on Phil Tufnell; most of the four sixes he hit off the Middlesex spinner went sailing over my head at deep long-on. One bounced so hard off the pavilion it rebounded all the way back to Tufnell, who casually bent down, picked it up and carried on bowling. But 246 to win proved to be 84 too many.

Defeat at home to New Zealand was the low point in my time as a player. Nasser Hussain had earned some plaudits for the start he had made as captain, but as he accepted the loser's cheque and the boos of the crowd, he must have wondered what he had let himself in for. The *Sun* recreated the famous 'Ashes' headline of long ago and announced the death of English cricket. I went to the Chelsea Ram, a pub close to our hotel, with Phil Tufnell and Bob Cottam to reflect on our defeat; with Tufnell ordering tequila chasers and photographers gathering outside, I thought it wise, in the circumstances, to leave early and sober rather than late and drunk, and I left Tufnell to feed the snappers' frenzy.

It is possible that Nasser Hussain would have continued to go around in circles, like others before him, if Duncan Fletcher had not come aboard as coach at the end of that season in time for the South African tour. He had actually been appointed at the beginning of the summer but had insisted on fulfilling his contract with Glamorgan, leaving Graham Gooch in temporary charge of the England team. Fletcher did not have an auspicious start. At the interview, Simon Pack greeted him with 'Hello, Dav' (Lancashire's Dav Whatmore was also in the running) and then Fletcher met his new captain only briefly before they went their separate ways for the summer.

When it came to coaching and coaches, I was very much a sceptic. I simply hadn't come across that many good ones. Often they were too keen to justify their role and overcoached; others made it clear coaching was more about their own ego and their reputation in the game than the teams and the players they purported to help. I thought the growing numbers of specialist coaches to be, occasionally, a bad thing; players too often used coaching as an excuse upon which to blame their poor form. My experience is that the best lessons are the ones you learn yourself and there is no substitute for watching and talking to good players. Generally, I think it easier for a coach to ruin a player than make him better. A good coach is an asset to any team but rather than be subjected to bad coaching I am in favour of no coaching at all.

Occasionally, I worried about England's players, especially the young and inexperienced ones, feeling under pressure to listen to various coaches prior to Test matches. A young player gets bombarded with enough advice anyway before his Test debut let alone taking on board advice from a coach he has never worked with before. A young player really needs to be left alone to sink or swim for a while. I watched with concern when Bob Cottam tried to change Andrew Flintoff's run-up the day before his Test debut. Bob is a good technician and I have no doubt the advice was sound, but was it really the right time for it? I remember John Crawley telling me how uncomfortable he felt with Graham Gooch constantly peering at him, like an ancient and valuable relic, during net sessions.

Even the experienced players were guilty sometimes of worrying too much about coaching and technique. Nasser Hussain's batting problems during the 2000–01 season started, in my opinion, not as a result of the pressures of captaincy, but primarily because of a search for technical perfection in the nets at the expense of worrying about runs in the middle. In England generally, we have a tendency to overcoach and worry too much about technique – it can turn naturally gifted teenagers, capable of playing occasionally brilliant innings, into stilted Test match players.

It was, therefore, with no great hope or expectation that I travelled to Lilleshall on 20 September for our fitness assessments ahead of the South African tour, and to meet our new coach for the first time. I sat down irritably to listen to Fletcher – his talk was to be followed by the punishing bleep test, which often caused severe back spasms for me, and the results of which were sure to advertise my advancing middle age. After the initial introduction he set up a blackboard and proceeded to write out an obscure mathematical formula that showed improved individual percentages would increase the output of the team as a whole. I looked around during this strange presentation; Gough's brow was furrowed, clearly confused, while Headley was busy sending text messages on his phone. It wasn't the most auspicious start for the new coach. But how wrong first impressions can be. Duncan Fletcher was, is, an outstanding England coach – very much the Cardinal Richelieu to Hussain's Louis XIII, the power behind the throne.

Hussain had the good sense to listen to Fletcher. He could have easily taken the view that Fletcher was less experienced than most of the team when it came to Test cricket, and relegated him to the background. But Fletcher had missed international cricket only by virtue of his nationality (Zimbabwe had not been given Test status when he played) rather than his ability, and he had been a hugely respected and successful captain of his country. Hussain listened to him and their partnership flourished. Fletcher, in turn, never criticised Hussain or the team, made suggestions rather than gave orders, and was self-assured enough to stay in the background and leave the glory to the captain and his players.

On his appointment some had expressed concerns about a foreigner coaching the national team. I thought it was Fletcher's great advantage. He was tarnished by neither the defeats nor the confusion of the past and came to the job with no preconceptions about players. Later he confided to me that during the

selection meeting for the South African tour, he had been astonished to hear selectors say that this player was 'a bad 'un' or that
player was 'selfish' and fully expected to be coaching a team of
troublemakers. He found that nothing was further from the
truth. He came to the job with an open mind and each player
felt he had been given a clean slate and a fresh start.

His great strength was man-management; he believed in talking to players and having faith in their judgement. One of his
first tasks was to set up a 'senior management' group. It was not
a novel thing – Graham Gooch and I had often coopted players
on to a tour committee – but Fletcher's management group was
more wide-ranging, and along with the captain and coach they
were responsible for running the show.

Before we left for South Africa, I met Fletcher in the airport
hotel and he asked me to join the group. I was happy to do so
but first I had to explain to him some of my concerns. After I
had given up the captaincy I was painfully aware that I had to
stay in the background and let the new captain get on with the
job in his own way with no perceived interference from me.
Between giving up the captaincy in 1998 and the forthcoming
South African tour my influence had been minimal. I was happy
to give advice if it was asked for, but players had to come to me
rather than the other way around. Fletcher understood, but said
he would still like me to be involved and I agreed.

In time, Fletcher used the management group to engage those
players who might otherwise have been recalcitrant. Graham
Thorpe was the classic example. Thorpe was a popular player in
the team, respected for his ability and his personality. I instinctively gravitated to the more interesting, complex characters
such as Thorpe. He was never a troublemaker but he certainly
viewed those in authority with suspicion and he did his best to
disrupt the occasionally fussy rules and regulations that teams
have to abide by.

In St Vincent on the 1998 West Indies tour, for example, the
whole team were invited on to Paul Getty's yacht. We turned

up dressed uniformly in our board-issue casual tops and shorts. Thorpe dressed differently quite deliberately and I overheard Getty asking David Lloyd, 'Is he not part of your team, then?' If the stipulation was black shoes, Thorpe would wear brown; if we had to wear our short-sleeves, Thorpe would wear long-sleeves, and so on.

To me, dress codes are fairly inconsequential; in the modern world where image is considered as important as substance they are a necessary evil. But the management had to think carefully about how to handle Thorpe's nonconformity because, of all the players I played with, he was the one whose state of mind most affected his play. A happy, contented Graham Thorpe is a world-class player, his presence beneficial to any team. If something off the field is eating away at him, he cannot put it to the back of his mind and concentrate on his cricket. The death of his friend Graham Kersey had a profound effect on him throughout the Zimbabwe tour of 1996–97, and his return home from India in 2001 is an indication that he has to have his life in order before he can commit himself fully to cricket.

Fletcher recognised this and was quick to include Thorpe on the management team for the tours of Pakistan and Sri Lanka in 2000–01. From poacher to gamekeeper, all of a sudden Thorpe found himself setting the kind of trivial regulations he had previously abhorred, and of course he was a shining example of conformity after that. Secretly, Thorpe liked having some influence, as his reaction to being overlooked for the captaincy at Old Trafford a year earlier had indicated. Fletcher and England reaped the rewards of this inclusive approach – he scored 284 runs at 56.80 in Pakistan and 269 runs at 67.25 in Sri Lanka, and was instrumental in both series wins.

Fletcher's successful management style was further illustrated to me directly that winter. During the last Test in Colombo, Nasser Hussain suffered a groin strain and sent a message to the dressing room asking whether he should come off or bat with a runner. Fletcher canvassed opinion. I thought Hussain should come off. His two main shots to the spinners were the sweep and the launch over mid-on and he was fit enough to play neither. Also I thought that his inability to score would seriously hamper Graham Thorpe, at the other end, who was our key player and whose game relied on a constant rotation of the strike.

My view was in the minority, and a runner was sent for. I felt strongly that it was the wrong decision and I rashly criticised Fletcher in front of the team. 'That could be a costly decision you've just made,' I said. He said nothing, but later that evening came knocking on my door. In a perfectly calm manner he told me that while I may have been right he didn't like the way I had spoken to him in front of the rest of the team. I agreed and apologised immediately and the matter was forgotten. Had he raised the matter during play, tensions were such that neither of us would have backed down and a damaging argument would have taken place. Instead, he made me fully aware that he wasn't happy with what had happened and didn't want a repeat, but he did so at a time and in a manner that resulted in an immediate apology rather than a heated argument.

At the end of October 1999, two months after our defeat by New Zealand, we arrived in South Africa for Fletcher's first series in charge. I was immediately struck by how committed he was, as Lloyd was before him, to fielding and fitness, and by the fact that he was tough and uncompromising. Fletcher's routines, like Lloyd's, were varied and intense. The game before the First Test was against a combined Northern Transvaal and Gauteng eleven on the high veldt in Pretoria. At the end of each day's play we would congregate for extra fielding practice, to get used to the altitude as much as anything else. Fletcher gave players sets of ten catches at a time, which at altitude was enough to get the lungs burning. Phil Tufnell always gave the impression that he was unfit; in fact, he was naturally one of the fittest members of our team although he was notoriously loath to show this in either fielding or fitness work. Halfway through his set of ten, Tufnell began to throw the ball back wildly out of Fletcher's reach. The ploy was obviously intended to slow down the procedure to give him more breathing space between catches. Fletcher halted the practice. He got some more balls and positioned somebody behind him for the wayward return throws, and then he proceeded to run Tufnell into the ground. He didn't stop at ten, and each throw was aimed tantalisingly out of the spinner's reach until Tufnell's legs and his lungs cried no more and he lay, foetus-like, crumpled in a heap on the ground. Fletcher calmly picked up his gear and walked in, leaving Tufnell to take the long walk back alone. The coach had made his point.

The First Test, days later, was in Johannesburg and never can a coach have experienced a more traumatic start to his tenure. On a capricious pitch and in murky light, Allan Donald and Shaun Pollock reduced us to 2–4 in the fourth over. All the experienced players (Butcher, Hussain, Stewart and me) were back in the shed, and Michael Vaughan and Chris Adams, both on debut, were at the crease. The dressing room was completely silent and in a state of intense shock – even those of us experienced in England's calamities had never seen anything quite like it. What Fletcher was thinking I have no idea, but the pulse of even this most phlegmatic of characters must have been racing. Yet he sat inscrutable, his features hidden behind his sunglasses; calmness, through triumph and disaster alike, would become his trademark. Inevitably, we lost the match heavily in four days. Fletcher conducted a controlled review. He insisted the extra practice was not a 'naughty boy net session' and afterwards he allowed the team to go to Sun City for a break, as planned. There was never a hint of panic.

As the series progressed, Fletcher developed serious concerns about Mark Butcher's lack of form. By the time the New Year's Test in Cape Town came around, Butcher's highest score for the series was 48, and his confidence was demonstrably low. At practice Fletcher motioned me over. 'Have you ever seen Marcus

Trescothick play?' he asked. I had, but not for about five years; I recalled a chubby, middle order left-hander who looked completely out of his depth against Wasim Akram sometime in the mid 1990s. 'I saw something in him last year that really made me sit up and take notice,' Fletcher continued. I had little to offer, except that he must back his own judgement in the matter. I thought no more of it.

Fletcher did back his own judgement and brought Trescothick into the England fold midway through the following summer. What Fletcher had seen I now saw clearly with my own eyes; I thought Trescothick the most promising newcomer to the England team I had seen, and welcomed him happily as my opening partner for the remainder of my career. By and large, Fletcher's judgement on players was sound; of those elevated to central contract status, only Chris Schofield, the young Lancashire leg-spinner, was a poor call.

South Africa wrapped up the series in Cape Town 2–0 and both teams flew to Pretoria for the final match of a now dead rubber. It was to be the Test in which match-fixing was finally proved to the world although the players did not know that then. Rain halted proceedings after South Africa had reached 155–6 on the first day and, like four years before, it didn't stop raining for another three days, leaving the last day for both teams to play out the seemingly inevitable draw. Certainly, on the fourth evening, there was no indication of the shenanigans to follow as most of us spent that night, and some of the following morning, in the bar at the Sandton Sun hotel, where we were staying.

Half an hour before play on that fifth morning, Hansie Cronje offered Nasser Hussain a game; if both sides would forfeit an innings, he would set England around 280 to win in eighty overs. Hussain called Stewart, Fletcher and me over. 'What do you think?' he asked. All of us thought it would be madness to agree to a game without first seeing how the pitch would play after three days of rain, and we deferred. After half an hour of play, it was clear the pitch was playing fine. I was sent off to see if the offer still stood. It did, and so Hussain went off to negotiate terms with Cronje. He came back with an offer of 249 in seventy-six overs. Again he sought our counsel. This time we thought it was too good to turn down; the pitch was true, there was no Allan Donald (he missed the match, suffering from gout) and it was by no means a stiff target. Game on.

When Chris Adams fended Nantie Hayward to Mark Boucher for 1 just short of the halfway stage, we were 102–4, Hussain was muttering darkly about being 'conned', and he sent Michael Vaughan out to bat with safety-first instructions. Then Cronje brought on the debutant and part-time bowler Pieter Strydom and our innings gained new momentum. Stewart's 73 and Vaughan's 69 took us to a position where only victory or defeat were contemplated by a now more boisterous Hussain. With the last pair at the crease we needed 9 from thirteen balls and a couple of swipes from Gough and Chris Silverwood saw us home.

For the first time in my life I felt completely flat at the moment of a Test victory. It wasn't that I suspected match-fixing, but a Test match victory is a thing that has to be earned; you need to put in the hard work to get twenty wickets and go through the almost inevitable emotional roller-coaster ride as the match swings this way and that, over five days, reaching its natural conclusion. That is why Test match victories are so special. We had worked hard on the final afternoon for our victory, but in essence the match had been gifted to us, and, as a result, I felt it was a hollow victory. As the players wandered over to the far side of the ground to share the triumph with the Barmy Army, I stayed in the changing rooms, sharing none of their joy. In the end, it wasn't just about winning.

Three months later, on the first day of the new English season at Fenner's, where Lancashire were playing Cambridge, the incredible story of Hansie Cronje and match-fixing hit the news. The events at Centurion Park were suddenly illuminated in a harsher light. Cronje hadn't declared for the good of the game but because he had been paid to ensure the match did not end in a draw. Suddenly his strange decision to open the game up became clear; he was trying to win the game but if he couldn't, he was to make sure he lost it – anything but a draw. My intuition about the game had been sound.

At the end of Nasser Hussain's and Duncan Fletcher's first tour together, my instinct was that the England team was in good hands. They had gelled well, and quickly gained the respect of the team. The team itself, however, looked as far away from success as ever before; the selectors had chosen new faces, some of whom were clearly not up to the task, and the final 2–1 scoreline was flattered by the farce at Centurion Park. Sometime during the tour, the ECB had announced that central contracts would be in place for the start of the summer, and Fletcher had spent much of the tour ruminating over their make-up. It was to be the final piece of the jigsaw.

19

SUCCESS AT LAST

The introduction of central contracts prior to the start of the 2000 season, whereby England's élite cricketers were contracted to the ECB as well as their counties, was the most important change, and biggest step forward, in my time as an England player. Throughout the 1990s there had been a constant battle between the counties and the national team; in whose interests was the game being run? At a stroke, the argument was settled in the national interest. Since the counties could only survive through monies garnered from international cricket, they bowed to the inevitable and gave away power. Central contracts gave Duncan Fletcher an advantage that no other England coach had had – ultimate control over his players.

The Acfield report in 1996 had previously considered central contracts. Despite the fact that I had recommended them in my captain's report at the end of the 1995–96 South African tour, and despite the fact that two former England captains, David Gower and Mike Gatting, sat on the committee, no recommendation was forthcoming. The report did recognise that England's greatest problem was the number of domestic games our cricketers played compared with the rest of the world. All told, for example, I played in exactly three times as many matches for Lancashire as Mark Waugh played for New South Wales (354 to 118). Despite this, the Acfield committee failed to recommend measures to ease the burden. England's coach could recommend a rest for his top players but he had no contractual control. He relied on the counties' goodwill. The coach was powerless to prevent his players playing too much and consequently getting injured, as Darren Gough did while playing for Yorkshire at the end of the 1997 season, so missing a vital West Indies tour.

At the start of the 2000 season all that changed. Fletcher decided upon twelve names initially – only Craig White and Chris Schofield raised eyebrows in the media – and he dismantled much of the squad that had optimistically been sent to South Africa. He could now plan ahead with purpose and players could push, at last, for conditions of employment commensurate with their status. Inevitably there were teething problems; counties demanded compensation for missing out on their best players, and when non-contracted players such as Dominic Cork were chosen for the Test team and no compensation was forthcoming, those counties made their concerns known. Given that it was such a radical change, however, things went remarkably smoothly.

The advantages were enormous. Fletcher was able to control how often his top cricketers played. This was beneficial especially for strike bowlers such as Darren Gough and Andrew Caddick who were fully fit, rested and therefore firing for every Test match of the summer. Both were ever present throughout the summer, sharing sixty-four wickets between them. Caddick, as Somerset's only bowler of real quality, was invariably overbowled when he played for his county. For example, he has bowled over 5,000 overs for Somerset in all competitions, five times as many as Glenn McGrath has bowled for New South Wales. Now that energy could be saved up for England.

Moreover, having shelled out over half a million pounds on central contracts, it was clear that the selectors' hand was already forced – given a close call between a contracted player and a non-contracted player, obviously the contracted player would get the nod. So the new system encouraged, almost forced, the selectors into the kind of stability that had long been missing.

For the West Indies series that summer, only seventeen players were used – the fewest for a five-Test home series since 1987. This reflected both the stability of selection and the fact that players were less likely to get injured once proper controls were in place on the amount of cricket they played.

Most importantly, the players began to think of themselves as England players first and foremost. Previously they had thought of themselves as county cricketers who occasionally played for England. Now they were England cricketers who occasionally were allowed to play for their counties. It was a critical change of attitude and ethos; at Test matches, a player no longer rushed to the teletext to see how his county was doing because his primary loyalty had changed. Now the England team *was* a team, almost a nineteenth county, travelling together, practising together and playing together – unity at last.

For those of us coming to the end of our careers, central contracts came ten years too late. I know I would have been a better player, and in better physical shape at the end of my career, had I had the benefits of central contracts at the beginning. Nevertheless, the administrators had finally got their act together – better late than never. With the Fletcher/Hussain partnership and a nucleus of Test cricketers of five years' experience or more (Stewart, Thorpe, Hussain, Gough, Caddick and me), all that was needed now was for the players to acquire the winning habit.

To that end, it helped that Zimbabwe arrived in April for a short, two-match Test series. It was a weak Test side, increasingly troubled by the political events back home, and they provided suitably meek opposition although our self-doubt was still obvious. After a comprehensive victory at Lord's we struggled at Trent Bridge. I had to come off my sick bed in the second innings, after a century in the first, to take us to safety. The draw maintained our 1–0 advantage, and I passed Denis Compton's record in the process for the most Test runs scored at Trent Bridge.

The West Indies arrived while the Zimbabwe series was in progress. They were a team that had toured badly in recent times, but normal service (against England at least) was resumed in the First Test at Edgbaston where they won comfortably by an innings and 93 runs. The Second Test, at Lord's, was the pivotal match of the summer. In hindsight it was one of the most important matches of my career, and the start of the team's turnaround. If we were to lose the game, I was sure we would lose the series. More than that, it would put undue pressure on Nasser Hussain, who would by that stage have lost three out of his first four series in charge, and defeat would have given added voice to those dinosaurs who were already grumbling about central contracts and the withdrawal of England's players from county matches.

Ironically, Alec Stewart captained England in the crucial encounter because Hussain had broken his thumb the week before. Stewart put the West Indies in to bat and by mid afternoon on the second day we had conceded a first-innings lead of 133. In the next two incredible hours, amid the kind of fervent atmosphere I had never experienced before at Lord's, we bowled out the West Indies for 54. It was their lowest innings total against England, Andrew Caddick taking five second-innings wickets for 16 runs.

On that second evening, as I sat in the dressing room reflecting on that passage of play, I remembered something Mike Selvey, the *Guardian*'s cricket correspondent, had said to me about Caddick. It was in Barbados in 1994 and Selvey predicted Caddick would be our second-innings hero. 'Why's that?' I asked. 'Because he's a glory hunter,' he said. It was a prescient comment from Selvey as Caddick did go on to be our match-winner in Barbados, and had often gone on to bowl much better in the second innings of matches generally. I didn't entirely agree with Selvey's analysis however. In this instance, I think Caddick felt the pressure and expectation an opening bowler feels when a captain inserts the opposition on the morning of a match, and he tightened up. In the second innings there was less pressure, the pitch was bouncier and more uneven, and Caddick brought us right back into the game.

Over the years we had always thought the West Indies vulner-able, in English conditions, to the typical English seamer who pitched the ball up with swing and seam. Here, though, Caddick hit the deck hard, generating pace and steep bounce; it was a reversal of all the years of being pounded by the West Indian quick bowlers. Now their batsmen were on the receiving end and they didn't like it; three were caught at short-leg by Mark Ramprakash off short-pitched deliveries, and the West Indian psychological dominance was finally broken.

We still needed 188 to win at the start of the third day, on an increasingly uneven pitch, against Courtney Walsh and Curtly Ambrose. Before he began his spell on the third morning, Ambrose walked down the pitch towards me and stared intently, as if he was looking for a lost coin, at the area to which he intended to bowl. Then he looked up at me with a huge grin, rubbed his hands together a few times, and walked back to his mark. At the start I was marooned at Ambrose's end; after twenty-seven balls I had still to get off the mark and a cluster of red marks worried the patch that Ambrose had stared at so intently. His grin, however, had turned to a grimace each time the ball passed the bat, which was frequently, without taking the edge.

Luckily, Michael Vaughan, a young player with an unflappable temperament, had replaced the injured and horribly out of form Hussain and he came to the wicket after Mark Ramprakash had been dismissed. Both of us missed more balls than we hit in the early stages of our innings; we laughed readily and shrugged off our inadequacy and the excellence of the West Indies' new ball attack, and agreed we should try to tuck in when the change of bowling came. It was tough going, though; in a short run chase Jimmy Adams could bowl Ambrose and Walsh for most of the time. In the circumstances – the nature of the wicket, the quality of the bowling and the importance of the game – I regard the 45 I scored that day as one of my best and most important innings for England.

When Alec Stewart departed at 140–5, the match was in the balance. Minutes later he was sitting beside me on the balcony and we were 140–6, Craig White having come and gone in a flash. 'Do you fancy us?' I asked him. Shortly afterwards, Nick Knight fenced and was caught behind – 149–7. Alec looked at me and shook his head. Dominic Cork had entered the fray and immediately looked positive, lofting Courtney Walsh over mid-off for four. I looked quizzically at Alec. 'I do now,' he said. So did I – Cork demonstrably had the attitude of a winner that day, and after his first aggressive shot I knew that victory was ours, provided he found someone to stay with him. That someone was Darren Gough, much to the relief of Matthew Hoggard, whose debut it was and who sat pale and nervous under his helmet in the far corner of the dressing room, chewing his chin-strap and unable to speak to anyone. As with the critical match at Old Trafford in the 1997 Ashes series, the scores had been levelled at 1–1, but the fortunes of the two teams were travelling in opposite directions.

Old Trafford, the next match, marked one hundred Test appearances for Alec Stewart and me. Although Stewart is five years older than me, our England careers had run virtually concurrently; I made my debut a series before him, but with the odd injury and omission we approached the milestone neck and neck. Our batting records were near identical too, both of us rapidly approaching 7,000 Test runs, he at a slightly better average, while I had one more 100 to my name. There, frankly, the similarity ended.

It is not that we don't get along. Although there may have been some early rivalry, I can hardly remember a cross word between us. But in character, temperament and style we are complete opposites. He is upright, clean-shaven, always sharply dressed, with an almost military bearing. I am more slouched, laid-back and have little interest in fashion. Alec is acutely aware of records, statistics and his place in the history of the game. I have little interest in those things. He is passionate, loves to be in the thick of any action on offer and has a narrow focus on sport and life. I am more detached, one of life's observers, and have a broader outlook on both. In twelve years of playing together I can scarcely recall us eating out together, on our own, once.

When Alec finally calls time on his outstanding career, I often wonder whether he will look back with regret at some of the missed opportunities that touring life offers. During the day on tour he would usually top up his tan by the hotel swimming pool, whereas I might be more curious about the places we visited. In the evenings he would religiously order chicken (no skin), vegetables (no sauce) and chips. I would often be in a local restaurant sampling exotic dishes, and usually paying the price for them the next day. Maybe that's why he's still playing and I'm not.

Whenever possible I tried to be adventurous on tour, not through any kind of intellectual snobbery, but because the opportunities were too good to turn down, and I also found that it helped my cricket. The Afghan restaurant, in the heart of Peshawar's bullet-ridden old city, where I occasionally dragged Hussain and Thorpe, was a favourite – dimly lit, with only cushions to sit on, and live music from an instrument George Formby would have loved. You could even sneak in some wine of your own, if you so wished, provided that it was disguised in a plastic water bottle and drunk out of teacups. It could be argued that we were unprofessional to go there. We went without our armed guards (Peshawar is notoriously dangerous) and the lack of chairs, and spicy food, could have had disastrous consequences for my back, or bowels, or both. But a four-month cricket tour can be so claustrophobic and overwhelming that I found it was essential to get out and forget about cricket, if only so that I could arrive at the ground the next day with a fresh and uncluttered mind. There is nothing worse than constantly stewing in your room over a false shot or a dropped catch, and there are only so many plates of egg and chips at the British High Commission that a man can eat.

The lack of common ground between Alec and me was obvious, not just to us, but to distant observers as well. Because of that, I suspect that people thought there was some latent animosity between us that we fought constantly to keep under control, and out of sight. It simply did not exist. A generous amount of mutual respect, I think, underpinned the relationship, and I have the highest regard for his achievements as a pugnacious opening batsman and continually underrated wicket-keeper.

At the crease we were equally different, yet complementary. He gripped the bat high, right at the top of the handle, with his hands together. I gripped it lower with my hands slightly apart. It gave him better timing and more power and allowed me more manoeuvrability and softer hands in defence, especially against spin. He liked to move back as his initial movement and dominate from the start; I preferred to play forward and build momentum gradually. It was a good contrast and the main reason why we performed so well together at the top of the order, before his wicket-keeping duties brought an end to our opening partnership.

Unlike me, Stewart graced his hundredth Test with a glorious century. The West Indies bowled too short, as they often did to Stewart. It was a mystery to me why they continually did so because it was so clearly one of his strengths. Here, as he had been in Bridgetown six years before, Stewart was fearless and responded with rasping cuts, pulls and back-foot punches. As he brought up his 100, the Lancastrian crowd rose to acclaim him, and they gave him an ovation the like of which I have heard neither before nor since at Old Trafford. It was rare for northerners to take a southerner to heart, but they surely did that day.

At Headingley the series swung decisively in our favour. Swing was indeed the thing. White, Gough and Caddick tucked into a West Indies batting line-up that was looking increasingly fragile and short of confidence. The match was over in two days, Caddick's four wickets in an over reducing the West Indies to 61 all out second time around. We went to The Oval knowing that victory against the West Indies was a formality if we kept our heads.

Since the Zimbabwe series, I had been having a quiet spell. It wasn't that I was out of form – only at Old Trafford had I played poorly – but it was tough going against Ambrose and Walsh on pitches that were bowler friendly. My modest returns resulted in whisperings that I was going to be omitted from the final game. My place was confirmed the day before the match and I looked forward to proving the doubters wrong.

The Oval pitch was also bowler friendly. After the first morning, deliveries dug into its loose surface, causing them to stop, and resulting in a surface that was two-paced and sometimes uneven. I instinctively felt it was the type of surface that would suit me. It demanded good judgement of length and sure shot selection, and benefited players such as Graham Thorpe and me, who manoeuvred the ball around and played late, rather than the big shot makers such as Stewart, Hick and Lara.

My intuition was right; I scored 83 and 108 in over twelve hours of batting. Only one other batsman scored a half-century in the match, and in our second innings my 100 was four times the next highest contribution. I needed my share of luck, however. In one over, Walsh beat my outside edge four times. After the third, he stood exasperated in the middle of the wicket, rubbed his hands together as if he was releasing some magic dust, and shouted 'Kazam!' and wandered back, more hopefully, to his mark. I played at and missed the next ball and this time he just lifted his eyes and hands to the heavens and trudged off to fine-leg. The ovation that greeted my 100 on Stewart's home ground, matched his on my home ground. I lifted my bat a third time to acknowledge the crowd and still it continued. It was really one of the most touching moments of my career.

The game encapsulated all that is good about cricket. As Curtly Ambrose walked to the crease for the last time, Nasser Hussain said to me, 'Shall we do something?' 'Absolutely,' I replied and without a signal from anyone the England team instinctively

acks, fissures and undulations. An unplayable pitch at Sabina Park led to the First Test of the 1997–98
ur being abandoned.

cision time. *Left to right:* M.A., Venkat, match referee Barry Jarman, Brian Lara and Steve Bucknor
pare to abandon the game.

On the brink of resignation, Antigua 1997.

A half century in Barbados 1998 brings a rare moment of relief.

Moments before my resignation speech in Antigua. Either side of me are Nasser Hussain and Alec Stewart, soon to jockey for position to be England's next captain.

classic confrontation with Allan Donald, Trent Bridge 1998.

eling the pain in Australia 1998–99. I really ought to have come home from that tour.

Above: An excellent partnership – Nasser Hussain and Duncan Fletcher.

Left: A rueful smile from Curtly Ambrose as he beats my outside edge again at Lord's 2001.

Below: Caddick giving Shivnarine Chanderpaul the treatment at Lord's. The West Indies' psychological dominance was broken in that match.

he Wisden trophy returns, and the people ·lebrate our triumph over the West Indies in 2001.

A match-winning performance at The Oval against the West Indies and a touching reaction from the crowd.

he one hundredth Test for Alec Stewart and me, Old Trafford 2001. The fullness in my face betrays the fects of the drugs (prednisolene) that I was on at the time.

Nasser Hussain and Graham Thorpe celebrate our amazing win in Karachi in 2001. By this stage, the sun had gone down and night was closing in rapidly.

Mark Butcher celebrates his match-winning innings against Australia in 2002. It was the best innings I have seen from an England player.

o regrets, but a tear or two. Bowing out at The Oval against Australia in 2002.

On holiday in Jamaica, 1998, with my girlfriend Isabelle.

lined up to give him a guard of honour in his last game. As he and his great mate Courtney Walsh left the field for the last time, the crowd rose to them. Ambrose symbolically removed his trademark white armbands, as if to say 'Enough', safe in the knowledge that his legs would have to do no more pounding. It was a wise decision. Australia, where they were due next, is no place for old bones.

On the final morning, as victory awaited us, masses of people filled The Oval. This was a different crowd, not the usual corporate set, or those who had pre-booked tickets. This was truly the people's crowd. They queued long and early down the Harleyford Road, ready to see a bit of history and the West Indian shackles broken, and Surrey wisely opened the empty hospitality boxes to increase capacity for those struggling to get in. Some could not gain entry, and settled for listening to the roars coming from inside. Walsh, finally, was lbw to Cork. Nasser Hussain fell to his knees, pope-like, with his head in his hands. The Wisden Trophy had come back to Lord's after twenty-seven long years of West Indian custody.

The team was beginning to look more settled and confident. Trescothick and Vaughan represented a new generation of batsmen to complement the old guard. Gough and Caddick were benefiting greatly from being withdrawn regularly from county cricket, and Craig White was flourishing under Duncan Fletcher's patronage. Only the spin department was a worry – doubly so since Pakistan and Sri Lanka, where spin dominated, were the venues for our winter tour.

I knew my time at the top was drawing to a close. I had another cortisone injection in my back the day before we left for Pakistan and Brad Williamson, my surgeon, indicated that he was unwilling to give me any more. I was, literally, on my last legs. But it was a tour that I desperately wanted to go on. Due to a quirk of the fixture list, we had not toured the sub-continent since India and Sri Lanka in 1992–93, and my limited involvement on that tour meant I had never really proved myself in Asia against spin. It was an omission I wanted to put right before I finished. Succeed there and I could say that I had scored runs in every part of the world.

Pakistan was sure to be testing. In Saqlain Mushtaq and Mushtaq Ahmed they had two of the best spinners in the world; the two, in fact, whom I had most difficulty reading from the hand. Mushtaq bowled with a high arm and lots of over-spin (unlike Shane Warne who bowled with a low arm and lots of side spin). It meant Mushtaq spun the ball less than Warne, but also that he was harder to pick, there being less difference between his leg-spinner and his googly. Saqlain was the hardest of all. He had developed a delivery that spun to the off with just a flick of his fingers. I rarely picked him out of the hand.

There are three ways to pick a spinner – from the hand, in the air, or off the pitch. From the hand is best as it is the earliest and it gives a batsman the most time to decide what shot he should play. Off the pitch is the least satisfactory, as it gives him the least time. When I struggled to read a spinner out of the hand, I merely watched the ball carefully in the air to see which way the seam was spinning. I assumed this was what most batsmen did until I heard Geoffrey Boycott and Sunil Gavaskar in conversation, when both of them admitted they never saw the ball spinning in the air. I checked this with Boycott the next time I saw him, and he confirmed it to me.

Good eyesight is clearly advantageous to a batsman. In a random eye test sometime in the mid 1990s, Andrew Caddick and I had scored top marks among the England team. Lancashire employed an eye specialist from time to time, whose message was simply that the eye could be trained and improved like any other muscle in the body. He had devised a number of exercises to improve our eye muscles. One involved focusing and picking out a number of letters on a record that was being played at 45rpm, simulating, if you like, the spinning ball. For a while I had religiously followed these exercises until a combination of boredom, laziness and scepticism won the day.

During the First Test at Lahore, Marcus Trescothick had great difficulty picking up which way the ball was reverse swinging. When I was on strike, however, I was able to see the ball clearly in the bowler's hand as he was running in to bowl. I was able to work out from where the shiny side was, which way the ball was going to swing. Trescothick could not; so during our first innings partnership of 134, we devised a method whereby, when Trescothick was on strike and I was at the non-striker's end, I would look for the shiny side and stand with my bat in my left hand for the inswinger (to him) and my right hand for the outswinger. This worked perfectly until Trescothick wrote about the ploy in his *Mail on Sunday* column the following summer. Thereafter Pakistan's bowlers ran up covering the ball with both hands, so that neither of us could see.

As well as being able to pick the spinners, at least in the air, I gradually got back to how I used to play spin at the start of my career. Our absence from the sub-continent for a decade, and the prevalence of seam-based bowling in England, meant I had become rusty. Gradually I lowered my stance to a more squat position. As a result, I felt closer to the ball and better able to pick up length, and I felt the rhythm of playing spin bowling coming back to me. I scored 73 in the first innings at Lahore and a match-saving 65* in the second at Faisalabad. Both matches were dull affairs, but we were hanging in and getting to grips with what was a new challenge for everyone. We hoped that the pressure on the home side in the final Test in Karachi, where Pakistan had never lost a Test, would be in our favour.

In reply to Pakistan's first innings of 405, I scored a nine-hour 100 to drag us to near parity. It brought howls of protest and derision from Michael Henderson of the *Daily Telegraph*. Had I scored so slowly batting first, that would have been fair enough, but I knew that the only way we could win the match batting second was to get up to their first-innings score, no matter how long it took. I shrugged off the criticism, knowing that by the fifth morning we were the only team that could win the match.

It needed Pakistan to panic in their second innings and collapse under pressure, which they did. By mid afternoon on the last day we needed 176 from a minimum of forty-four overs. At lunchtime I had overheard Hussain, Thorpe and Fletcher debating whether I should be dropped down the order in the second innings run chase. Frankly, it pissed me off. As a batsman, you play according to the situation, and that was why I had cut out all risk in our first innings. I knew I had the shots for the second-innings scramble. They relented and I got us off to a little flier with a run a ball 26. As I walked off for tea, I turned to Inzamam-ul-Haq and said, 'We're going to beat you, you know.' He shook his head and said in his sonorous way, smiling. 'No, no. We'll never let you finish the match. It will get too dark.' Then he turned to his colleagues and said something in Urdu, at which they all laughed. The implication was, I think, that I was being wholly naïve if I thought Pakistan would let the match go to its natural conclusion. Inzi and his colleagues wandered off for their tea looking totally unconcerned.

I was out shortly after the break. Thereafter Moin Khan did everything in his power to slow proceedings down; the bowlers were consulted after every delivery, and there were field changes every ball. There was even the old shoelace ploy. Then as darkness fell, Moin complained to umpire Bucknor that his fielders could not see the ball. Bucknor stood firm. At 5.30 the sirens from the local mosque sounded to indicate that the sun had gone down, and that the fast for the day (it was Ramadan) was over. We still needed a dozen runs, with Thorpe and Hussain at the crease.

The physio's room next to the main dressing room was a northern enclave; Michael Vaughan, Darren Gough and I were camped there, aware of the cricketing superstition that dictates you can't move seats while things are going well. The atmosphere was tense in a kind of will-we won't-we way, but also lighthearted. Vaughan was running a book on how long each over would take, while the dollar signs were whizzing in front of Gough's eyes. 'It will add a hundred grand to my benefit year if we can win this!'

The light faded rapidly. I am not sure that any eye exercises could prepare a batsman for batting in pitch darkness against Waqar Younis. From the side, I could see only shapes and shadows. I certainly couldn't see the ball, and so it looked as if Graham Thorpe was playing shadow shots for a while. I'm certain he couldn't see the ball. Then with 6 runs needed to win, we heard the sound of leather on willow, and looked about wildly. Inzamam at deep cover sensed the ball was coming his way and stood imploringly with his arms outstretched, his feet wide apart. The ball passed by five yards to his right and still he stood motionless.

At the moment of victory we rushed next door to join the rest. Craig White was brandishing his bat around like a madman, and belted me on the end of the nose. Andrew Caddick replicated the ritual champagne moment in this alcohol-free zone by opening a bottle of fizzy pop over everyone. The presentations, minutes later, took place under a clear night sky, with the moon and the stars now shining brightly. Inzamam had tears in his eyes. I received the man of the match award, and we became the first England team to win a Test in Pakistan for thirty-nine years.

Throughout this run of success Nasser Hussain had been in horrible form. It started with an overemphasis on technique and nets and continued through a couple of sloppy shots against Zimbabwe. By the time he completed a pair at The Oval against the West Indies, his game, and mind, were shot to pieces. In Pakistan things got no better. The team had been winning, though, and so the pressure had not really started to mount. The general perception, however, as we prepared for the second half of the winter in Sri Lanka, was that he needed runs desperately.

During the international matches, he rarely let his poor form affect his captaincy. But after we were defeated in the searing heat of the First Test at Galle, another match in which Hussain failed with the bat, it was clear that he was close to the end of his tether. He was looking tired and drawn, and struggling to sleep at night, taking instead to wandering the corridors of the hotel in the early hours of the morning. After the match he came to my room. He wasn't sure, he said, how long he could continue in his present frame of mind, and he wanted to know the feelings of the team. I told him, honestly, that the team were all behind him and willing him to do well. I tried to offer the kind of support Graham Gooch had given me during my troubles in 1994. I also told him that he might consider dropping down the order, if not now, then certainly in the summer. For a highly strung character such as Hussain, batting at number three rarely gives you time to get the captaincy in the field out of your system. A move to number five would give him more breathing space.

The Asgiriya Stadium, Kandy, the scene for the Second Test, at least held some happy memories for Hussain. It was here in 1987, on our England Young Cricketers tour, that he had demolished Sri Lanka Young Cricketers with 170. It was at the same venue in 2001 that he finally emerged from the doldrums; his 109 didn't have the brilliance or fluency of his innings fourteen years before, but back then we were all innocent – naïve, unencumbered and unaware of the funny tricks that cricket can play on your mind.

We won a fractious match. Sri Lanka's captain, Sanath Jayasuriya, was caught off a bump ball and given out. Halfway to the pavilion, he flung away his gloves and helmet in disgust. Then Graeme Hick was caught legitimately and given not out. He hung around a while longer until finally dismissed for a tortured duck. 'Shit,' he said on his return, 'I'd have walked for the catch, if I'd known I was going to make such a prick of myself afterwards.' He was another having a bad trot, and it was good he could continue to laugh at himself. Later, I caught a legitimate catch at slip and, amid all the confusion, it was referred to the third umpire who gave it not out. Although there was a history of bad blood between the teams, emanating from a one-day international in Adelaide in 1998, in this instance the warring came from the players' frustrations with the standard of umpiring.

Graham Thorpe was our match winner in the Third Test in Colombo. I knew from his time at Lancashire that Muralitharan had a mental block bowling to left-handers, and Trescothick and Thorpe had taken advantage of this throughout the tour. Gradually Thorpe imposed a kind of dominance over Muralitharan, in the same way that Brian Lara did a year later. In the first innings, Thorpe scored an undefeated 113, and in the second, when we were wobbling chasing 74, he scored 32*. By the end, Muralitharan was bowling without any hint of his usual confidence. While Muralitharan has a kind of freakish brilliance, he lacks Shane Warne's craftiness and know-how.

Chaminda Vaas had my number throughout the Sri Lankan series, and I contributed little to our victory, but I could look back on a year in which I had top scored in three of the four series we had won. Nasser Hussain, despite his poor run of form, could reflect with pride on a team transformed. It had been a stormy passage at times but now he, and I, had beaten every Test-playing country in a Test series, bar Australia. As the light faded in Colombo, the England team – a proud and committed England team – did the now customary lap of honour. The Barmy Army seemed excited too, and optimistic, as cries of 'Bring on the Aussies!' reverberated around the stadium.

20

BOWING OUT

There are few, if any, fairytale endings in sport. My plan was to bow out at The Oval with 100, Australia vanquished, the Ashes ours at last and a career fulfilled. Given our progression in the last year, and Australia's failure on the sub-continent (where we had succeeded), it was not an unreasonable dream. Duncan Fletcher and Nasser Hussain did their utmost to play down expectations, but the country would have none of it and Australia's visit was eagerly anticipated. In the end, the 2001 Ashes series proved to be the most one-sided that I played in and, as you will be aware by now, that was quite an achievement.

Before the First Test, the battle between Glenn McGrath and me was seen as pivotal to the outcome of the series. McGrath was a bowler against whom I had struggled before. Strangely, the first time I played against him in Brisbane in 1994, he bowled so moderately that I thought him the least impressive of the Australian bowlers I had seen. He was dropped immediately after that game, and although he returned for the last Test in Perth and bowled much better, I didn't think at that stage he was someone to lose sleep over.

When Australia came to England in 1997, McGrath was very much their spearhead, and as I was playing moderately at the time, he began to cause problems for me. I had a tendency to go across my crease when I was playing badly, instead of moving down the pitch. McGrath got so close to the stumps and bowled so straight that I found, as a result, I was playing across the ball too often. During that series he dismissed me seven times.

On our next tour of Australia a year later, my back problems meant I was a sitting duck for his bouncer, which was invariably straight and head high. I played the game before the First Test in complete spasm and needed four cortisone injections to ensure my place in the starting line-up in Brisbane. I played on throughout the series until my withdrawal in Sydney but was stiff and immobile at the crease for much of the time. McGrath preyed on this weakness and I was suckered in to taking on his bouncer, rather than evading it, with disastrous results.

When a bowler dismisses you so often it becomes a mental problem. On paper there was no reason why I should not have been successful against McGrath. After all, Shaun Pollock was virtually a carbon copy – quickish, close to the stumps, plenty of bounce and just doing a little with the ball either way – and he had dismissed me just six times in three full series. But bad memories of a bowler prey on your mind and near the end of my career I felt I was less mentally strong than before and they were therefore harder to overcome. The Australians were quick to remind me of my frailty and rarely an innings went by without some mention of it from the slips – 'Come on McGrath, let's make it number thirteen!'

I was more nervous than usual, therefore, as I padded up before both captains went out to toss at Edgbaston. I knew we would be batting – Nasser wanted to bat first and I had noticed Steve Waugh's new policy of inserting the opposition, almost regardless, during their home series against the West Indies. Mark Taylor had nearly always batted first; Waugh recognised that, with Shane Warne no longer the force of old, his team's strength now lay in pace not spin, and he preferred to give his quick bowlers the first chance to exploit whatever was in the wicket.

My mouth was so dry with nerves that I had to call for a drink in the second over after Jason Gillespie dismissed Marcus Trescothick. Throughout the series Trescothick struggled with

Gillespie in the same way that I did with McGrath. Gillespie pitches the ball a yard further up than any other international opening bowler and, as Trescothick moves his feet less than any other opening batsman, it was the first time I had really seen the Somerset man troubled in Test cricket. Over the next few Ashes series that will be a key confrontation.

Nasser Hussain was feeling as tense as I was in the build-up to the match. The edifice that he and Duncan Fletcher had been trying to build was beginning to crumble at an unfortunate time. He was recovering from a broken finger sustained against Pakistan earlier in the summer and there were fresh injuries to Graham Thorpe and Michael Vaughan. The day before the match we practised on some poor wickets and Hussain exploded during his net. He was still simmering when his team-talk took place.

The injuries created a hole where the middle order should have been and the selectors gave a debut to Usman Afzaal of Nottinghamshire. On the morning of the match I wished him good luck.

'Thank you, Sir,' he replied, looking at me with star-struck eyes, no doubt in the same way that I had looked at David Gower over a decade earlier.

'There's no need to call me Sir, we're on the same side.'

'Okay, Sir.'

Two winters earlier, on an internal flight in South Africa, I had sat next to a young player's girlfriend and had observed her A level revision. I was definitely beginning to feel like the elder statesman in the team, despite the fact that I was only thirty-three and years younger than Alec Stewart.

On the first morning of the series I played confidently and well. I escaped McGrath's clutches although as the series wore on he would definitely win that battle, dismissing me six times in all. The Australians had talked up Brett Lee but when he came on he bowled at medium pace and I pulled him hard in front of square during a century stand with the recalled Mark Butcher.

After lunch, our revamped middle order was blown away. Australia replied after tea and a pumped-up Michael Slater, all emotion and aggression, took 18 off Darren Gough's opening over. I wandered past him and said, 'I see you've been on the Prozac again, Slats.' I realised that Test cricket, of the type played by this Australian team, was not the same Test cricket that I had been introduced to in 1989.

In the second innings we faced a heavy innings defeat. Jason Gillespie hit Nasser Hussain on the hand and Hussain's fragile fingers betrayed him again. Alec Stewart had captained previously in Hussain's absence but during the triangular series against Pakistan and Australia, Stewart had taken a fair amount of personal criticism. As Hussain retired hurt, I sat next to Stewart and looked at him quizzically. Without a word he looked at me, smiled, and shook his head. I laughed – we were both thinking the same thing. With Hussain and Thorpe injured, and Stewart unwilling, I left Edgbaston knowing that the selectors would come knocking on my door.

When I resigned the captaincy on Antiguan soil in 1998, I promised myself that, in the unlikely event of being asked, I would never take on the challenge again. After all it wasn't as though my tenure had been prematurely curtailed – fifty-two games was ample opportunity to try to make a difference. As I have said, I was acutely aware of the need to stay in the background and let whoever was captain get on with the job without distraction. For that reason I had declined to take the reins again at Old Trafford in 1999 when Nasser Hussain was injured for the first time.

The day after the Test, a Monday, I went to fish the Derbyshire Wye and to think things through. I had been introduced to fishing by John Barclay on our 1996 South African tour, and had found it to be the perfect antidote to the pressure of international sport. Content with my own company and possessing patience in abundance, I was ready made for it. That is not to say I was any good – as Barclay and trout the world over, from the

Drakensburg in South Africa to Lake Taupo in New Zealand, would testify.

As I jointed my rod in anticipation, I realised that I was in a unique situation. The obvious candidate, Thorpe, was injured and not certain to play at Lord's while Stewart and Butcher had publicly ruled themselves out that morning. That left Marcus Trescothick and me. I knew how much Duncan Fletcher wanted to avoid burdening Trescothick at this stage of his career and so I was not surprised, halfway through a blank and fishless day, to get a call from the coach to see if I would help out. I told him I would.

Three days later, David Graveney confirmed that the selectors wanted me to captain the team at Lord's. As in 1993, my appointment followed an innings defeat by a rampant Australian team. Once more I found myself thrust into the media spotlight and felt the keen sense of anticipation of a challenge ahead. I immediately spoke to the senior players – Thorpe, Trescothick, Stewart, Caddick and Gough – to gauge their reaction and get their feelings about the team for the Second Test. The consensus was that we needed to strengthen our bowling attack. At the management meeting prior to the First Test, both Marcus Trescothick and I had argued for an extra seamer. Craig White had only just returned from injury and had bowled little and we argued that, on seamer-friendly wickets, he and Ashley Giles were insufficient support for Caddick and Gough. The general feeling, and one that I agreed with, was that neither White nor Dominic Cork (who seemed to have temporarily lost his swing) were adequate third seamers although either was fine as a fourth. To a man, we felt that Martin Bicknell, as an experienced and in form pitch-up swing bowler, would be the perfect foil for the more aggressive Gough and Caddick. I relayed our thoughts to the selectors.

As I travelled to Old Trafford on the Sunday for our National League match against Durham, I listened to the radio announcement of the Test team with more interest than I had done for a while. To my surprise, Chris Silverwood and Alex Tudor were selected in the squad; Silverwood had not really figured in our discussions and days earlier Tudor had been considered too big a fitness risk for a five-day game. David Graveney rang me to say that they wanted to give Dominic Cork one last chance at his favourite hunting ground.

In the event, the selectors shied away from selecting Bicknell, a thirty-two year old who had looked innocuous the day before during the Benson & Hedges final. That was their prerogative. David Graveney and Geoff Miller are two of the best selectors to serve English cricket in recent times. At times, however, the selection process still lacks transparency and is confused: where does the ultimate responsibility for selection lie, and what precisely is the input of the captain and coach?

At Lord's I felt that there were two areas in particular that needed immediate surgery. The fielding at Edgbaston had been sloppy and we needed more intensity. Somehow we also had to box more cleverly in the field. We had to move quicker between attack and defence to strangle Australia's aggressive instincts – their publicly stated intent was to score at more than 4 runs an over – and make them choke on their arrogance.

I was hopeful that my captaincy skills wouldn't be too rusty; although I hadn't captained any team for over two years I always asked myself, in every game, what moves I would be making. It kept my mind sharp if nothing else. As I walked to the toss with Steve Waugh, I felt a keen sense of anticipation, but nothing like the excitement I had felt on captaining my country for the first time in 1993. After all, I was a stand-in only, and I didn't feel it was my team in the same way as I had between 1994 and 1998.

We struggled to 121–4 on a dank and dismal first day. After we had been bowled out for 187 on the second, there was, at least, some immediate improvement in the field. By bowling straight at Michael Slater we denied him room to free his arms and play his shots. Denying Slater width was like starving a man of oxygen, and he scored just 25 out of the first 100 (Hayden and Ponting were dismissed cheaply) before, asphyxiated, he tried to swat Caddick to square-leg. At the end of the second day Australia led by 68 with five wickets in hand.

The next day, as a window of opportunity presented itself, we dropped Adam Gilchrist four times on his way to a match-winning 100. We had begun to drop catches at the start of the summer against Pakistan, but four in one session was excessive even by our standards. Who knows why we suddenly became butter-fingered? Perhaps the injuries had created an unsettled slip cordon. More likely, I think, was that the fielders realised that Gilchrist was an explosive batsman. A dropped catch could prove to be disastrously expensive, and their hands unconsciously tensed up and became harder. Soft and relaxed hands are the keys to good catching.

We had to win at Trent Bridge to keep the series alive and I worked doubly hard on my batting before the match. I got there a day early, and stayed behind each day for extra practice. I felt that in the first two Tests I had played well on difficult wickets, and that a big score was around the corner. McGrath bowled the second ball of the match to me; it pitched halfway down and I dropped my hands to let the ball pass harmlessly by. It didn't bounce as much as I anticipated and it brushed my back forearm. I immediately feared the worst and looked up to see John Hampshire raising his arm. All that preparation and hard work for nothing.

I sat in the dressing room disconsolate. After a while, Duncan Fletcher came up to me and said, 'I don't want to hear your views on technology ever again!' I laughed; it was a running joke between us. Fletcher is adamant that an increased use of technology to help umpires with lbws and caught behinds, as well as line decisions, will improve the percentage of correct decisions and make the game fairer. I am against it. Of course, in the moments immediately after a bad decision, it is easy to wish for a different outcome, but on balance I still disagree with Fletcher.

Umpires, like players, are human and will make mistakes, and without mistakes it would be a dull game indeed. The essence of the game lies in its human element – the frailties, the errors and the often irrational emotional responses that characterise us as living, feeling beings rather than automatons. A batsman must learn to accept his fate – the unplayable delivery, the brilliant catch, a spiteful pitch, a poor decision. These things are beyond his control and how he copes with these setbacks is part of the challenge of the game. Life is not fair – why should cricket be any different?

In any event, there is no guarantee that increased technology will produce an error-free nirvana. Recently, umpires have been able to refer uncertain catches to the third umpire for confir-mation. This extension of the third umpire's role has led to more, not less, controversy and a greater number of errors than before. It may be an old-fashioned viewpoint but I believe that things do even themselves out, and that good teams and good players come through in the end. That the umpire's decision is final is the basic tenet around which the game is based; increased use of technology would further weaken umpires' authority, and therefore the game itself.

As I sat stewing in the Trent Bridge changing rooms, I some-how had to put the disappointment to one side. I had a team to lead, and runs to score next time around. After being bowled out for 185 in just over half a day, we, in turn, reduced Australia to 105–7 by its end. As we left the field to a rousing reception, I dreamed briefly of what could be, and what might have been. The next day Australia scrambled to 190 and I set out to put the duck in the first innings behind me. On 51 I pushed forward to a Shane Warne leg-break that spun and missed my outside edge by an inch or so. There was a huge appeal. Not again, surely? This time Venkat raised the crooked finger of doom and again I was sent on my way. Of course, it was hard to take, but walking back to the pavilion, my wry smile reflected the fact that I had more than paid my dues for the let-off against Allan Donald at this very ground three years earlier.

My unfortunate departure, and Marcus Trescothick's bizarre dismissal – he swept Warne only to see the ball bounce up off short-leg's ankle – sparked a collapse that left Australia needing only 158 for victory. At 88–3 with Steve Waugh stretchered off after ripping his calf, they were wobbling. At this point, Australian teams of the past might have panicked, but now Damien Martyn and Mark Waugh played a flurry of shots and they eased past the victory target. Halfway through another Ashes series, the outcome had been decided.

This realisation, and the knowledge that, for one or two of us, our Ashes hopes were over for good, left a dressing room that was sombre and silent. Nasser Hussain had gone home a day earlier, and somebody had to say something, so I tried to capture the mood. I acknowledged that the end was approaching for one or two, but that for others, such as Trescothick and Tudor, this defeat should signal the start of a quest. Australia represented the benchmark to aim at. It was no disgrace to lose to them now, and overhauling them was a challenge worth pursuing. It wouldn't be straightforward but then nothing worth achieving is ever easy.

Knowing what to say is sometimes hard as well. At least my inadequate words brought some closure to the first half of the summer. We could move on afresh. Besides, I believed in what I was saying. The Australians *had* taken the game on to a new level that summer. The aggressive batting of their middle and lower-middle order was the best that I had seen. Although their catching and bowling was a little overrated, they deserved the plaudits as one of the very best teams of the modern age.

Despite the fact that my international career started with a 4–0 defeat by Australia and ended with a 4–1 defeat, ashes to ashes if you like, there is no doubt in my mind that England have also improved in that period. Central contracts have given the England team a better chance of success than before but I still feel that we can do more. I talked with Duncan Fletcher about the need for a more hands-on approach to managing

England players but he did not agree. His coaching background is in a country (South Africa) where there is an in-built culture of self-motivation and hard work. I am not sure that this exists sufficiently in English cricket yet. Players go away after each Test and are left to their own devices for a week; not all will do the training or practice expected of them.

There ought to be a national facility where the England coach can work with the players, and where those injured or recovering can be sent for treatment. It is right to rest players and withdraw them from county games; it is also the perfect time to do some quality practice and preparation, given the right kind of facility and complete contractual control over the players.

Graham Thorpe's injury during the Ashes series was a case in point; once injured he left England's control and returned to Surrey. There was little further communication between the player and the England set-up. Steve Waugh, under constant supervision from the Australian physiotherapist, got fit in half the time. The time has come to centralise completely the management of England players, by placing our élite cricketers under contract to the ECB alone, rather than to England and their counties. It would prevent that kind of *laissez-faire* attitude to Thorpe's injury and recovery. It would result in a more professional and successful system.

As the majority of the team left Trent Bridge, I stayed behind with Alec Stewart to reflect on the series and share a beer with some of the Aussies. Shane Warne came up for a drink and I discussed retirement with him. He cautioned against it; he too had felt that way a year earlier and had found a second wind and was now enjoying his cricket more than ever. Suddenly from behind came a familiar voice. 'Oi, arsewipe, fancy a beer?' I didn't have to look around to know who it was. Merv Hughes was leading a tour group and judging by his spreading girth, he was certainly enjoying retirement. I accepted the beer.

During the next few days there was inevitably some harsh criticism of my captaincy. It didn't really matter now, but irritatingly I was still niggled by it. In fact, I had captained well at Trent Bridge; in bowling out Australia for 190 in the first innings it was the only time in the whole series that we were competitive in the field. In the other three games that I did not captain, Australia's first innings scores were 576, 447 and 641–4 declared.

Thankfully, however, Hussain recovered in time to take his rightful place at the head of affairs for the next Test at Headingley. Before that, Lancashire had a semi-final to play against Leicestershire at Grace Road. As I was driving there, Hussain phoned me. 'There's a problem,' he said. 'Butch has been seen out late during the Trent Bridge Test. The selectors are livid and want to drop him for a game. What do you think?' I told him I thought the selectors harsh. We had no formal curfew rules and he wouldn't be the first England player to have stayed out beyond midnight during a Test match. Besides, after a difficult year in which his private life had been confused and his cricket a mess, Butcher was now feeling good about himself and his game. A ban would knock him back badly. Hussain agreed and no doubt managed to persuade the selectors to change their minds.

Nine days later at Headingley, as we chased 315 for victory, Butcher played the best attacking innings I had seen in thirteen years as an England player. Earlier, I had gloved a McGrath lifter and I sat on the balcony alone to watch our innings. Butcher immediately appeared calm and confident, his judgement of length superb. As the ball lost its hardness and bounce, he began to attack the Australian bowlers. It soon became apparent to me that something special was in the offing and, despite the cold, I sat glued to proceedings.

Butcher's success was a touching tale. He had spent the previous winter in the wilderness, working with his father, Alan, to restore his confidence and technique. In the early part of the summer he had languished in Surrey's second eleven; at Didsbury against Lancashire seconds, he was dismissed first ball and he walked off with the air of a man who had had his fill of the game. Now, at Headingley, he was cutting, pulling and driving his name into the history books. Butcher is one of cricket's characters, interesting and curious about life. It was good to see him finally break free from the shackles of mediocrity.

Adam Gilchrist was Australia's stand-in captain and had no answer. As Butcher passed 150 and we closed in on the target, the balcony gradually filled up. Nasser Hussain appeared and as Butcher square-drove Warne towards the cover boundary to clinch victory, I turned to our jubilant captain whose arms were aloft. 'All right, Brearley?' I joked. 'You're a lucky bastard.' He knew and I knew that without the rain on the fourth day, Australia would have been well out of reach and a whitewash a formality; and that this unlikely victory would further enhance his burgeoning reputation. He looked at me and winked. 'I'll keep conning them for a while yet,' he said.

Before my final Test at The Oval, both the Ashes and my retirement had been decided. Going into the game I felt deflated and flat, like a balloon that had been popped. It was so difficult to concentrate. During Australia's mammoth first innings, I found myself fielding at deep square-leg in front of the Archbishop Tenison's School; there were already two fielders behind square but I wandered yards to my right to make it three. Thankfully, neither Hussain nor the umpires noticed my error. One wag in the crowd did. 'Oi, Atherton, don't you know the rules?' he bellowed.

I wasn't the only one having a difficult match. Phil Tufnell had been recalled to his favourite hunting ground but had taken a mauling. Darren Gough and Alec Stewart had signalled their intention not to tour India, and were flapping about whether they would be allowed to go to New Zealand. It was an awkward time for Gough. He had recently fallen out with Yorkshire and the Ashes series had been a disappointment for him. When the second new ball came around, Hussain ignored the disgruntled

Yorkshireman. 'Right then, I'll bowl at medium pace to a ring of fielders like a change bowler should,' he quipped with a twinkle in his eye.

Alec Stewart was unhappy that his first winter off for a decade or more was going to be held against him. As I walked into the dressing room on the final morning, he was in the middle of a blazing row with Duncan Fletcher and Nasser Hussain. Fletcher, generally calm and fair, had a look in his eyes and I thought it wise to leave the dressing room and let them sort it out. I recalled similar scenes, at this very ground, against Pakistan five years earlier. Nasser probably had the same headache I had back then.

Meanwhile Australia had progressed serenely to 641–4 and had enforced the follow-on. On the Sunday evening I had played my final innings and now, as the team went out to prepare for the final day, I stayed in the dressing room for treatment. It was almost as if I was physically removing myself now that my contribution was done. I looked upon the match situation, and the problems, dispassionately, from a distance.

I was determined to enjoy my last day, however. Mostly, I watched on television from my corner in the dressing room trying to commit to memory a place I might never see again. To my left, Nasser Hussain's gear was strewn as messily as mine; to my right was Mark Butcher's locker with its inscription 'heavy drinking can cause confusion' – was that the basis of his brilliance days before? Opposite was Duncan Fletcher's clipboard with tactical advice on how to dismiss Australia's batsmen; next to Adam Gilchrist's name there was still a question mark. It didn't matter – at The Oval we couldn't even get him in for a second innings, never mind out.

In the afternoon Graham Thorpe hobbled in. 'I'm sorry to have missed your last game, Athers, but I'm proud to have played with you.' At the end, Duncan Fletcher gave a small speech of thanks for my efforts over the last fifteen years, and urged everyone to come to the dinner in my honour that night. I was getting a little emotional. Phil Tufnell sauntered over with a fag in his mouth and a sad look on his face. I took his limp, outstretched hand and awaited his eulogy. 'Athers . . . I bowled all right, didn't I? Jesus, I've gone for 170 on a "Bunsen" but I bowled well . . . didn't I?'

EPILOGUE

Mostly this book has been written at 'Riverrun', a remote cottage on the banks of the mighty Essequibo River in Guyana, South America. It is a place of strange creatures – the howler monkeys who provide a constant primordial backdrop and the 'six o'clock beetle' whose shrill cry at sun-up and sun-down announces each day's beginning and end; a place of strange people too – Orlando Fernando, Mr Duck and Mr Five – but that, I suppose, is another story.

It is also a quiet and peaceful place. For the local Amerindian population the rhythms of life are as simple and constant as the tide which ebbs and flows each day, a world away from the hustle and bustle of international cricket that has fulfilled me for the last fifteen years. As the moon rises over 'Shanklands' on the far side of the river, its light illuminating everything, it is clear that there is a life beyond cricket.

This winter, in between writing stints, I've enjoyed doing things that previously I haven't been able to do. I travelled with the players and directors of Manchester United to watch a Champions League match in Munich. I was intrigued by the restraints imposed on the players, a world away from the kind of freedom cricketers enjoy on tour. I sat next but one to Bobby Charlton on the return flight and, as we took off in freezing temperatures, I wondered how often he had flashbacks to that terrible night in Munich nearly half a century ago.

I went to both Cheltenham National Hunt festivals, in November and March. I backed a horse called Wemyss Quest in the three-mile novice hurdle in November, only to see it set off as if it was a five-furlong sprint and then pull up with two circuits to go. On a bitterly cold Gold Cup day in March, I watched from the royal box as Best Mate jumped his rivals into the ground.

The fishing rods are ready for action and a week in Russia on the Umba Peninsula awaits. In time, there will be plenty of fish to catch, horses to back, sports to watch, books to read, articles to write, places to go and friends to see. Every sportsman needs a hinterland; after all, 'what do they know of cricket, who only cricket know?'

That famous quote from the Caribbean writer C.L.R. James has been a leitmotif throughout my career. With the international cricket calendar increasingly crowded, and the dangers of fame and celebrity everywhere, I have desperately tried to stay grounded, keep a sense of perspective and stay interested – always a human being first and a cricketer second. In the end, I suppose, for the élite who play international cricket the game is inevitably all-consuming. For the rest, the 400 or so county cricketers in this country, I've come to realise that the narrow focus imposed by professional sport is a bad thing for those who play it and for the sport itself.

If this book has, to some extent, kept my life beyond cricket hidden, that is entirely my fault. The decision to write an autobiography at the grand old age of thirty-three wasn't easy in the first place. I felt that the one thing of note, and of real interest, that I've done is to play for and captain England.

A month after this book was finished my first son, Joshua, was born. He weighed 7lb 11oz and has long limbs and big feet. It is, of course, the defining moment of anybody's life and it changes everything. I hope to see more of him growing up than I might have done had I still been playing.

Of course, I still have an involvement in the game. I write on cricket for the *Sunday Telegraph* and I am thrilled to have been given the opportunity to join Channel 4's award-winning team. In their own way, and in a different sphere, Channel 4 and their production company Sunset and Vine are as dedicated and professional as any team I played in. The meetings I sat in prior to my 'debut' for them opened my eyes – maybe if I'd had the opportunity to do that while I was still playing my occasionally truculent relationship with the media would have been different. Maybe not.

On my first morning for Channel 4 at Lord's I wandered up to the entrance to the media centre. At the door was my boyhood hero David Gower, now of Sky Sports and 'They Think It's All Over'. He had forgotten his media pass and the doorman wouldn't let him in. 'Don't you know who this guy is?' I protested on David's behalf, as I showed my pass and prepared to enter. The doorman looked nonplussed for a moment and then his face brightened. 'Yeah! You're that comedian off the BBC!' How quickly people forget!

On my first day I made sure I sat in the box whenever Richie Benaud was commentating. During the afternoon Michael Slater was on air and was all of a muddle. He wanted to use the past tense of the word 'sneak', but wasn't sure whether it should be 'snuck' or 'sneaked'. He turned to the doyen of commentators, who was eating a sandwich and studying the form. 'Hey, Rich,' he whispered, 'can I use the word snuck, or is it sneaked? Whadya think?' Richie finished his sandwich and then ticked his fancy. Then, in characteristic fashion, he raised an eyebrow and half turned to Slater. 'Michael,' he said, 'quite a few "ucks" spring to mind but "sn" is not one of them.' Masterful.

Some sportsmen fall into the trap of thinking that they are irreplaceable. As I write this I have just seen my replacement at the top of the order, Michael Vaughan, score a Test century at Lord's, something I never managed to do. He is a Mancunian and a solid citizen – head still, feet moving forward and back according to length, a high elbow the fulcrum of his play, orthodox and stylish, a seamless transition. No, I don't think I shall be missed at all.

England Tour to South Africa and the World Cup 1995–96, Captain's Report

Selection

Contrary to the previous winter, I felt this was a well-selected squad. Bearing in mind the summer success against the West Indies, the selectors decided to keep faith with the players who had performed well. The only area of discussion on the batting front was whether to select a third opener. The feeling was that neither Gallian nor Knight at the moment had the necessary class, and would benefit from another A tour where they were likely to get more cricket. Ramprakash, on the back of an excellent domestic season, was preferred. Unfortunately, the move backfired. I felt the bowling possessed good variety: pace (Malcolm, Gough), left-arm (Ilott), swing (Cork, Martin) and two kinds of finger spin. Qualities the selectors were looking for were a good attitude, an aptitude for hard work and an ability to 'tough out' what was likely to be a tough tour with plenty of fast bowling. The fielding, while not as good as South Africa's, was adequate and few chances were spilled. There was little press or public criticism of the squad selected. It was a harmonious squad and one that gelled well together with a good back-up team of Barclay, Morton, Bell, Ashton *et al.*

One point for future discussion is the number of players we

take on tour. On all recent tours there have inevitably been one or two players who play very little cricket. On a full four-month tour I can see why we need a full complement of sixteen players. But on a modern tour, aside from international cricket, there is very little other cricket and whether we can reduce the number who tour needs to be considered carefully.

Finally, in September, the selectors decided to bring out four players to join the squad for the one-day internationals in South Africa in preparation for the World Cup. While it was necessary for these players to get some cricket, as they were wintering in England, it made life extremely difficult in South Africa. The problems of running two campaigns at once were many: for the final two Tests we had twenty-two players – an unmanageable number. We had to tell certain players who were playing in the final Test match that they were going to be travelling home – hardly ideal preparation for the Cape Town Test. In many ways, with the World Cup coming on the back of the South African tour, these problems were inevitable, but it reflects badly on the planning by the overseas committee that a prestigious once-every-four-years tournament should follow an arduous four-month tour.

Planning and preparation

I am a firm believer that planning and preparation are the best means to achieving success. As per last winter, because the tour followed so quickly on the back of the domestic season there was little time to prepare. Is it only a coincidence that England teams of late have played their best overseas cricket in the West Indies where adequate preparation time is allowed? Future planning needs to discuss whether we can achieve shorter tours and give more time for preparation. I agree a full five-match tour of Australia is necessary but is it necessary every winter? Shorter tours would allow more rest/preparation, which I believe would lead to greater success.

A comparison with the South African team might serve a purpose here. They had five months off prior to our tour – a series they viewed as of the utmost importance. In that time they prepared as a team together with a series of training camps that included all aspects of cricket, physical, technical, mental etc. Their view was that the longer the series went, the more tired we would become in comparison with their fresh legs. This was borne out. While I mention this, I realise the inherent problems in giving our players enough rest. However, it illustrates the different approaches in preparation by the two sides, which is probably reflected in the final result.

Itinerary

Before I try to point out the faults in the itinerary I should mention that it was better than a few of recent memory. There was certainly good preparation time prior to the First Test and the squad benefited from practising at altitude on the high veldt. The fact that there was a four-day game between each Test was good and I also like an itinerary where the one-day internationals are in one batch, unlike Australia.

However, there were some negatives, which hopefully the next touring party to South Africa will avoid. If the First Test is at altitude, it is imperative that the game immediately prior to it is at altitude as well. The games in between the Test matches need to be at good grounds against good opposition. Prior to the Third Test we were at Paarl and prior to the Fourth Test we were at Pietermaritzburg. Neither venues or opposition were of the quality needed prior to a Test match.

While I accept that this touring party was the first to South Africa for thirty years and there were political considerations as well, it is vital that we stand up for ourselves and don't get pushed around by foreign cricket boards. How we accepted seven one-day internationals in a fortnight all at different venues is a mystery to me. If there was one overwhelming reason for the unsuccessful second half of the winter, it was this fortnight period – it induced fatigue from which we were not to recover. We were playing against a fresher side and the defeats in this period were extremely damaging to our confidence and morale, which continued into the World Cup period. The well-being of our players should be of paramount importance and it angers me that our board should adhere to the wishes of the South African board at the expense of our physical well-being.

Performance

South Africa were an extremely well-drilled side and to beat them at home would have been a considerable achievement. I felt the two sides were evenly matched and that it would be a close series which we would narrowly win by a match or so. We recognise that we have certain limitations in our bowling: the lack of a top-class fast bowler and wrist spinner. But within those limitations, I thought we performed well. Dominic Cork was our strike bowler and had an outstanding series: around him the others performed to par and we were disciplined. South Africa never exposed our limitations and topped 400 only once. Our fielders, again while not as naturally gifted as South Africa's, backed up our bowlers and few chances were spilled. In all, we had a fairly tight grip on the game in the field.

It was in the batting department, an area where I expected few problems, that we struggled. Five players (Atherton, Stewart, Hick, Thorpe and Smith) have career Test averages of around 40 and I envisaged us posting some challenging scores. Only at Centurion Park, however, did we bat well as a unit and if a reason is to be sought for our ultimate failure then it must be here. Certainly Atherton, Stewart, Thorpe and Hick ought to be a nucleus for years to come, but maybe we need to look to the younger element: certainly Crawley needs an extended chance. Overall the batting was disappointing, all the more so as this was our perceived strength.

We were unfortunate with the weather at Centurion Park. We posted a challenging score only to be thwarted by the rain. At the Wanderers we underperformed but managed a draw – a good sign as this was surely a match we would have lost a few years ago. Similarly at Port Elizabeth we secured an honourable draw and looked as likely to win the match as lose it. Rain affected the third match at Durban. For the deciding Test, we gambled on a fifth bowler – a gamble well worth taking but one that ultimately backfired. All in all, it was a hard-fought series, narrowly going to South Africa but one in which we competed all the way.

One-day internationals

As mentioned previously, the nature of the itinerary and the comings and goings of players presented huge difficulties. We also made some mistakes: in trying to prepare for the World Cup, too many changes were made to the side and not enough importance was given to getting into a groove and getting a winning run together. We failed to adapt to the fifteen-over rule well enough: I feel the absence of such a rule in England puts us at a huge disadvantage and I'm glad to see that we've rectified this. I must also admit to being completely drained at this stage. Tiredness and disappointment over the Test result played its part. Certainly during the second half of the winter, my batting form declined along with the general form of the side. Again, fatigue was a crucial factor.

Management

The back-up team were excellent and a pleasure to work with. Both Wayne Morton and John Barclay were well respected and appreciated by the team, who I am sure would welcome their involvement again. Malcolm Ashton seemed an excellent choice as scorer and eased the financial burden on the manager.

Raymond Illingworth has a knowledge of cricket and cricketers second to none in England. I feel that after some early hiccups I have established a good working relationship with him. However, having talked to him both prior to and after the tour, I did not feel that he wanted the involvement of touring again. Touring is an arduous business and I feel that the team needs a younger full-time coach. This is in no way 'back-stabbing' Raymond, who I assume will remain as Chairman of Selectors, as I have spoken to him personally about it.

But I do feel that the team has suffered from the lack of a full-time and permanent coach. The team needs a coach who will run a good practice efficiently, enthusiastically and innovatively, while at the same time having good technical expertise and being a positive influence around the dressing room.

While the two specialist coaches were dedicated to their task I do not feel that this is the way forward. Certainly if specialists are required, then the coach ought to have a budget to employ them whenever the situation arises. But I do not feel the presence of specialist coaches for two days prior to a Test match or for the first match of a tour is a professional approach.

For the domestic 1996 season and beyond, the employment of the right man as coach is the most pressing concern. It is a vital role.

Fitness/physical

For the first time in my career we took a doctor, Phillip Bell, on tour. Phillip was well liked and respected by the players. It was apparent, however, that other than routine medical treatments (stitches, malarials etc) there was little for him to do. I know that Phillip has specialist sports medicine training and it seems to me that unless we utilise that more, it is difficult to justify the role of a doctor on tour if restricted merely to perfunctory medical tasks. Obviously my lack of medical knowledge inhibits me here but this is something that Wayne Morton and Phillip can discuss with the board in future.

Wayne Morton proved himself to be an exceptional physio-therapist. Clearly he ought to be involved with the England team for many years to come and have complete control over the physical well-being of the team.

Although we suffered fewer injuries than on the previous tour, we do suffer more than other teams (we were the only team to send two players home from the World Cup). Clearly this is no mere accident; it is a result of overplaying. Obviously, the problems that Dominic Cork experienced during the World Cup were as a result of the amount of overs he was asked to bowl throughout the calendar year. Considering especially the need to look after our premier players (in particular fast bowlers), it seems to me the sooner we can ensure these players are under TCCB contracts all year round the better. I do not see this as diminishing county cricket, merely a common-sense reaction to the ever-increasing demands placed on international players.

South Africa – a comparison

It was an extremely interesting tour to South Africa and I offer a comparison with them only as a means of achieving greater success for England.

In the short time that they have been re-involved in international cricket, South Africa have formed themselves into not the best but the most professional of teams. Obviously our systems differ but the quicker we can match their efficiency the better.

Their strengths are: strong management/team structure; an innovative coach who runs a quality practice; they are fresh and well prepared for each series; and they have good press management – they lead rather than are led by their press.

In all these areas we can improve. I do not want to get too negative because, in preparation, I believe we are only behind Australia/South Africa – but the point is that we want to be the best. Obviously the board cannot play for the players but they can give the players the very best environment in which to perform and give them the very best chance of success.

The World Cup

Naturally, for all involved, the World Cup was an extreme disappointment. While I went with a positive and optimistic attitude, in hindsight the damage to our campaign had already been done. The period of the one-day internationals in South Africa turned a confident team into a fatigued team lacking in confidence. This was only ten days before the World Cup campaign started, and the scars remained and were difficult to remove.

We felt that the first week in Lahore was a crucial week. We trained and practised hard. While the quality of the practice facilities was decidedly average, the team coped well. Contrary to public perception, this was not a whingeing team and the need not to get upset by the difficult nature of the sub-continent was constantly emphasised by the management.

In many ways, the intensity and quality of the practice sessions were the best of the winter, but as I have said the damage had been done. Only early wins would strengthen our fragile confidence and so the early defeat by New Zealand and the early dropped catches were, in hindsight, extremely damaging.

We failed to adapt as well as other teams to the fifteen-over rule, and I think its introduction into our domestic cricket will be beneficial by the time the next World Cup comes around.

Finally, while this winter finished on an extremely disappointing note, it should not be forgotten that for the first three months of the winter it was perceived that we were on an upward curve, having drawn with the West Indies and reaching Cape Town with a chance of winning the winter series. Amid all the doom and gloom that must not be forgotten. It was a long and arduous winter and I would like to thank all the management and back-up for their continuing support during some trying times.

M.A. ATHERTON
April 1996

CAREER STATISTICS

Compiled by Vic Issacs

TEST CAREER

Series by series

	M	I	NO	Runs	HS	Avge	100	50	Ct	Overs	Mdns	Runs	Wkts	Avge	Best	SR
Australia in England, 1989 (Drawn 1, Lost 1)	2	4	0	73	47	18.25	–	–	1	8	0	34	0	–	–	–
New Zealand in England, 1990 (Won 1, Drawn 2)	3	5	0	357	151	71.40	1	3	3	10	6	17	0	–	–	–
India in England, 1990 (Won 1, Drawn 2)	3	6	0	378	131	63.00	1	3	3	28	3	161	1	161.00	1/61	168.00
England in Australia, 1990–91 (Drawn 2, Lost 3)	5	10	1	279	105	31.00	1	1	5	15	2	70	0	–	–	–
West Indies in England, 1991 (Won 2 Drawn 1, Lost 2)	5	9	0	79	32	8.77	–	–	3	–	–	–	–	–	–	–
Pakistan in England, 1992 (Won 1 Drawn 1, Lost 1)	3	5	0	145	76	29.00	–	2	5	–	–	–	–	–	–	–
England in India, 1992–93 (Lost 1)	1	2	0	48	37	24.00	–	–	2	–	–	–	–	–	–	–
England in Sri Lanka, 1992–93 (Lost 1)	1	2	0	15	13	7.50	–	–	1	–	–	–	–	–	–	–
Australia in England, 1993 (Won 1, Drawn 1, Lost 4)	6	12	0	553	99	46.08	–	6	1	–	–	–	–	–	–	–
England in West Indies, 1993–94 (Won 1, Drawn 1, Lost 3)	5	9	0	510	144	56.66	2	2	3	–	–	–	–	–	–	–
New Zealand in England, 1994 (Won 1, Drawn 2)	3	4	0	273	111	68.25	2	–	2	–	–	–	–	–	–	–
South Africa in England, 1994 (Won 1, Drawn 1, Lost 1)	3	6	0	207	99	34.50	–	2	1	–	–	–	–	–	–	–
England in Australia, 1994–95 (Won 1, Drawn 1, Lost 3)	5	10	0	407	88	40.70	–	4	4	–	–	–	–	–	–	–
West Indies in England, 1995							1	3								

England in South Africa, 1995–96 (Drawn 4, Lost 1)	5	8	1	390	185*	55.71	1	2	2	–	–	–	–	–	–	–
India in England, 1996 (Won 1, Drawn 2)	3	5	1	263	160	65.75	1	1	2	–	–	–	–	–	–	–
Pakistan in England, 1996 (Drawn 1, Lost 2)	3	5	0	162	64	32.40	–	2	3	7	1	20	1	20.00	1/20	42.00
England in Zimbabwe, 1996–97 (Drawn 2)	2	4	0	34	16	8.50	–	–	2	–	–	–	–	–	–	–
England in New Zealand, 1996–97 (Won 2, Drawn 1)	3	4	1	325	118	108.33	1	2	1	–	–	–	–	–	–	–
Australia in England, 1997 (Won 2, Drawn 2, Lost 3)	6	12	1	257	77	23.36	–	2	2	–	–	–	–	–	–	–
England in West Indies, 1997–98 (Won 1, Drawn 2, Lost 3)	6	11	0	199	64	18.09	–	1	5	–	–	–	–	–	–	–
South Africa in England, 1998 (Won 2, Drawn 2, Lost 1)	5	10	1	493	103	54.77	1	3	2	–	–	–	–	–	–	–
England in Australia, 1998–99 (Won 1, Drawn 1, Lost 2)	4	8	0	110	41	13.75	–	–	2	–	–	–	–	–	–	–
New Zealand in England, 1999 (Drawn 1, Lost 1)	2	4	0	133	64	33.25	–	1	1	–	–	–	–	–	–	–
England in South Africa, 1999–00 (Won 1, Drawn 2, Lost 2)	5	8	0	225	108	28.12	1	1	3	–	–	–	–	–	–	–
Zimbabwe in England, 2000 (Won 1, Drawn 1)	2	3	0	225	136	75.00	1	1	2	–	–	–	–	–	–	–
West Indies in England, 2000 (Won 3, Drawn 1, Lost 1)	5	9	0	311	108	34.55	1	1	2	–	–	–	–	–	–	–
England in Pakistan, 2000–01 (Won 1, Drawn 2)	3	6	1	341	125	68.20	1	2	2	–	–	–	–	–	–	–
England in Sri Lanka, 2000–01 (Won 2, Lost 1)	3	6	0	129	44	21.50	–	–	2	–	–	–	–	–	–	–
Pakistan in England, 2001 (Won 1, Lost 1)	2	3	0	98	51	32.66	–	1	6	–	–	–	–	–	–	–
Australia in England, 2001 (Won 1, Lost 4)	5	10	0	221	57	22.10	–	2	7	–	–	–	–	–	–	–

Opponents

	M	I	NO	Runs	HS	Avge	100	50	Ct	Overs	Mdns	Runs	Wkts	Avge	Best	SR
Australia	33	66	2	1900	105	29.68	1	15	22	23	2	104	0	–	–	–
India	7	13	1	689	160	57.41	2	4	7	28	3	161	1	161.00	1/60	168.00
New Zealand	11	17	1	1088	151	68.00	4	6	7	10	6	17	0	–	–	–
Pakistan	11	19	1	746	125	41.44	1	6	16	7	1	20	1	20.00	1/20	42.00
South Africa	18	32	2	1315	185*	43.83	3	8	8	–	–	–	–	–	–	–
Sri Lanka	4	8	0	144	44	18.00	–	–	3	–	–	–	–	–	–	–
West Indies	27	50	0	1587	144	31.74	4	6	16	–	–	–	–	–	–	–
Zimbabwe	4	7	0	259	55	37.00	1	1	4	–	–	–	–	–	–	–
TOTAL	115	212	7	7728	185*	37.69	16	46	83	68	12	302	2	151.00	1/20	204.00

Opponents as captain

	M	I	NO	Runs	HS	Avge	100	50	Ct	Overs	Mdns	Runs	Wkts	Avge	Best	SR
Australia	15	30	1	964	88	33.24	–	9	9	–	–	–	–	–	–	–
India	3	5	1	263	160	65.75	1	1	2	–	–	–	–	–	–	–
New Zealand	6	8	1	598	118	85.42	3	2	3	–	–	–	–	–	–	–
Pakistan	3	5	0	162	64	32.40	–	1	3	7	1	20	1	20.00	1/20	42.00
South Africa	8	14	1	597	99	45.92	1	4	3	–	–	–	–	–	–	–
West Indies	17	32	0	1197	144	37.40	3	5	11	–	–	–	–	–	–	–
Zimbabwe	2	4	0	34	16	8.50	–	–	2	–	–	–	–	–	–	–
TOTAL	54	98	4	3815	185*	40.58	8	22	33	7	1	20	1	20.00	1/20	42.00

Captaincy record in Test matches

Matches 54: won 13 (24%), lost 21 (39%), drawn 20 (37%)

Dismissals breakdown

	B	Ct	Ct(wk)	C&B	St	LBW	RO	HW	Os
Australia	9	23	19	1	1	9	1	1	7
India	2	4	3	–	–	3	–	–	1
New Zealand	1	6	4	1	–	4	–	–	1
Pakistan	4	5	6	–	–	3	–	–	1
South Africa	6	12	8	1	–	3	–	–	5
Sri Lanka	–	1	2	1	–	4	–	–	–
West Indies	9	15	17	–	–	7	2	–	5
Zimbabwe	1	4	–	–	–	2	–	–	–
TOTAL (205 dismissals)	32	70	59	4	1	35	3	1	20

Bowlers who have dismissed Atherton most often in Tests

19	G.D. McGrath	Australia
17	C.E.L. Ambrose	West Indies
17	C.A. Walsh	West Indies
11	A.A. Donald	South Africa
10	S.K. Warne	Australia
6	S.M. Pollock	South Africa
6	Waqar Younis	Pakistan

Test centuries

151	v New Zealand	Nottingham	1990
131	v India	Manchester	1990
105	v Australia	Sydney	1990–91
144	v West Indies	Georgetown	1993–94 (c)
135	v West Indies	St John's	1993–94 (c)
101	v New Zealand	Nottingham	1994 (c)
111	v New Zealand	Manchester	1994 (c)
113	v West Indies	Nottingham	1995 (c)
185*	v South Africa	Johannesburg	1995–96 (c)
160	v India	Nottingham	1996 (c)
118	v New Zealand	Christchurch	1996–97 (c)
103	v South Africa	Birmingham	1998
108	v South Africa	Port Elizabeth	1999–00
136	v Zimbabwe	Nottingham	2000
108	v West Indies	The Oval	2000
125	v Pakistan	Karachi	2000–01

Test record at each ground

	M	I	NO	Runs	HS	Avge	100	50	Ct	Overs	Mdns	Runs	Wkts	Avge	Best	SR
AUSTRALIA																
Adelaide	3	6	0	227	87	37.83	–	2	2	–	–	–	–	–	–	–
Brisbane	3	6	0	133	54	22.16	–	1	3	2	0	16	0	–	–	–
Melbourne	3	6	0	73	44	12.16	–	–	3	5	1	17	0	–	–	–
Sydney	2	4	1	263	105	87.66	1	2	1	8	1	37	0	–	–	–
Perth	3	6	0	100	35	16.66	–	–	2	–	–	–	–	–	–	–
ENGLAND																
Birmingham	9	18	2	664	103	41.50	1	6	9	9	5	17	0	–	–	–
Leeds	10	18	0	529	99	29.38	–	5	11	7	1	20	1	1/20	20.00	42.00
The Oval	12	24	0	859	108	35.79	1	7	5	8	0	70	1	1/60	70.00	48.00
Lord's	15	27	0	852	99	31.55	–	7	8	2	1	11	0	–	–	–
Manchester	10	18	0	729	131	40.50	2	3	10	20	3	90	0	–	–	–
Nottingham	11	19	1	1083	160	60.16	5	3	6	7	0	24	0	–	–	–
INDIA																
Mumbai	1	2	0	48	37	24.00	–	–	2	–	–	–	–	–	–	–
NEW ZEALAND																
Wellington	1	1	0	30	30	30.00	–	–	–	–	–	–	–	–	–	–
Auckland	1	1	0	83	83	83.00	–	1	–	–	–	–	–	–	–	–
Christchurch	1	2	1	212	118	212.00	1	1	1	–	–	–	–	–	–	–
PAKISTAN																
Lahore	1	2	0	93	73	46.50	–	1	–	–	–	–	–	–	–	–
Faisalabad	1	2	1	97	65*	97.00	–	1	1	–	–	–	–	–	–	–
Karachi	1	2	0	151	125	75.50	1	–	1	–	–	–	–	–	–	–

Ground	M	I	NO	Runs	HS	Avge	100	50	Ct						
SOUTH AFRICA															
Durban	2	2	0	3	2	1.50	–	1	–	–	–	–	–	–	–
Johannesburg	2	4	1	194	185*	64.66	1	–	2	–	–	–	–	–	–
Cape Town	2	4	0	116	71	29.00	–	1	2	–	–	–	–	–	–
Port Elizabeth	2	4	0	217	108	54.25	1	1	2	–	–	–	–	–	–
Centurion Park	2	2	0	85	78	42.50	–	1	–	–	–	–	–	–	–
SRI LANKA															
Kandy	1	2	0	18	11	9.00	–	–	1	–	–	–	–	–	–
Galle	1	2	0	77	44	38.50	–	–	–	–	–	–	–	–	–
Colombo (SSC)	2	4	0	49	21	12.25	–	–	2	–	–	–	–	–	–
WEST INDIES															
St John's	2	3	0	163	135	54.33	1	–	–	–	–	–	–	–	–
Georgetown	2	4	0	145	144	36.25	1	–	1	–	–	–	–	–	–
Bridgetown	2	4	0	175	85	43.75	–	2	2	–	–	–	–	–	–
Port-of-Spain	3	6	0	141	49	23.50	–	–	5	–	–	–	–	–	–
Kingston	2	3	0	85	55	28.33	–	1	–	–	–	–	–	–	–
ZIMBABWE															
Harare	1	2	0	14	13	7.00	–	–	–	–	–	–	–	–	–
Bulawayo	1	2	0	20	16	10.00	–	–	2	–	–	–	–	–	–

Milestones

Test debut:	v Australia at Nottingham	1989	
1000 runs	v Australia at Adelaide	1990–91	(12th Test)
2000 runs	v West Indies at Kingston	1993–94	(30th Test)
3000 runs	v Australia at Melbourne	1994–95	(42nd Test)
4000 runs	v South Africa at Johannesburg	1995–96	(53rd Test)
5000 runs	v Australia at Birmingham	1997	(68th Test)
6000 runs	v Australia at Adelaide	1998–99	(87th Test)
7000 runs	v Pakistan at Lahore	2000–01	(103rd Test)

FIRST-CLASS CAREER SEASON BY SEASON

			M	I	NO	Runs	HS	Avge	100	50	Ct	Overs	Mdns	Runs	Wkts	Avge	Best	SR
1987	England	Lancs/Camb. U/Comb. U/ MCC	21	35	4	1193	110	38.48	2	4	7	162.5	16	544	9	60.44	3-72	–
1988	England	Lancs/Camb. U	16	27	4	1121	152*	48.73	4	3	15	269.1	42	807	11	73.36	3-32	–
1989	England	Lancs/England/Camb. U	18	33	3	941	115*	31.36	1	4	16	405.4	89	1137	28	40.60	3-58	–
1989–90	Zimbabwe	England A	2	3	0	250	122	83.33	2	–	3	44.2	15	107	3	35.66	3-4	3
1990	England	Lancs/England	20	31	4	1924	191	71.25	7	12	24	433.3	103	1398	45	31.06	6-78	3
1990–91	Australia	England	11	22	2	577	114	28.85	2	2	10	79.1	10	330	6	55.00	3-27	–
1991	England	Lancs/England	14	23	3	820	138	41.00	3	2	9	–	–	–	–	–	–	–
1992	England	Lancs/England	21	37	6	1598	199	51.54	5	7	24	74.1	9	343	4	85.75	2-109	–
1992–93	India	England	4	8	1	238	80*	34.00	–	2	4	–	–	–	–	–	–	–
1992–93	Sri Lanka	England	1	2	0	15	13	7.50	–	–	1	–	–	–	–	–	–	–
1993	England	Lancs/England	19	32	1	1364	137	44.00	3	9	14	5	0	8	1	8.00	1-8	–
1993–94	W. Indies	England	7	12	0	704	144	58.66	3	3	4	–	–	–	–	–	–	–
1994	England	Lancs/England	16	27	2	899	111	35.96	2	4	14	7	2	10	0	–	–	–
1994–95	Australia	England	10	20	1	755	88	39.73	–	6	8	2	0	6	0	–	–	–
1995	England	Lancs/England	18	31	1	1323	155*	44.10	4	6	14	1	0	1	0	–	–	–
1995–96	S.Africa	England	9	15	2	587	185*	45.15	1	5	3	–	–	–	–	–	–	–
1995–96	W. Indies	Lancs	1	2	0	144	117	72.00	1	–	–	–	–	–	–	–	–	–
1996	England	Lancs/England	15	26	1	963	160	38.52	1	7	8	12	2	35	1	35.00	1-20	–
1996–97	Zimbabwe	England	4	8	1	102	55	12.75	–	1	3	–	–	–	–	–	–	–
1996–97	N. Zealand	England	6	9	2	354	118	50.57	1	2	7	–	–	–	–	–	–	–
1997	England	Lancs/England	16	28	0	853	149	32.80	2	5	8	1	0	7	0	–	–	–
1997–98	W. Indies	England	9	16	0	312	64	19.50	–	1	10	–	–	–	–	–	–	–
1998	England	Lancs/England	13	24	2	874	152	39.72	2	3	9	–	–	–	–	–	–	–
1998–99	Australia	England	8	15	1	438	210*	31.28	1	1	3	–	–	–	–	–	–	–
1999	England	Lancs/England	9	15	2	578	268*	44.46	1	2	4	–	–	–	–	–	–	–
1999–00	S.Africa	England	9	15	0	603	108	40.20	1	4	7	–	–	–	–	–	–	–
2000	England	Lancs/England	18	29	1	1068	136	38.14	3	6	15	–	–	–	–	–	–	–
2000–01	Pakistan	England	5	9	1	399	125	49.87	1	2	3	–	–	–	–	–	–	–
2000–01	Sri Lanka	England	5	9	0	283	85	31.44	–	1	4	–	–	–	–	–	–	–
2001	England	Lancs/England	11	21	1	649	160	32.45	1	3	17	–	–	–	–	–	–	–
TOTAL			336	584	47	21929	268*	40.83	54	107	268	1496.5	288	4733	108	43.83	6-78	3

Series by series

	M	I	NO	Runs	HS	Avge	100	50	Ct
Texaco Trophy in England v India, 1990 (Lost 2)	2	2	0	66	59	33.00	–	1	2
Benson & Hedges World Series in Australia, 1990–91 (Lost 2)	2	2	0	41	33	20.50	–	–	1
England in New Zealand, 1990–91 (Won 1, Lost 2)	3	3	0	60	34	20.00	–	–	–
Texaco Trophy in England v West Indies, 1991 (Won 3)	3	3	1	168	74	84.00	–	2	–
England in West Indies, 1993–94 (Won 2, Lost 3)	5	5	1	243	86	60.75	–	2	1
Texaco Trophy in England v New Zealand, 1994 (Won 1)	1	1	0	81	81	81.00	–	1	–
Texaco Trophy in England v South Africa, 1994 (Won 2)	2	2	0	68	49	34.00	–	–	–
Benson & Hedges World Series in Australia, 1994–95 (Won 2, Lost 2)	4	4	0	114	60	28.50	–	1	1
Texaco Trophy in England v West Indies, 1995 (Won 2, Lost 1)	3	3	0	227	127	75.66	1	1	4
England in South Africa, 1995–96 (Won 1, Lost 5)	6	6	0	146	85	24.33	–	1	1
Wills World Cup in India/Pakistan/Sri Lanka, 1995–96 (Won 2, Lost 4)	6	6	0	119	66	19.83	–	1	–
Texaco Trophy in England v India, 1996 (Won 2, No Result 1)	3	3	0	20	13	6.66	–	–	–
Texaco Trophy in England v Pakistan, 1996 (Won 2, Lost 1)	3	3	0	96	65	32.00	–	1	1
England in Zimbabwe, 1996–97 (Lost 3)	3	3	0	66	25	22.00	–	–	2
England in New Zealand, 1996–97 (Won 1, Lost 2, Tied 1)	4	4	0	94	43	23.50	–	–	1
Texaco Trophy in England v Australia, 1997 (Won 3)	3	3	1	118	113*	59.00	1	–	1
Emirates Triangular Tournament in England, 1998 (Lost 1)	1	1	0	64	64	64.00	–	1	–

Opponents

	M	I	NO	Runs	HS	Avge	100	50	Ct
Australia	6	6	1	200	113*	40.00	1	1	3
India	5	5	0	86	59	17.20	–	1	3
Netherlands	1	1	0	10	10	10.00	–	–	–
New Zealand	10	10	0	269	81	26.90	–	1	1
Pakistan	4	4	0	162	66	40.50	–	2	–
South Africa	9	9	0	214	85	23.77	–	1	1
Sri Lanka	2	2	0	86	64	43.00	–	1	–
United Arab Emirates	1	1	0	20	20	20.00	–	–	–
West Indies	11	11	2	638	127	70.88	1	5	5
Zimbabwe	5	5	0	106	26	21.20	–	–	2
TOTAL	**54**	**54**	**3**	**1791**	**127**	**35.11**	**2**	**12**	**15**

Opponents as captain

	M	I	NO	Runs	HS	Avge	100	50	Ct
Australia	5	5	1	192	113*	48.00	1	1	2
India	3	3	0	20	13	6.66	–	–	1
Netherlands	1	1	0	10	10	10.00	–	–	–
New Zealand	6	6	0	176	81	29.33	–	1	1
Pakistan	4	4	0	162	66	40.50	–	2	–
South Africa	9	9	0	214	85	23.77	–	1	1
Sri Lanka	1	1	0	22	22	22.00	–	–	–
United Arab Emirates	1	1	0	20	20	20.00	–	–	–
West Indies	8	8	1	470	127	67.14	1	3	5
Zimbabwe	5	5	0	106	26	21.20	–	–	2
TOTAL	**43**	**43**	**2**	**1392**	**127**	**33.95**	**2**	**8**	**12**

Captaincy record in one-day internationals

Dismissals breakdown

	B	Ct	Ct(wk)	C&B	St	LBW	RO	Os
Australia	–	1	2	–	–	2	–	–
India	–	1	2	–	–	2	–	1
Netherlands	1	–	–	–	–	–	–	1
New Zealand	4	3	1	–	–	–	2	1
Pakistan	2	1	–	–	–	1	–	–
South Africa	1	4	3	–	–	–	1	2
Sri Lanka	–	1	1	–	–	–	–	–
United Arab Emirates	1	–	–	–	–	–	–	–
West Indies	3	5	1	–	–	–	–	–
Zimbabwe	–	2	2	–	–	1	–	–
TOTAL (51 dismissals)	12	18	12	–	–	6	3	4

One-day international centuries

127	v West Indies	Lord's	1995 (c)
113*	v Australia	The Oval	1997 (c)

One-day international record at each ground

	M	I	NO	Runs	HS	Avge	100	50	Ct
AUSTRALIA									
Adelaide	1	1	0	33	33	33.00	–	–	–
Brisbane	1	1	0	26	26	26.00	·	–	–
Melbourne	1	1	0	14	14	14.00	–	–	1
Sydney	3	3	0	82	60	27.33	–	1	3
ENGLAND									
Birmingham	4	4	1	200	81	66.65	–	2	–
Leeds	3	3	0	18	7	6.00	–	–	3
The Oval	3	3	1	218	113*	109.00	1	1	1
Lord's	4	4	0	217	127	54.25	1	1	2
Manchester	4	4	0	158	74	39.50	–	2	–
Nottingham	3	3	0	97	59	32.33	–	1	2
INDIA									
Ahmedabad	1	1	0	1	1	1.00	–	–	–

One-day international record at each ground (*continued*)

	M	I	NO	Runs	HS	Avge	100	50	Ct
NEW ZEALAND									
Wellington	2	2	0	69	43	34.50	–	–	1
Auckland	2	2	0	43	34	21.50	–	–	–
Christchurch	2	2	0	19	19	9.50	–	–	–
Napier	1	1	0	23	23	23.00	–	–	–
PAKISTAN									
Peshawar	2	2	0	30	20	15.00	–	–	–
Faisalabad	1	1	0	22	22	22.00	–	–	–
Karachi	1	1	0	66	66	66.00	–	1	–
Rawalpindi	1	1	0	0	0	0.00	–	–	–
SOUTH AFRICA									
East London	1	1	0	6	6	6.00	–	–	1
Bloemfontein	1	1	0	85	85	85.00	–	1	–
Durban	1	1	0	17	17	17.00	–	–	–
Johannesburg	1	1	0	0	0	0.00	–	–	–
Cape Town	1	1	0	35	35	35.00	–	–	–
Port Elizabeth	1	1	0	3	3	3.00	–	–	–
WEST INDIES									
Arnos Vale, St Vincent	1	1	1	19	19*	–	–	–	–
Bridgetown	1	1	0	86	86	86.00	–	1	–
Port-of-Spain	2	2	0	92	51	46.00	–	1	1
Kingston	1	1	0	46	46	46.00	–	–	–
ZIMBABWE									
Harare	2	2	0	43	25	21.50	–	–	2
Bulawayo	1	1	0	23	23	23.00	–	–	–
TOTAL	287	279	23	9343	127	36.49	14	59	111

Record in all domestic one-day matches

	Overs	Mdns	Runs	Wkts	Avge	Best	SR
TOTAL	135.2	4	711	24	29.62	4-42	1

INDEX

319